Power and Economy in Early Classic Period Hohokam Society: An Archaeological Perspective from the Marana Mound Site

edited by
James M. Bayman, Paul R. Fish, and Suzanne K. Fish

with contributions by
Frank E. Bayham, James M. Bayman, Margaret E. Beck,
Michael J. Boley, Sergio F. Castro-Reino, Christopher Descantes,
Paul R. Fish, Suzanne K. Fish, Michael D. Glascock,
Deanna Grimstead, Karla Hansen-Speer, Cory Harris,
Karen G. Harry, Abigail L. Holeman, R. Emerson Howell,
Jeffrey A. Homburg, Phillip O. Leckman, Elizabeth Miksa,
Christopher Roos, Robert J. Speakman

Arizona State Museum
THE UNIVERSITY OF ARIZONA.

Arizona State Museum Archaeological Series 207

Arizona State Museum
The University of Arizona
Tucson, Arizona 85721-0026
Copyright © 2013 by the Arizona Board of Regents
All rights reserved.
Printed in the United States of America

ISBN (paper): 978-1-889747-85-9
Library of Congress Control Number: 2013941021

ARIZONA STATE MUSEUM ARCHAEOLOGICAL SERIES

General Editor: Richard C. Lange
Technical Editors: Laura Burghardt, Alicia M. Vega

The *Archaeological Series* of the Arizona State Museum, The University of Arizona, publishes the results of research in archaeology and related disciplines conducted in the Greater Southwest. Original, monograph-length manuscripts are considered for publication, provided they deal with appropriate subject matter. Information regarding procedures or manuscript submission and review is given under Research Publications on the Arizona State Museum website: *www.statemuseum.arizona.edu/research/pubs.* Information may be also obtained from the General Editor, *Archaeological Series*, Arizona State Museum, P.O. Box 210026, The University of Arizona, Tucson, Arizona, 85721-0026; Email: langer@email.arizona.edu. Electronic publications and previous volumes in the Arizona State Museum Library or available from the University of Arizona Press are listed on the website noted above. Print-on-demand versions of the lastest Arizona State Museum Archaeological Series may be obtained from several booksellers on-line.

The Arizona State Museum *Archaeological Series* is grateful to the many donors and supporters who continue to make this publication possible.

Cover: Drawing by Pamela Key, Pamela Key Studios, Los Angeles, California.

Contents

Figures

Tables

Foreword

This volume introduces the research design for investigations undertaken at the Marana Mound site (AZ AA:12:251 [ASM]) following the conclusion of the Northern Tucson Basin Survey (NTBS) in 1990, a brief summary of major findings at this Early Classic center, and selected studies on more focused topics. Results of the previous NTBS survey have been published in a variety of venues, including journal articles, book chapters, monographs, and graduate student theses and dissertations. Comprehensive summary publications are *The Marana Community in the Hohokam World* edited by Suzanne K. Fish, Paul R. Fish, and John H. Madsen (1992a), *The Northern Tucson Basin Survey: Research Directions and Background Studies* edited by John H. Madsen, Paul R. Fish, and Suzanne K. Fish (1993), and *Between Desert and River: Hohokam Settlement and Land Use in the Los Robles Community* by Christian E. Downum (1993).

The selected studies in this volume are an outgrowth of archaeological field classes and field schools that were held at the Marana Mound site during spring semesters between 1990 and 2003. The contributions were initially presented at a symposium at the 69th Annual Meeting of the Society for American Archaeology (SAA) in Montreal, Canada, in 2004, and have been modified over the intervening years. As of this writing, studies of Marana collections continue and some of the findings reported here undoubtedly will be refined by this ongoing research as well as future analyses. In the meantime, these studies offer valuable insights on the organization of Hohokam society during the Early Classic Period (ca. AD 1150-1300) from the perspective of one uniquely well-preserved locale—the Marana Mound site.

Acknowledgments

We, most of all, wish to acknowledge the insights and efforts of our numerous graduate assistants who had supervisory roles in the Marana Mound site investigations. These individuals include Gavin Archer, Nicole Arendt, Margaret Beck, Michael Boley, Trixi Bubemyer, John Carpenter, John Chamblee, Sara Chavarria, Christopher Doolittle, Christian Downum, Michael Faught, Tina Fortugno, Emiliano Gallaga, Douglas Gann, James Gittings, Karla Hansen-Speer, Chris Hardaker, Cory Harris, Karen Harry, Matt Hill, Abigail Holeman, Maren Hopkins, R. Emerson Howell, Daniela Klokler, Phillip O. Leckman, Stacy Lengyel, Arthur MacWilliams, Anna Neuzil, Todd Pitezel, Christopher Roos, Barbara Roth, Guadalupe Sanchez de Carpenter, Miriam Stark, and Ruth Van Dyke. Numerous archaeologists and other experts have also advised, collaborated closely, and supervised aspects of Marana Mound research, including Frank Bayham, Ronald Beckwith, Mary Bernard, Curtiss Brennan, Jeffrey Dean, William Deaver, David Doyel, Michael Glascock, William Harrison, Jeffrey Homburg, Joseph Joaquin, Lambert Jose, Elliott Lax, John Madsen, Charles Miksicek, Elizabeth Miksa, Hector Neff, Nancy Odegaard, David Stephen, Ben Sternberg, Christine Szuter, Lynn Teague, Henry Wallace, John Welch, and Stephanie Whittlesey. Most figures in this volume and those used elsewhere in Marana publications are the products of Ronald Beckwith and Phillip Leckman. The Marana fieldwork and analysis would never have been possible without the assistance of countless members of the Arizona Archaeological and Historical Society and numerous students employees, University of Arizona and University of Hawai'i field school participants and other volunteers. We thank Pamela Key, Pamela Key Studios, Los Angeles, California for her thoughtful rendering of the Marana Platform Mound as it appeared around A.D. 1275. Funding for the Marana Mound Project came from the National Science Foundation Senior Research and Dissertation Improvement grant programs, Curtiss and Mary Brennan Foundation, Wenner Gren Foundation, University of Missouri Reactor Facility, American Anthropological Association Small Grant Program for Specialized Analyses, U.S. Department of Education, University of Arizona Foundation, Arizona State Museum, and University of Hawai'i. Finally, thanks to Douglas Craig and an anonymous reviewer for suggestions that improved the manuscript and to Richard C. Lange, Alicia M. Vega, and Laura Burghardt whose unflagging efforts produced the volume.

Chapter 1
Introduction: The Marana Mound Site

Suzanne K. Fish
Paul R. Fish
James M. Bayman

INTRODUCTION

The appropriate characterization of societal complexity and political economy across the vast Hohokam domain is far from settled. Nevertheless, Hohokam and other societies of the late prehispanic Southwest were undeniably middle range and regional sequences exhibited increasingly large-scale and complex configurations over time. Along with developments surrounding Chaco Canyon on the Colorado Plateaus and Casas Grandes in Chihuahua, Hohokam Classic period socio-political organization is often considered one of the three most prominent examples of regional complexity in the adjoining U.S. Southwest and Mexican Northwest (e.g., Cordell 2012; Lekson 2009; Plog 2008). Hohokam attributes contributing to this perception include maximally dense and permanent populations, the largest prehispanic canal systems north of Peru (Doolittle 1990: 79) and other forms of intensive agriculture, multi-site territorial and political entities known as "communities," and the erection of relatively massive public architecture.

The Hohokam trajectory is marked by changing civic-territorial institutions that parallel developments in residential and social organization. These institutions are subsumed by the Southwestern concept of the community, which has archaeological expression in spatial patterns and symbols (e.g., Adler 1994; Doyel and Lekson 1993; P. Fish and Fish 1994; S. Fish and Fish 2000; Wilcox and Sternberg 1983). A Hohokam community, as defined in this volume, consists of a set of interrelated sites within a bounded territory that also contains a center with public architecture of a kind and/or magnitude not duplicated in other community sites (S. Fish and Fish 1994). The integration of population and settlements throughout is symbolically embodied in the communal structures for observances on behalf of all members.

The functions associated with central sites, and with public or ceremonial precincts within these sites, are key factors in assessing leadership, inequality, and complexity. Communal storage and food preparation, ritual observances, astronomy and calendrics, production and consumption of high value craft items, and architecturally differentiated residence in association with community centers and their public architecture are cited in recent studies (e.g., Bayman 2002; Bostwick and Downum 1994; Crown and Fish 1996; Doyel 2000; Elson 1998; P. Fish and Fish 2000; Harry and Bayman 2000; Howard 1992; Lindauer and Blitz 1997). The creation of symbols of social and territorial commonality in the form of platform mounds would have bestowed a unique status on community centers and those who officiated in communal activities (Fish and Yoffee 1996; S. Fish and Fish 2000).

The internal structure and distributional profiles of community centers are essential elements in the further elucidation of Classic period hierarchical organization and political economy. Southwestern societies present a powerful challenge because leaders and elites are not readily visible in the archaeological record. Although there is unequivocal evidence for appreciable centralized and coordinated effort in some spheres, leaders are not distinguished by easily recognized indicators such as lavish wealth displayed in residences or mortuary treatment, restricted prestige goods and exclusive insignia, evidence of institutionalized coercion, or individualized prominence in art or iconography. Previous Marana Mound site studies and intra-community comparison have identified many of the ritual, political, and economic variables by which inhabitants of this center were distinguished from other Early Classic community members (e.g., Bayman 1994, 1995, 1996a,b; Fish et al. 1989, 1992b; P. Fish and Fish 2000; Harry 1997, 2003; Harry and Bayman 2000). Most of the research reported in this volume seeks to investigate the nature and degree of differentiation among the primary social and residential units and public precincts within this community center.

There are few opportunities, however, to obtain more than fragmentary evidence of this kind. Long-term occupations create complicated records in a majority of central settlements while most have suffered extensive damage from agricultural and urban development. The Marana Mound site represents an unusual opportunity to examine comprehensive distributions of important variables at multiple scales. As a result of regional survey, this site can be precisely placed in the context of an aggregating community settlement system (S. Fish and Fish 1990; Fish et al. 1989, 1992a). Fortuitous circumstances of preservation without plowing, urban development, and extensive vandalism afford a unique view of total site layout. The absence of earlier or later occupations provides an uncompromised record of the Early Classic Tanque Verde phase (see P. Fish and Fish 2000).

In the Tucson Basin, Sedentary period dates for beginnings of mound constructions paralleling those in the Phoenix Basin have not been identified (Wallace and Holmlund 1984; Fish and Fish 1991; Doyel 2000). Thus, formal positioning between preceding ballcourts and the earliest forms of Hohokam platform mounds is not present at any Tucson site, and, indeed, in only one case was an earlier ballcourt site (Martinez Hill) chosen as a location for Classic mound construction. The Marana Mound site configuration therefore should represent tangible correlates of the social and ideational concepts underlying the new modes of public architecture and compound residence appearing in the Early Classic period.

THE MARANA CLASSIC PERIOD COMMUNITY

The Early Classic period Marana Community covered 146 km^2 and the Marana Mound site (AZ AA:12:251 [ASM]) was constructed at a central point within it. Six zones of differentiated productive and residential remains encompass all environmental settings of the northern Tucson Basin. Total habitation site area in the Marana Community increased from 2,000,000 m^2 in the Preclassic period to 6,000,000 m^2 in the Early Classic period, implying that trends in community aggregation involved some level of population relocation from surrounding Tucson settlements (Fish et al. 1989, 1992a).

Construction of the Marana platform mound in a geographically central position that offered floodwater farming opportunities of moderate productivity would have promoted communal concern with an architectural symbol to integrate the expanded population of the Classic period Community. Densely settled, but without immediate access to prime irrigated land, Marana Mound inhabitants would have had high stakes in a comprehensive and dependable system of subsistence exchange (see Chapter 5, Hansen-Speer, this volume), balanced by a site emphasis in craft manufacture (Fish and Fish 1990; Fish and Donaldson 1991). The nature of intra- and inter-community exchange and the role of mound site residents in it are critical to understanding the political economy of the Marana Community. Systems of prestige goods circulating predominantly among elites are not readily apparent: however it is likely that higher value items concentrated in centers were broadly manipulated to reinforce obligations in goods and services (Bayman 1995, 1997, 2002; Bayman and Shackley 1999)

MARANA MOUND SITE INVESTIGATIONS

A Tiered Sampling Program

Differentiation among social constituencies at the Marana Mound site was approached through a sampling design focusing on: mapping, systematic collection for surface artifact distributions, extensive testing of trash mounds, outlining of compounds, outlining and excavation of rooms, and investigation of the mound precinct. Some previously published results will differ from data and interpretation in this volume because they were based on earlier, less complete data sets. The following chapters are based on varied samples, as specified by the author.

Evidence for differential material advantages and competitive strategies was sought in four realms; evidence bearing on each realm had previously been identified and encountered during previous work:

Access to and consumption of exotic or high value items, including value created through application of labor such as craft production or architectural investment.

Economic activities beyond ordinary subsistence production and consump-

tion, such as specialized agricultural production and craft manufacture.

Involvement in external exchange, whether with regard to the Marana Mound site, the Marana Community, or the region.

Participation in communal or integrative observances as signaled by ritually related items and features or associated activities such as feasting and the preparation of fermented beverages.

Site Mapping and Site Layout

In the mound site, covering an area more than 1.5 km long and 0.5 km wide, features are not deeply buried and are well represented by surface indications. To characterize this expansive community center, we have necessarily depended on different levels of sampling. A grid of 50 m squares served as the basis for systematic collections of surface artifacts over the entire site and architectural mapping. The site map shows low mounds of melted structural adobe, cobble and gravel alignments, and trash mounds in patterned arrangements (Figure 1.1).

Although it is notoriously difficult to detect Hohokam adobe architecture from the surface, the Marana Mound site map can be justified as an accurate approximation of layout at the height of a relatively short occupation. Among the tens of thousands of local decorated sherds from surface and excavated proveniences, designs are exclusively of the Tanque Verde phase. Infrequent intrusive ceramics, primarily Casa Grande Red-on-buff, McDonald Corrugated, Pinedale Black-on-white, San Carlos Red, Gila Black-on-red, and Tularosa Black-on-white, are chronologically compatible with the Early Classic period between A.D. 1150 or 1200 and 1300. No Red-on-brown or Red-on-buff sherds of Preclassic age are pres-

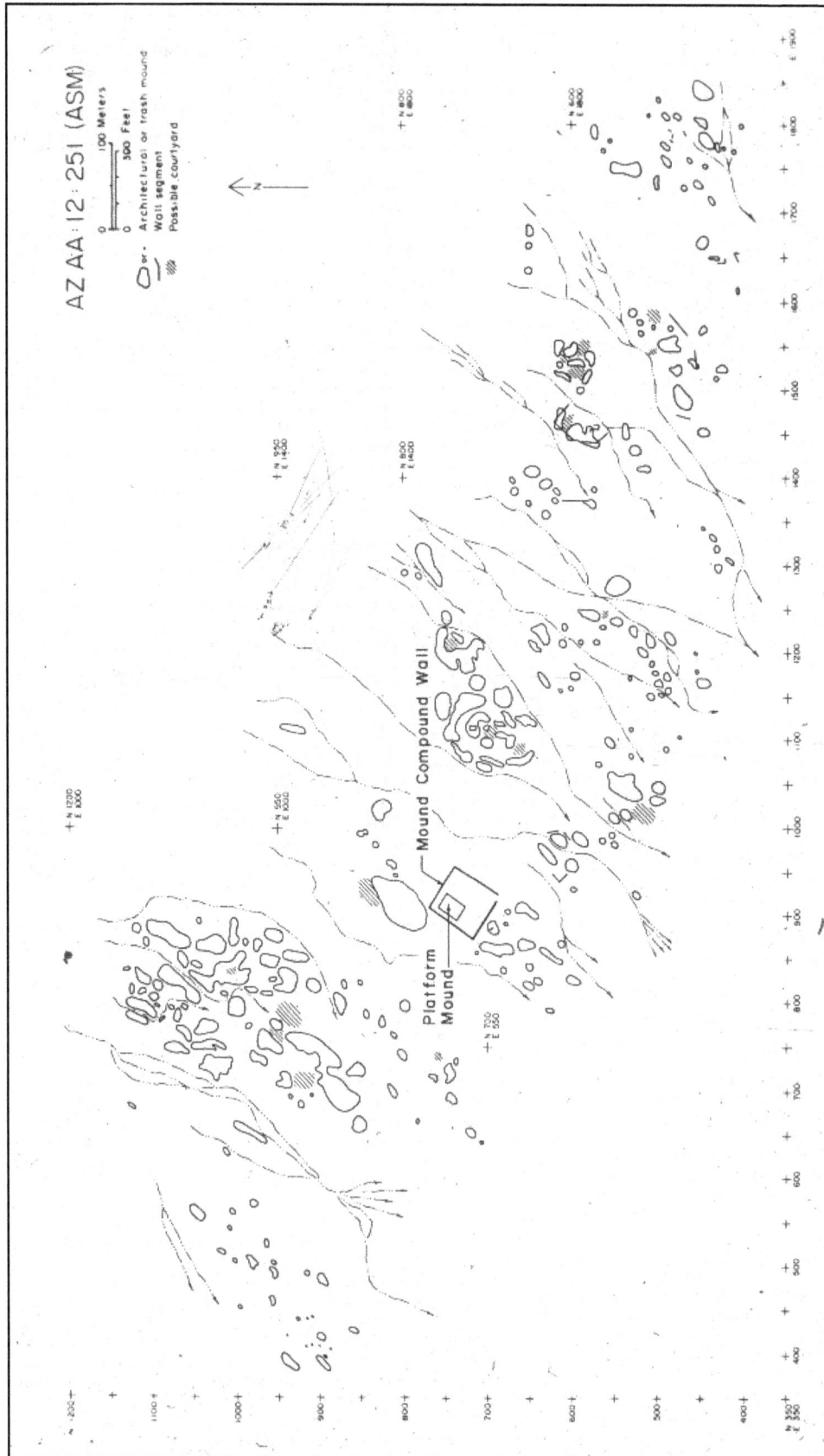

Figure 1.1. Map of the Marana Mound site showing low mounded accumulations of melted adobe and the platform mound in its compound.

ent. Pinto Polychrome and subsequent Salado wares, as well as the Maverick Mountain and Tucson polychromes, also are absent. Several archaeomagnetic and radiocarbon determinations from both the platform mound and structures in residential compounds indicate occupation within a narrow interval during the first half of the thirteenth century. Likewise, non-cutting tree-ring dates from four rooms in three compounds date from A.D. 1220 to 1260. Although there is extensive evidence for remodeling within rooms, actual superimposed structures occur only in two cases of an earlier and later structure that overlap within the same residential footprint. Only a few rooms appear to be trash filled, and most excavated rooms contained a variety of functional items in floor assemblages that could have been readily removed for use elsewhere.

Generally regular spacing between compounds and the remodeling/rebuilding episodes within each further suggest a majority were occupied contemporaneously. Surface artifact densities closely conform to the mapped limits of structural remains and their associated trash deposits (Bayman and Sanchez 1998); virtually all site inhabitants appear to have lived in compounds with extended occupations. Extensive backhoe and hand testing in areas with few surface artifacts and architectural indications revealed no isolated structures.

Confidence in our ability to distinguish compounds by means of patterning in subtle surface relief and other visible correlates of architectural remains rests upon a correspondence between surface patterns and subsurface features demonstrated through excavation (Figure 1.1). Alignments of rocks that served as pegs to bond adjacent adobe courses provide surface indications of some walls. The orientations of other walls are marked by linear concentrations of deflated gravels, accumulated from inclusions in the adobe matrix as the walls melted. The exposure of the walls

of multiple compounds and the outlining of rooms confirmed the relationship of site microtopography and other surface markers to shallowly buried architecture. Excavation further confirmed the unusual size of many compounds and the patterned exterior arrangement of trash mounds (Figures 1.2 and 1.3).

More complete outlined walls for 5 compounds (Figures 1.4 and 1.5) enclose between 2350 and 5500 m², up to several times the area of most reported residential compounds in the Phoenix Basin (for example, see compound sizes in Sires 1987:178-179), Tonto Basin, and other Hohokam regional sectors. The continuity of exposed compound walls and the strong patterning of trash mounds around compound exteriors (e.g., Figure 1.3) suggests that they were typically planned and executed as unitary rather than accretionary constructions (but see an argument for an exception in Harris, Chapter 4, this volume). Eleven rooms were wholly or partially excavated in Compound 1, an exceptionally large outlined enclosure that is believed to have contained more than 20 rooms. Smaller compounds would have had fewer rooms, but probably at least 10 to 15.

Early Classic period compounds and Late Classic compounds at a variety of relatively small Hohokam sites average around 1500 m² (Sires 1987). Similarly the single identified Early Classic residential compound at Gibbon Springs is 2000 m² (Slaughter and Roberts 1996:78); the one at Whiptail Ruin is 1200 m² (Gregonis and Hartmann 2011:14), and the one at Los Morteros, Locus 12 is about 700 m² (Wallace 1995:197). These Tucson Basin compounds are either below or at the low end of the range of corresponding compound areas at the Marana Mound site. At Late Classic period Los Muertos and Pueblo Grande, two large and extensively excavated Phoenix mound centers, compounds range from 800 m² to slightly over 2100 m² (Haury 1945; Mitchell and Foster 1994). The largest Marana compounds could

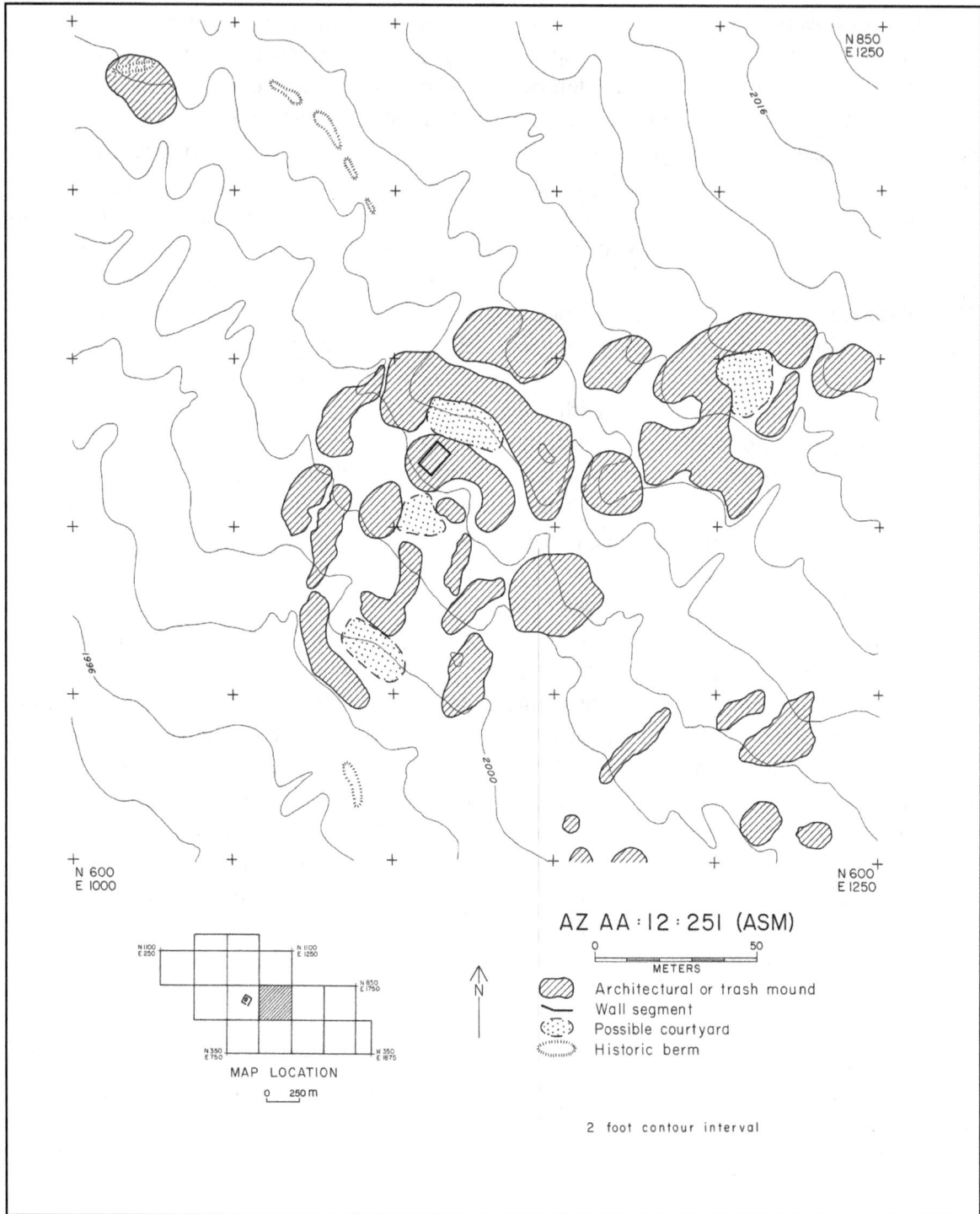

Figure 1.2. The configuration of mounded adobe melt that comprises Compound 1 and the trash mounds that surround it, as mapped prior to excavation.

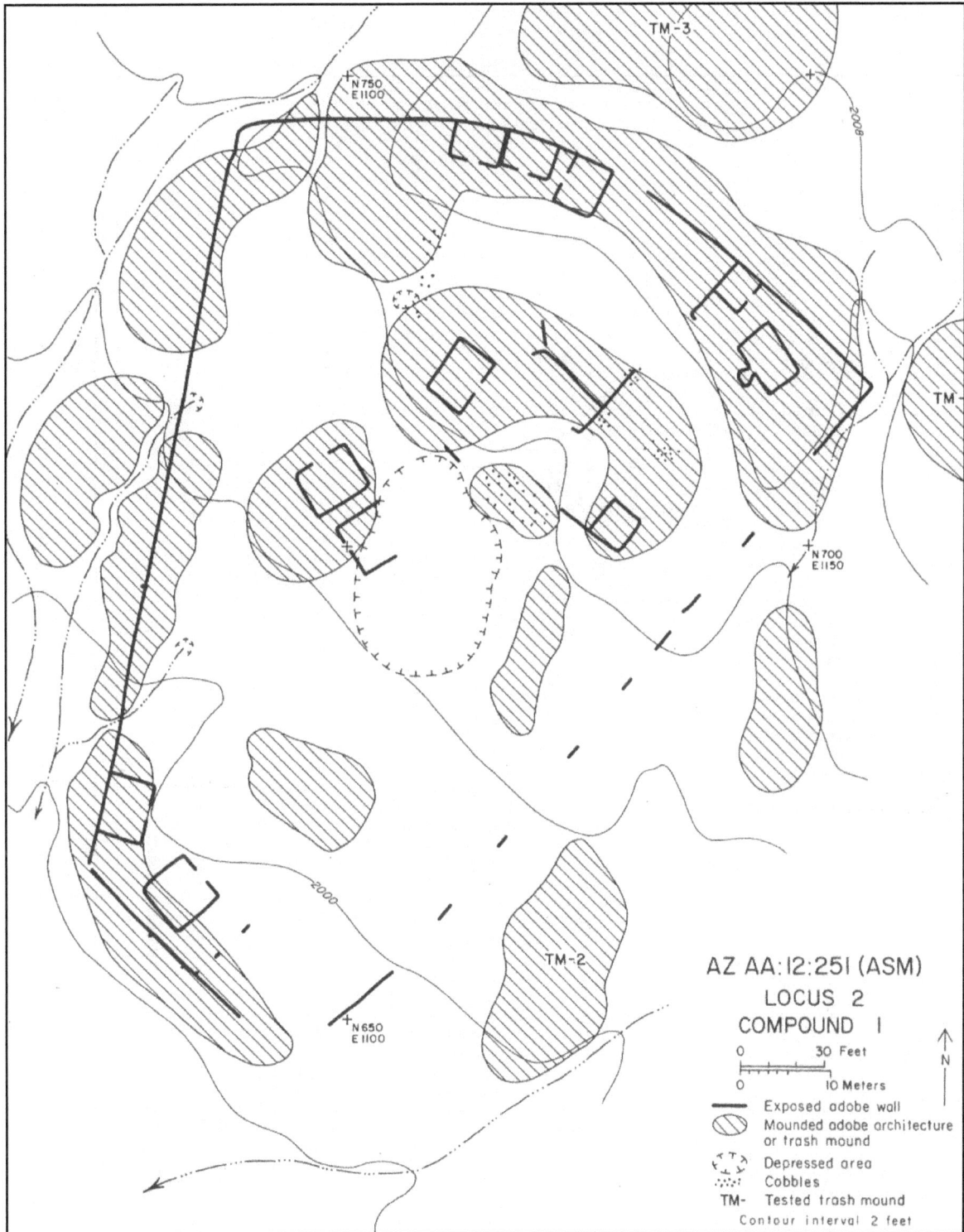

Figure 1.3. Outline of Compound 1 and its associated trash mounds in the central portion of Figure 1.2. Less than one half of total estimated rooms were excavated or outlined.

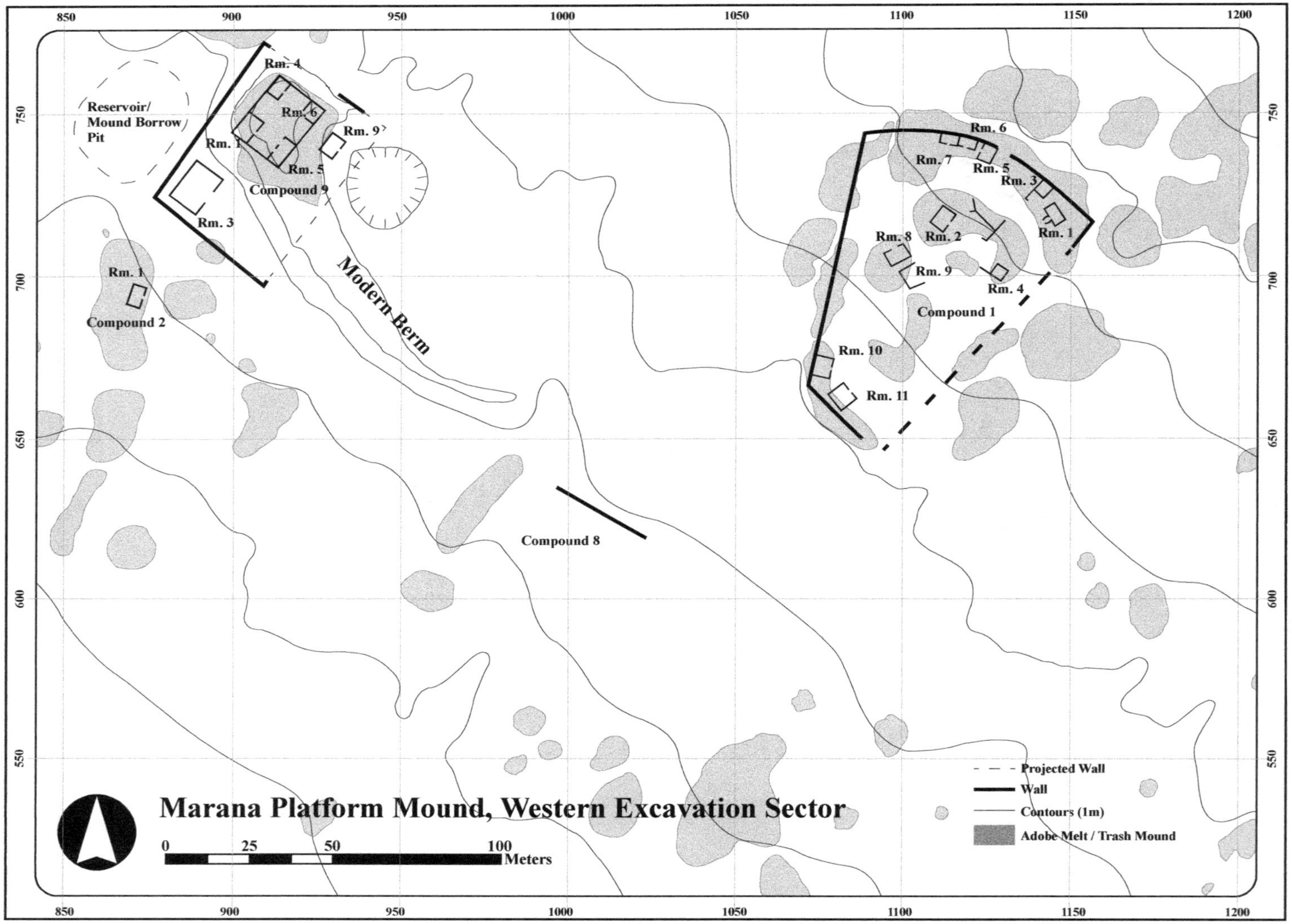
Marana Platform Mound, Western Excavation Sector
Reservoir/
Mound Borrow
Pit
Rm. 4
Rm. 6
Rm. 1
Rm. 9
Rm. 5
Compound 9
Rm. 3
Rm. 1
Compound 2
Modern Berm
Compound 8
Rm. 6
Rm. 7
Rm. 5
Rm. 3
Rm. 1
Rm. 8
Rm. 2
Rm. 9
Rm. 4
Compound 1
Rm. 10
Rm. 11
Projected Wall
Wall
Contours (1m)
Adobe Melt / Trash Mound
0
25
50
100
Meters
850
900
950
1000
1050
1100
1150
1200
750
700
650
600
550

Figure 1.4. Detailed map of the western sector of the Marana Mound site containing the platform mound compound (Compound 9) and residential compounds 1, 2, and 8.

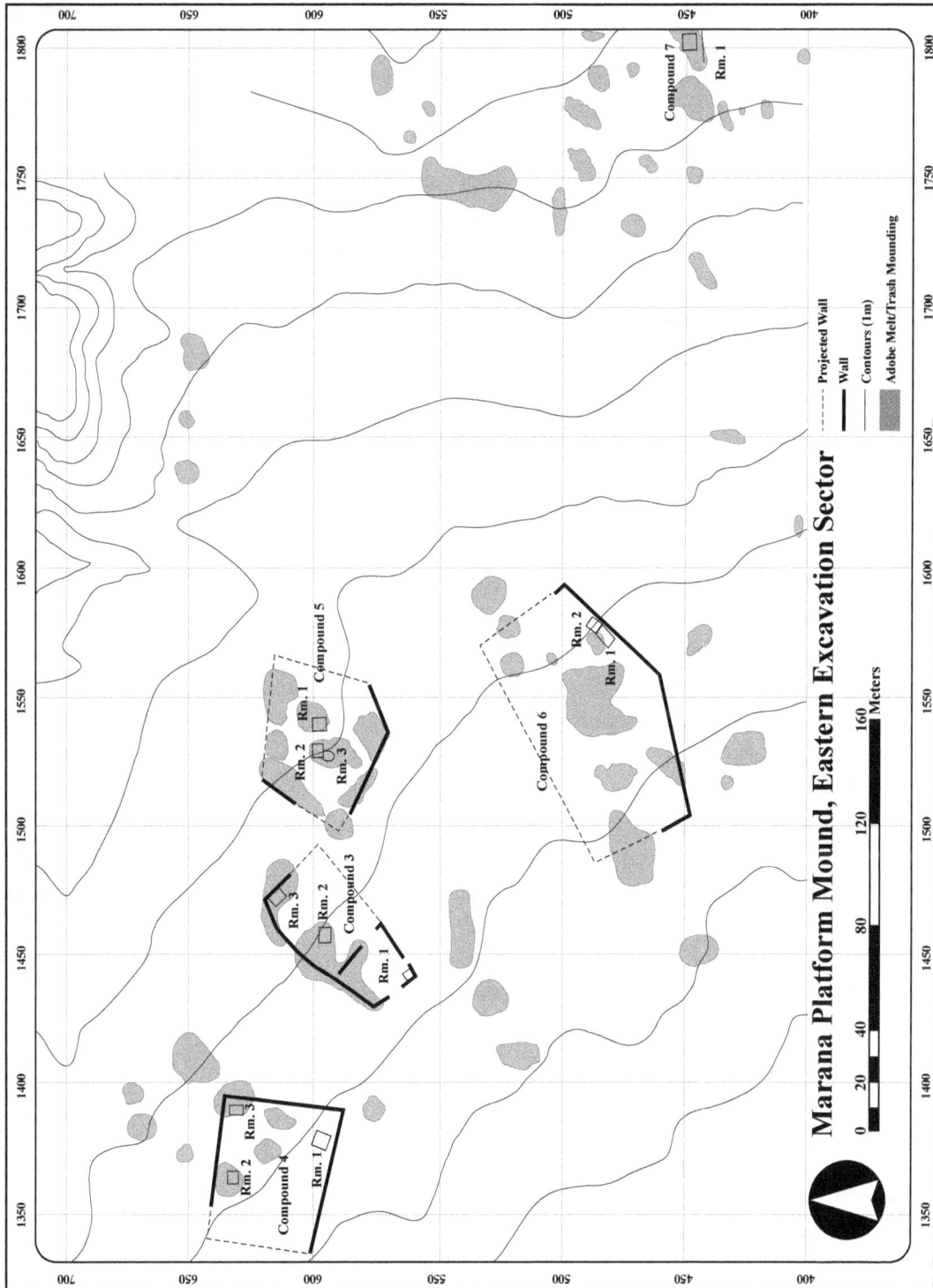

Marana Platform Mound, Eastern Excavation Sector

Figure 1.5. Detailed map of the eastern sector of the Marana Mound site containing Compounds 3, 4, 5, 6, and 7.

accommodate two to several compounds in this size range. Perhaps internal subunits identified within some Marana compounds (see outlined wall segments in the northeast corner of the excavated compound in Figure 1.3) correspond to one of these smaller compounds elsewhere.

The site map provides a reasonable basis for estimating numbers of compounds and, as a further stage of inference, site population. To estimate minimal compound numbers, an outline of the largest compound with its associated trash mounds was superimposed over adobe remnants across the entire site area until all mapped surface indications could be accounted for as parts of plausible compounds. This method suggests at least 35 to 40 compounds at the site. At a very conservative ratio of 15 persons to a 15-room compound, site population totals would range between 525 and 600 people. A more likely 30 persons per 15-room compound would raise the maximum number of residents to 1050-1200 persons. Large open courtyard areas within compound walls have yet to be extensively tested. In keeping with public buildings constructed solely at the community center, extramural space in mound site residential compounds may have accommodated visitors from outlying community settlements and perhaps more distant villages during centralized civic and religious events.

Trash Mound Excavations

Patterned trash disposal by Marana Mound residents created multiple trash mounds outside and adjacent to compound walls. Archaeologists (e.g., Henderson 1987a; Howard 1985; Gregory 1984) often cite trash mounds as one of the facilities shared by Preclassic courtyard groups (sets of three to five pithouses opening onto a common courtyard that are often equated with a household of closely related kin). Sires (1987) suggested continuity between

preceding courtyard groups and analogously arranged rooms in superimposed, typically small compounds of the Phoenix Basin. In the largest Marana compounds, subunits can be discerned by similarly inward-oriented sets of rooms and by sets of rooms divided off internally by walls that were less substantial than exterior compound walls. These subunits likely represent single, or, possibly in some cases, multiple member households. If occupants of the subunits deposited their debris in only one of the exterior trash mounds, each would provide an artifactual profile of that household group or groups. Together, the trash mounds ringing the compound represent the disposal behavior of its residents as a whole (Bayman 1994; and see Beck and Roos, Chapter 2, this volume).

Screened excavations of about 2 m^2 in 22 trash mounds spanning the site provide intra-site comparisons among compounds and possibly among individual member households. The abundant trash mound assemblages reveal generally comparable access to exotic and valuable materials and participation in craft manufacture as inferred from production tools and debris (Bayman 1994, 1995, 1996a,b). Trash mound tests produced artifact distributions resembling those of surface collections and other excavated contexts. For example, decorated ceramics occur in roughly equal percentages on the site surface (20.4 percent), in trash mounds (19.0 percent), and among whole vessels in a sample of excavated room floors (20.3 percent). Likewise, surface and trash mound ratios of obsidian and shell to sherds are similar (Bayman and Sanchez 1998: 81-83).

Residential Rooms

A wholly and partially excavated sample of 22 rooms in seven residential compounds provide data on construction styles, artifact assemblages, and modes of structure closure or abandonment for comparison within the Marana Mound site and elsewhere in the Marana Community. The excavated adobe residential rooms are standardized in terms of posthole, hearth, and doorway placements, and in low amounts of calcium carbonate additives (Howell and Homburg, Chapter 3, this volume). Although floors range from slightly depressed to as much as 75 cm below the original ground surface, true pithouses with adobe reinforced walls appear rare at the mound site.

With the exception of one room with small cobbles mixed into the adobe matrix of its above-ground walls and a second room with relatively thin post-reinforced walls, all other coursed adobe residential structures that were investigated followed the same pattern: an adobe wall was built below ground inside a pit. A separate above-ground wall was set slightly back from the wall in the pit so that its weight was not resting directly on the lower wall. A narrow shelf, sometimes retaining plaster remnants, usually could be discerned connecting the "up" wall rising from the ground surface and "down" walls in the pit. Hayden (1957:17) documented this arrangement at University Indian Ruin; architectural records from Whiptail Ruin (Gregonis and Hartmann 2011) also appear to show instances of a similar construction technique. Modern plowing and other relatively shallow ground disturbance would destroy such "up" walls arising from the prehispanic ground surface. It is probable that these kinds of coursed adobe rooms in currently disturbed situations would be usually interpreted as pithouses or houses in pits.

Almost all mound site rooms showed evidence of heavy to light burning, often associated with a major remodeling episode when an existing floor ceased to be used. Residents deposited clean fill of sufficient depth to cover assemblages placed on the existing floor and then established a new floor above it. They also re-plastered the burned walls, sometimes reconstructing new floor features on the new floor in the previous position. Up to a maximum of five sequential refloorings allowed residents to perform major, symbolic remodeling while continuing to reside in a persistent house footprint. With each re-flooring, the height of the floor increased from original depth below ground to a near-surface level in a few instances.

Charred wood identifications reveal frequent use of Douglas and white fir, ponderosa pine, pinyon, and juniper as structural elements. Ranging between 11.4 and 35 m^2, residental rooms have a median size of 23.5 m^2. In terms of room size, predominant coursed adobe architecture, use of conifer posts and vigas, and positioning of floor features, these structures are similar to contemporary counterparts at Los Morteros (Wallace 1995), Gibbon Springs (Slaughter and Roberts 1996), Whiptail (Gregonis and Hartmann 2011), and Muchas Casas (Bostwick 1987; Hackbarth 1987).

The sample of 22 rooms from seven residential compounds (see Figures 1.4 and 1.5) is not adequate for comprehensive intra-site or intra-compound comparison of all relevant variables. However, rich assemblages in most residential rooms variously revealed generalized habitation functions, indications of specialized storage in the form of numerous large jars and large floor pits, craft production tool kits and debris, and evidence for ritual activities such as sets of antler headdresses (P. Fish and Fish 2000). It is clear from a sample comparison that Marana Mound site rooms are marked by more extensive and intentionally placed floor assemblages when compared with those at several contemporary villages. Only one out of 17 fully excavated residential rooms at the Marana Mound site lacked an appreciable floor assemblage, while a much higher proportion of excavated rooms at contemporary Tucson Basin sites did not contain floor artifacts fitting these criteria (e.g., Bostwick 1987; Gregonis and Hartmann 2011; Hackbarth 1987; Slaughter and Roberts 1996; Wallace 1995). On the other hand, none of the Marana Mound site residential assemblages contained a full range of intact domestic equipment; for example, no room contained a metate of normal size and the sole intact metate recovered was atypically small. Instead, a variety of ceramic vessels and tools for the production of crafts such as pottery, shell jewelry, and agave and cotton fiber were commonly emphasized. The consistent richness and specialized nature of these floor assemblages at the mound site indicate distinctive room abandonment practices that were much less common in the surrounding community settlements and another contemporary site (P. Fish and Fish 2000).

Platform Mound Precinct

The compound wall surrounding the Marana platform mound is 75 cm in width and encloses 2,500 m². The walls of all mound structures are also more massive than walls in residential compounds. The platform mound was approximately 20 by 20 m in area, 3 m high, and located in the northwest corner of its compound. This placement is similar to Escalante Ruin (Doyel 1974) and fits Gregory's (1987: 194-195) category of western placement, one of two standard positions of mounds along the Salt and Gila rivers.

At approximately 20 by 20 m in area and 900 m³ in volume, the Marana platform mound is of small magnitude by Hohokam standards (see Doelle et al. 1995: 385-439; Minnis 1989: 278-279; Neitzel 1991: 206-211 for comparative estimates of mound volumes). Because Hohokam platform mounds are often enlarged by sequential construction stages, the relatively limited occupational span at Marana may be a factor in the mound's modest final area and volume. However, the Marana platform mound

volume is substantially larger than the initial stage of the late Sedentary period Gatlin mound west of Phoenix on the Gila River (Wasley 1960:248). It is comparable to Las Colinas Mound 8 in Phoenix after the third construction phase of Early Classic date (Gregory and Abbott 1988:10) and to the final size of the Early Classic period Mound B in Compound B at Casa Grande on the Gila River south of Phoenix (Doelle et al. 1995:393).

An intact pre-mound adobe room with a plastered floor approximately 2.25 m below the summit was incorporated into the internal mass of the platform mound at the time of its construction. An exploratory trench exposed a corner of this room with well-preserved walls extending up almost to the mound surface. The floor had sparse artifacts but was covered by a dense layer of white powdery ash. Current information is insufficient to determine if more than one room might be encompassed in mound fill, as is the case at the Late Classic period University Indian Ruin (Hayden 1957) and Martinez Hill (Gabel 1931) in the Tucson Basin and at some Tonto Basin (Craig and Clark 1994) and possibly San Pedro Valley (Lindauer 1992: 52) mound sites.

A massive retaining wall more than 1.5 m thick around the perimeter gave the mound a rectangular shape and vertical sides (see artist's reconstruction in Figure 1.6), and supported more than 3 million pounds of earthen fill; no internal cell walls have been identified. The outer retaining wall consists of two separate but conjoined constructions, each 75 cm in width. It is unclear whether this two-part construction sequence was planned at the onset of mound construction to facilitate drying of the first wall before the second was built. Alternatively, the second wall could have been added when it was determined that a single wall was insufficient to fully support the weight of fill.

Although the platform mound was a

relatively modest Hohokam monument, a community-wide effort would have been required to construct it. A local Tucson landscaping company (All Terrain Landscaping) estimated that it would require 1,500 man-days to hand-excavate and transport the mound's earthen fill from a large barrow pit located outside the compound walls. A series of adobe and plaster preparations attest to repeated refurbishing of the exterior surface of the mound's retaining wall. An upper wall atop the mound enclosed four rooms (Figure 1.6). The height of these rooms above the mound platform would have created a total vertical height of more than four meters. The rooms' flat tops would have provided a view over much of the surrounding basin as well as offering a towering stage for public communications (Leckman, Chapter 10, this volume).

The wall surrounding the top of the platform mound was of unusual width at 60 cm. The means of entry is unknown. It enclosed the four mound-top rooms in an inward-facing arrangement and served as the fourth, back wall

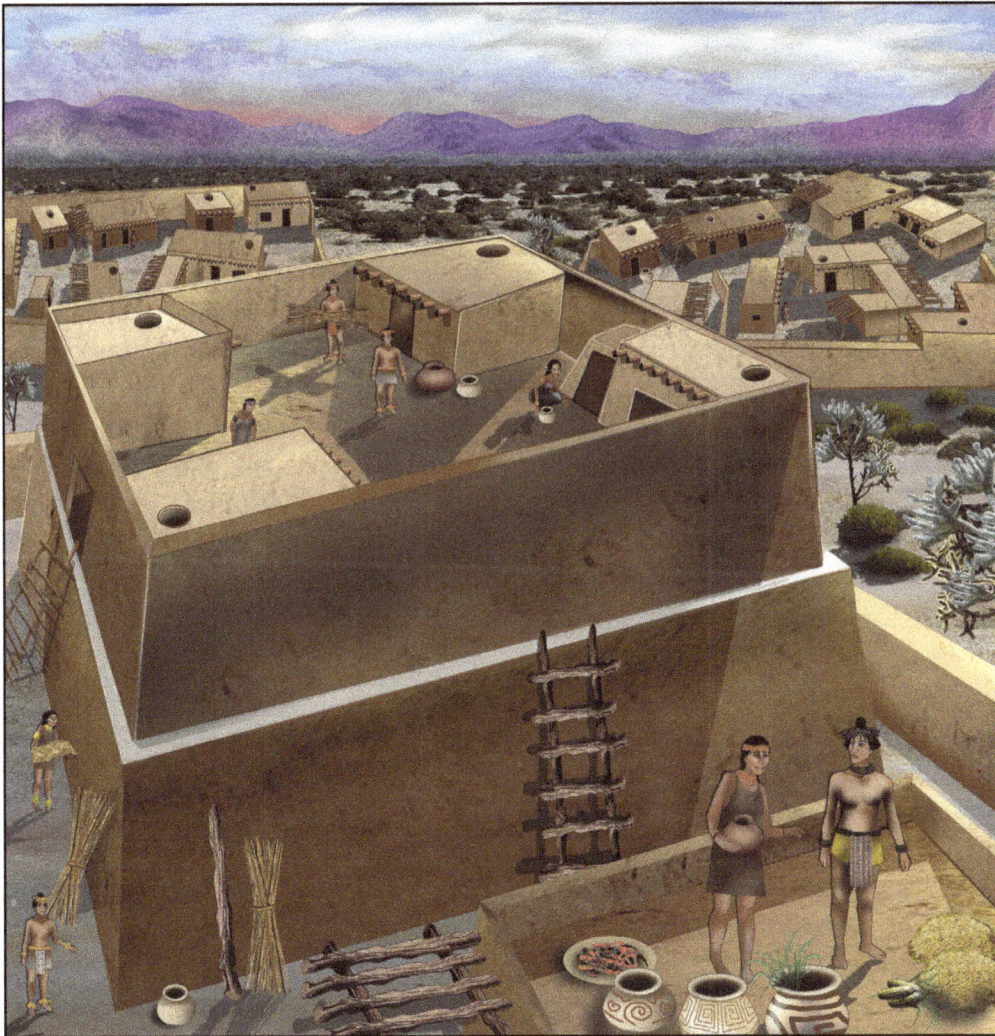

Figure 1.6. Artist Pamela Key's reconstruction of the Marana Platform Mound and nearby residential compounds (Courtesy of Pamela Key Studios, Los Angeles).

of each. The base of the wall enclosing the top rested on mound fill and was positioned just inside the exterior retaining walls below.

Current investigations have outlined rooms in the southwest and northwest corners of the mound summit and exposed wall segments of matching rooms in the other two heavily disturbed corners. Testing of presumably unroofed space between the rooms encountered no contemporary extramural features. However, excavations in post-occupation deposits of adobe melt in these summit areas and on the current slope of the mound have disclosed small hearths, abundant large faunal remains, and artifacts related to return visits after the cessation of mound use and occupation of the site.

The intact floor of the northwest mound-top room yielded only a few shell disk beads. In the partially damaged southwest room, the floor assemblage included a large Casa Grande Red-on-buff jar, a mountain sheep horn core, and a grooved axe placed in the hearth. Both rooms are within the size range of residential compound structures (19.9 m² and an estimated 32.2 m², respectively) and mirror placement of a clay-lined hearth, doorway, and post supports. As in the excavated residential compounds, structural wood includes fir and ponderosa pine. Although residence in these structures neither can be ruled out nor verified in any absolute sense, the trash mound associated with the platform mound precinct contained midden materials virtually indistinguishable from residential trash mounds throughout the site (Bayman 1994:91-92).

Two decidedly non-residential rooms were excavated to the south and east of the platform mound within its compound. The large room (38 m² floor area) to the east of the platform mound was intentionally decommissioned by removing all support timbers; a large segment of burned roofing rested on the floor but the overall heavy burning may have involved addi-

tional nonstructural fuels (Figure 1.7). A small ashy fire pit and concentrations of mostly rabbit remains suggest feasting or provisioning of the work party charged with dismantling the structure (Bayham and Grimstead, Chapter 6, this volume). Except for a reconstructable *Datura* effigy vessel, usable floor artifacts were absent. Over 170 small postholes in the southern half of the room suggest internal features such as looms, room dividers, or other furniture. The presence of a small hearth with a much larger one behind immediately in front of the door is an unusual feature among Marana Mound site structures.

The room south of the platform mound, with 102 m² of floor area, is among the largest Hohokam rooms ever excavated. The heavily plastered floor was 65 cm below ground surface and was distinguished by the numerous small sherds that were trampled into it. Its large hearth and two huge postholes follow the typical floor feature pattern for Marana rooms. Projectile points and small pieces of turquoise in the floor's numerous adobe mixing pits and the basalt boulder mortars positioned to brace the post in each of the massive postholes appear to represent ritual offerings or otherwise specialized inclusions. Similarly large structures within platform mound precincts were present at Escalante Ruin (Doyel 1974:132), also with small sherds trampled into the floor (Doyel 1974:91-92), and at Las Colinas (Gregory 1988:34).

A series of large, shallow, lightly oxidized hearths (Figure 1.8) were situated on the interior surface of the mound compound, just inside and in alignment with its southwest wall, to the southeast of the largest room. Superimposed hearths, interspersed with sequential re-plasterings of the interior compound surfaces, imply continuity in function. Similar specialized hearths were found within mound compounds also containing very large rooms at Escalante (Doyel 1974:132), and Las Colinas (Gregory

Figure 1.7. Room 9, Compound 9 (Platform Mound Compound). The hearth in the lower left (south) corner rests in roof-fall and is correlated with one of the bone concentrations discussed in Chapter 6. The faunal remains likely reflect provisioning or feasting during the decommissioning of this structure.

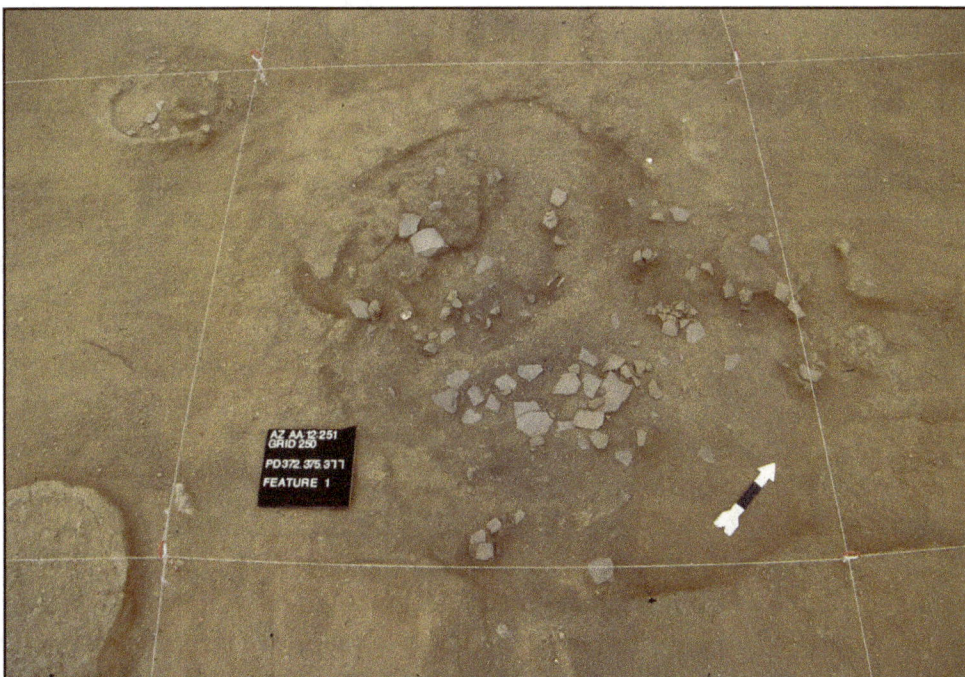

Figure 1.8. One of the large, shallow hearths with multiple, superimposed use episodes in the mound compound. The circular features to the left of the hearths are puddling pits used in plastering the massive compound wall and/or the plastered interior surface.

1988:34). Doyel (1991) has suggested that these hearths might have been used to encourage the fermentation of saguaro wine for annual ceremonies as recorded for the Tohono O'odham. Haury (1976:155) offered the same interpretation for 23 oxidized hearths under Mound 38 at Snaketown. Given that pits for saguaro wine fermentation are located inside O'odham round houses, an even more probable use of these Marana extramural thermal pits would have been to reheat feasting foods initially cooked elsewhere. A variety of food remains in them and cobble firedogs in one of the large, shallow hearths are compatible with such a function.

CONCLUSIONS PENDING FUTURE ANALYSES

The Marana Mound site stands out from other contemporary settlements in its community in a variety of ways. It is the largest and one of the few with compound architecture. It produced almost the only distant trade wares and, along with three other larger sites, significantly more decorated pottery. A neutron activation sourcing study suggested that these largest sites participated in a common ceramic exchange network that differed from the acquisition patterns and ceramic sources of other community settlements (Harry 1997, 2003). Marana Mound site residential floor assemblages on the whole are distinctive in the number and variety of items, and the high frequency of artifacts linked to craft production and personal ornamentation (P. Fish and Fish 2000). Comparison of trash mound contents with those at other settlements showed greater consumption and production of exotic items such as obsidian and shell and tools associated with agave production and crafts (e.g. Bayman 1994, 1995, 1996a). Imported items and manufacturing activities were concentrated at the mound site compared to other settlements.

The scale of exotic materials and craft production at the Marana Mound site does not indicate an advanced degree of specialization according to current conceptualizations. However, the concentration of these items and activities at the center help elucidate the political economy of the community and the competitive strategies of resident groups even though true prestige goods are not evident. Higher status individuals may not have directly or fully controlled the production, consumption, and redistribution of valued goods, but they undoubtedly manipulated their circulation through use in integrative rituals, intra-community exchange, and the creation of social obligations.

Internal differentiation within the community center, on the other hand, is much less readily apparent. An obvious model for the spatial partitioning of the site according to residential group status would be the location of compounds nearer and more distant from the platform mound. None of the trash mound measures for higher value and exotic items, craft manufacture, basic ceramic shapes and sizes, and gross designs (Bayman 1994; Bubemeyer 1993; Doolittle 1992) revealed substantial patterned inequalities in consumption and production between near and distant compounds, or among other site segments. Analyses of these broad material categories produced parallel results, but do not begin to exhaust potential variation related to social distinctions and competitive strategies.

ORGANIZATION OF THE VOLUME

The studies in this volume are relevant to four major topical themes including depositional consequences of artifact discard (Chapter 2, Beck and Roos), architectural investment and spatial organization of the mound site (Chapter 3, Howell and Homburg; Chapter 4, Harris;

and Chapter 10, Leckman), food production and consumption (Chapter 5, Hansen-Speer; Chapter 6, Bayham and Grimstead), and craft economies (Chapter 7, Holeman; Chapter 8, Harry and others; Chapter 9, Boley). Although Chapter 10 by Phillip Leckman is certainly relevant to the second theme, it is explicitly focused on functions of the platform mound and its probable role in integrating the larger community.

Chapter 2

From Households to Middens: Refuse Deposition Patterns in Two Settlements

Margaret E. Beck
Christopher Roos

INTRODUCTION

We describe here the movement of trash from source locations to middens, comparing ethnoarchaeological patterns of midden placement and use to an archaeological case. During the 2001 field season of the Kalinga Ethnoarchaeological Project in the Phillipines, the senior author observed refuse flow from households in the village of Dalupa and outlined some principles of midden catchment and accumulation (Beck 2003; Beck and Hill 2004, 2005). We use these midden formation principles here to better understand trash mounds at the Marana Platform Mound site (AZ AA:12:251[ASM]) in the northern Tucson Basin. Our work supports previous attempts to link midden deposits with their source households at AZ AA:12:251 (ASM) and other sites within the Marana Community so that midden artifacts can be used in comparing households or other social groups (Bayman 1994, 1995, 1996b).

Although not all of the specifics of the Kalinga model can be applied, some interesting patterns emerge through the comparison. Dalupa residents follow least-cost principles in their use of existing middens. Marana residents probably did as well. Factors controlling the placement of these middens differ between Kalinga and Hohokam settlements, however. These factors are probably the same factors affecting village layout and residence patterns and may include social structure, the nature of the cooperative economic groups, and cultural norms.

We start by describing the Kalinga research and principles of midden formation and placement in Dalupa. We then shift to Hohokam sites in central and southern Arizona, briefly describing evidence for Preclassic Hohokam community structure (prior to A.D. 1150) and trash disposal before addressing the Early Classic period Marana Platform Mound site (A.D. 1150-1300). We conclude by evaluating differences in ceramic accumulation between Kalinga and Hohokam middens.

MIDDEN FORMATION: AN ETHNOARCHAEOLOGICAL PERSPECTIVE

The research described here is part of a larger study of midden formation and midden ceramic assemblage formation (Beck 2003), conducted as part of the Kalinga Ethnoarchaeological Project (KEP). The study community was Dalupa, a village within the Pasil Municipality, Kalinga Province, the Philippines, located at approximately 17° 23' N latitude and 121° 11' E longitude in the Central Cordillera region of northern Luzon (Figure 2.1). The Kalinga in the Pasil Municipality have been studied by archaeologists since 1973, when William Longacre initiated the KEP (Longacre 1974,

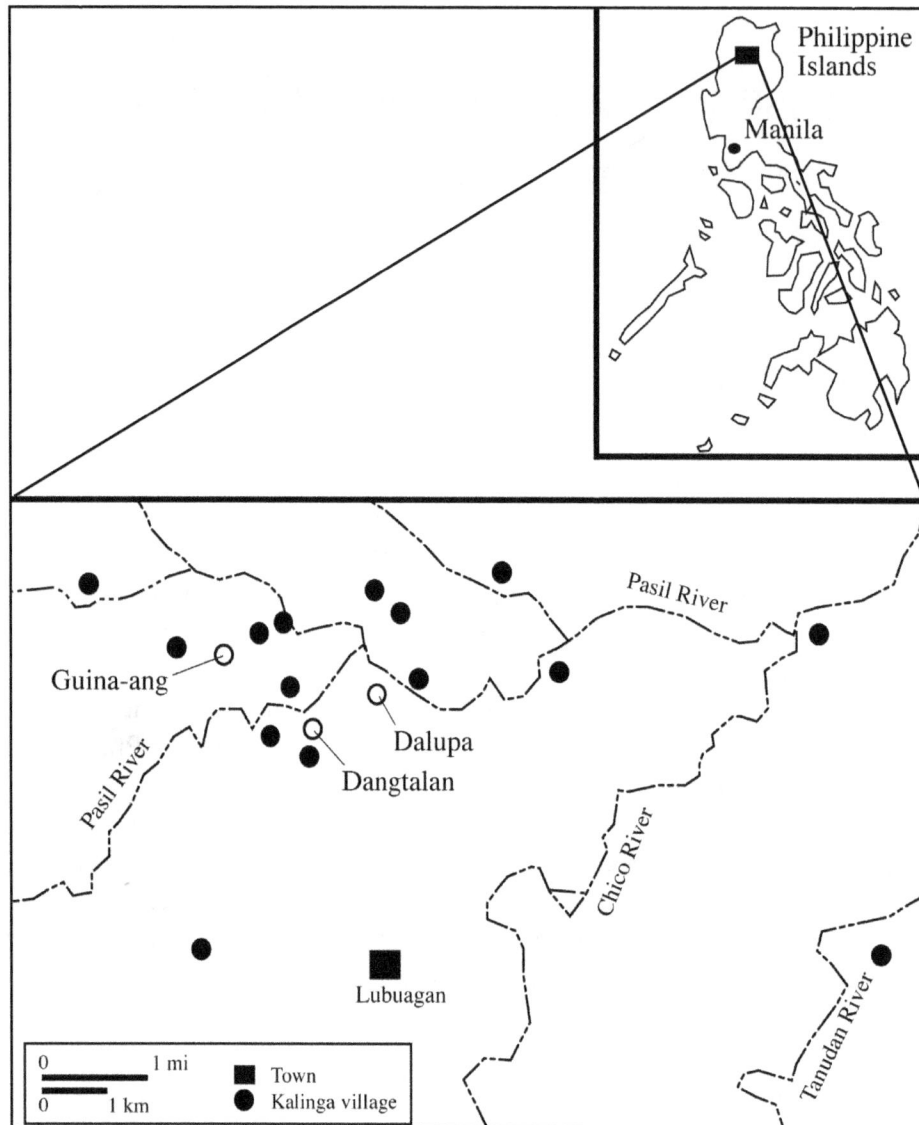

Figure 2.1. The Dalupa study area.

1981; Longacre and Skibo 1994). Extensive ethnoarchaeological research has been conducted in Dalupa by Miriam Stark (Longacre and Stark 1992; Stark 1991a, 1991b, 1992, 1993, 1994, 1995, 1999; Stark and Longacre 1993; Stark et al. 2000).

The Study Community

Dalupa's residential area (Figure 2.2) covers roughly 10 acres on a steep mountain face approximately 600 m above sea level. Artificial terraces provide the only flat surfaces for occupation and agriculture. Motor vehicles cannot be driven within Dalupa, or even to Dalupa, but must stop in the community of Ableg, about 1 km away.

Residents are primarily subsistence farmers, cultivating rice and vegetables and keeping domestic animals such as water buffalo, pigs, dogs, and chickens. In 2001, Dalupa had 380 residents in 71 houses. Typically each house

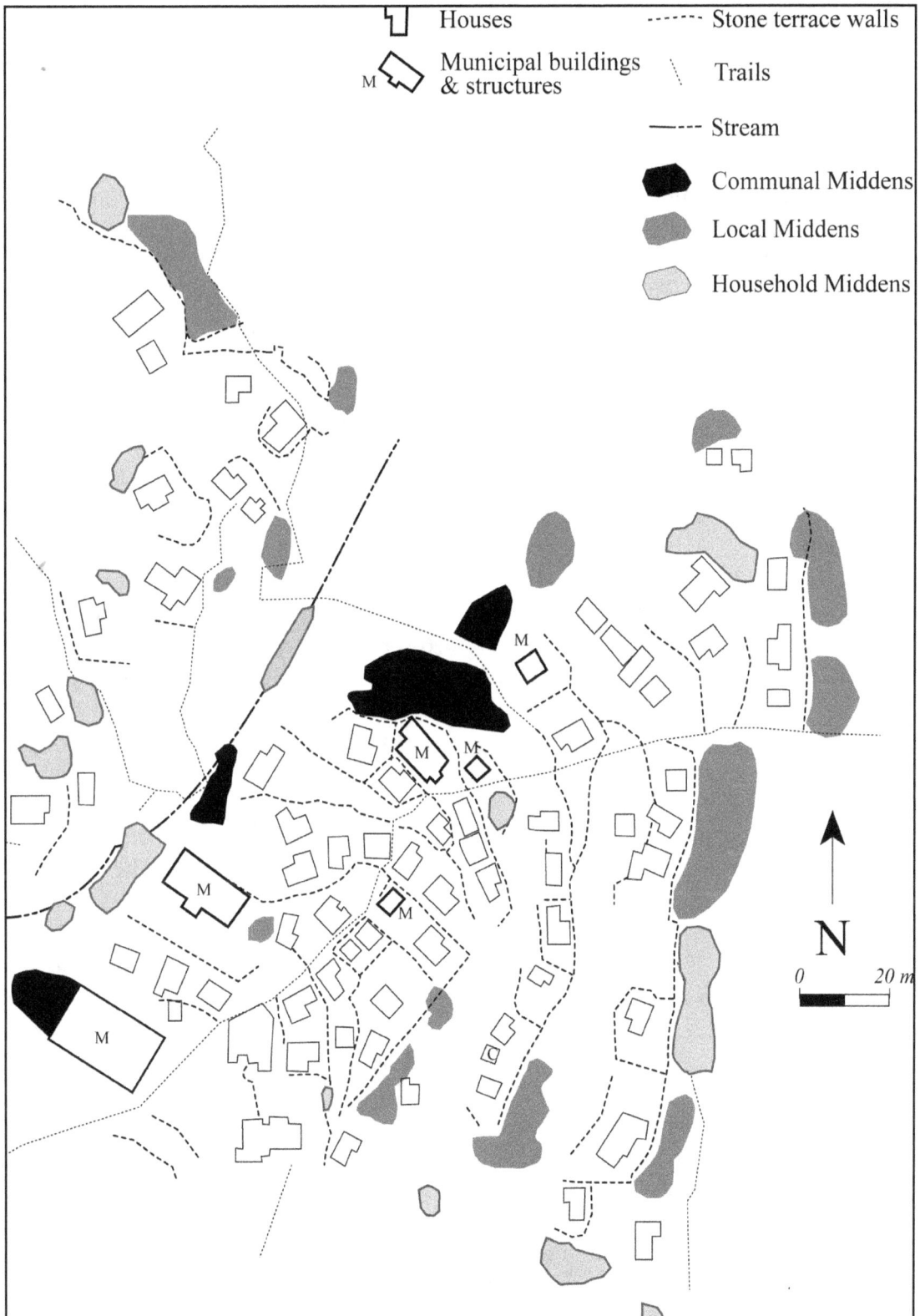

Houses
Municipal buildings
M   & structures
Stone terrace walls
Trails
Stream
Communal Middens
Local Middens
Household Middens

N
0   20 m

Figure 2.2. Dalupa in 2001.

structure was occupied by a nuclear family, perhaps with one or more extended family members. The number of people living in a house ranged from 1 to 12, with an average of 5.4 and a median of 5. In the Kalinga area, people coresiding in a single house are considered to be a household (Takaki 1977:56) and cooperate in the basic household activities of production, distribution, transmission, and reproduction (Wilk and Netting 1984).

Each house sits on a house lot, partially defined by terrace edges and often further marked with a low rock border or bamboo fence. Barriers between house lots are not substantial and people frequently walk through the yards of other homeowners. Almost all of the houses are set on a wooden platform mounted on stilts about 1.5 to 2 m above the ground. The space beneath the house platform is used to store large objects such as storage jars for wine. Domestic animals often sleep here as well.

Household waste is usually collected in a metal can or other container that is periodically carried to the midden and emptied. A few activities, such as winnowing rice in a basket to remove the chaff, produce so much debris that they may be conducted over the midden. Relatively large discarded objects, such as broken ceramic vessels, may be carried directly to a midden.

Midden Identification and Description

A midden is an "occupation deposit relatively rich in refuse. . . and with evidence for the deliberate and sequential accumulation of refuse at one location" (Needham and Spence 1997:80). This definition is similar to Wilson's (1994:44) "secondary refuse aggregate" or "localized, high-density deposit," which appears with formalized deposition. For Needham and Spence, formality is demonstrated by repeated use of the same feature for secondary discard. "In situ deposits are essential to the confident interpretation of [an archaeological] midden, since it requires evidence. . . of episodic dumping" (Needham and Spence 1997:80).

There were 32 active middens in Dalupa in 2001 (Beck and Hill 2004, 2005). These covered an estimated 10 percent of the residential area. KEP researchers were allowed to map and record 27 (84 percent) of the active middens. We interviewed 70 of the 71 households in Dalupa each week, asking what they discarded the previous day and where they put it. Discard locations were described in terms of named landmarks, and we could match most responses to defined middens. As a result, we have data on which middens each household used over the course of the project.

Dalupa households use between one and three middens for disposal of daily household waste. Of 69 households with sufficient data, 41 (61 percent) report use of one midden. Another 24 households (35 percent) apparently use two middens, and the remaining four households (6 percent) distribute their trash among three middens. Even when using multiple middens, households tend to concentrate their refuse in one midden, referred to here as the primary midden for that household. The primary midden was used in an average of 90 percent of discard episodes (range 43 to 100 percent; median 94 percent).

Middens can be categorized as household, local, or communal middens based on the number of contributing households. Household middens (n = 11) receive trash from a single household. As noted above, this does not guarantee that all of that household's trash is deposited in that household midden. Local middens (n = 15) receive contributions from two to five households, and communal (n = 4) middens collect refuse from six or more households (8 to 19 in the Dalupa sample). No household informant reported contributing to two active middens. The number of contributing households has a strong linear relationship with the number of contributing people ($r^2 = 0.96$), indicating that the number of contributing households is an appropriate way to classify intensity of midden use.

Households generally follow least-cost principles and use the midden closest to them. The mean distance to a communal midden is 35 m, compared to 11 m for local middens and 7 m for household middens. These differences are statistically significant, according to an ANOVA test for distance by midden type ($F = 32.381$; $df = 3,104$; $p < .0001$). Settlement density and activity area location are important factors affecting how many households share a midden and how far residents must carry their trash. Households on the edges of residential areas or situated next to the terrace edges can dispose of their trash around their house or in nearby unoccupied lots, creating household or local middens. Local middens tend to cluster around shared work areas. Six of the fifteen local middens (40 percent) are adjacent to water faucets, which serve as communal work areas for bathing and washing activities. Residents in densely occupied areas are forced to carry trash farther to one of the communal middens. Communal middens surround the densest areas of Dalupa and are also directly associated with a water faucet or another shared use space.

Similar spatial patterning of single and multiple-household extramural middens has been inferred in archaeological settings (Howard 2000:191). Different midden types might be distinguished archaeologically based on deposit size. In Dalupa, median values for area (68, 140, and 153 m²) and density (6.8, 8.5, and 15.6 artifacts per m²) increase with increasing numbers of contributing households. When the two variables are plotted against each other (Figure 2.3), middens tend to cluster by type. Artifact richness may also help distinguish

types. Artifact classes numbering 266 were defined for the diverse modern material culture in the Kalinga middens, with up to 49 classes in any individual midden (Beck 2003: Tables 3.1, 3.5-3.8). The median number of artifact classes increases with increasing numbers of contributing households, although there is considerable overlap in the distributions (Figure 2.4).

Household middens are best suited for studies of households and usually provide good samples of domestic refuse. Of the eleven household middens in Dalupa in 2001, nine were primary middens. The percentage of discard episodes ranged from 8 to 100 percent, with a mean of 82 percent and a median of 94 percent. A household midden should be archaeologically recognizable because of its relatively small size and its status as the closest midden for only one household.

General Principles

Two characteristics of midden composition and use in Dalupa may be applied to the interpretation of ancient archaeological sites. First, household, local, and communal middens exhibit differences in area, surface artifact density, and artifact richness. All three of these variables tend to increase with increasing numbers of contributors. Although the nature of the differences is probably a broader pattern, the exact values may depend on the specifics of local material consumption, and values from Dalupa may not be comparable to middens in other settings.

Second, Dalupa residents follow least-cost principles in their use of existing middens, allowing connections between structures and activity areas to the nearest midden. Archaeologists should be able to reconstruct sources of midden refuse if contemporaneous features can be identified.

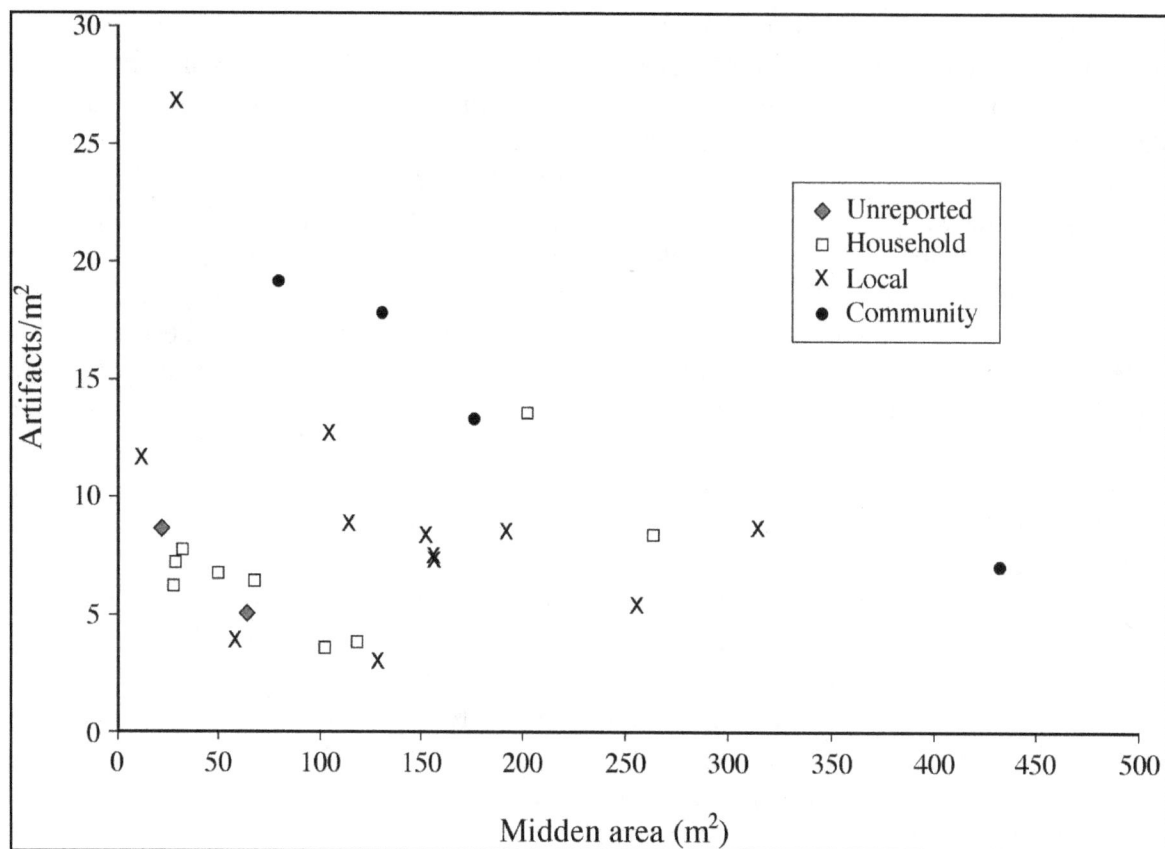

Figure 2.3. Area and artifact density by midden type.

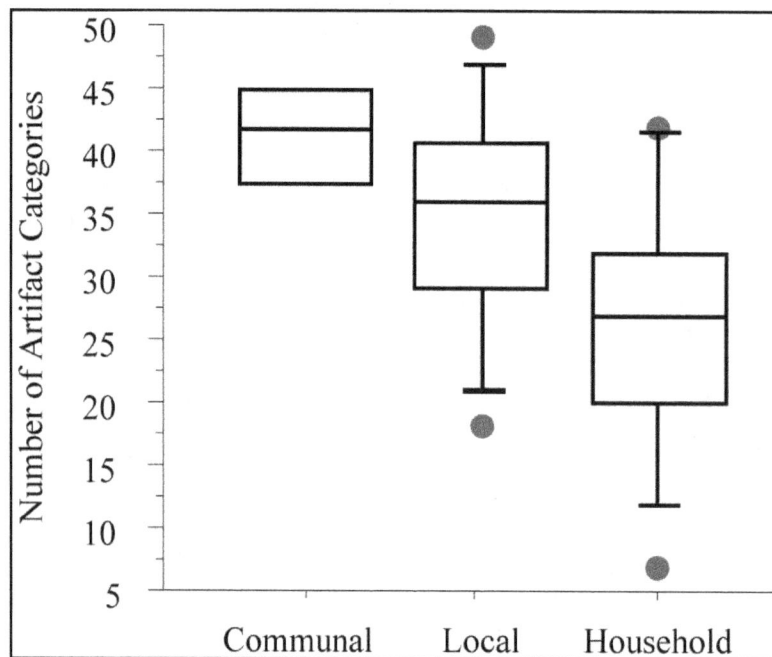

Figure 2.4. Artifact richness by midden type.

HOHOKAM MIDDENS: THE PRECLASSIC PERIOD

Previous authors (Gregory 1984; Henderson 1987a; Howard 1985, 2000; Wilcox et al. 1981) have described the general structure of Preclassic Hohokam settlements, predating roughly A.D. 1100. Defined units are:

1. the domestic unit or individual domestic structure, presumably housing a single nuclear family. The correlate to this in the Kalinga region is a square or rectangular structure, also housing a single nuclear family.

2. the house cluster made of several contemporaneous pithouses with entries opening on to a common courtyard area. Facilities such as activity areas, middens, and burial areas may be associated with the house clusters. Middens associated with house clusters would be considered local middens under the Dalupa model.

3. the village segment made of several house clusters. Henderson (1987a:10) argues that facilities are usually shared on the level of the village segment rather than the house cluster. In effect, she is arguing for a tendency toward communal rather than local middens.

4. the community or village made of "multiple village segments along with key communal features or structures such as ball courts, platform mounds, or plazas" (Henderson 1987a:13).

One apparent difference between Preclassic Hohokam communities and Dalupa is a greater tendency among the Hohokam to share middens regardless of settlement density. House clusters, for example, seem to share local middens despite adequate space for multiple household middens. Although it is possible that small household middens are not being identified archaeologically, one recently excavated hamlet supports the idea of more inclusive midden sharing. At AZ U:11:252 (ASM) near Queen Creek in Pinal County, Arizona (Figure 2.5; Wegener et al. 2002: See Figure 2.7), one communal midden seems to have been shared by two house clusters. The size of this midden, which extended to a depth of 1.25 m in the center, suggests that it was the primary midden for most or all of the households at the site. Distances to the midden from house entryways ranged from 5 to 21 m (with a mean of 12 and median of 11). Thus, most residents would have carried trash for distances that are generally comparable to distances to local and communal middens in Dalupa.

What accounts for these differences in midden placement and catchment? One possible explanation is different levels of integration between individual residences. The basic economic unit, the household, probably includes multiple house structures with different functions. Community structure for the Preclassic Hohokam has been argued to reflect social organization and descent rules, with village segments representing lineages (Henderson 1987a,b; Rice 1987a,b). Households may be physically and economically integrated along kinship lines, and residents of house clusters or village segments may have seen themselves as a cooperating unit of production.

In contrast, the residents of a single structure in Dalupa seem to be more independent from the residents of other structures. The primary unit is the individual house, symbolized by the physical delineation of house lots. Although there is a tendency for family members to live close together, residence within Dalupa is not rigidly organized by kinship (Beck and Hill 2004). Kinship is bilateral among the Kalinga (Dozier 1966), and kinship groups are somewhat fluid over time.

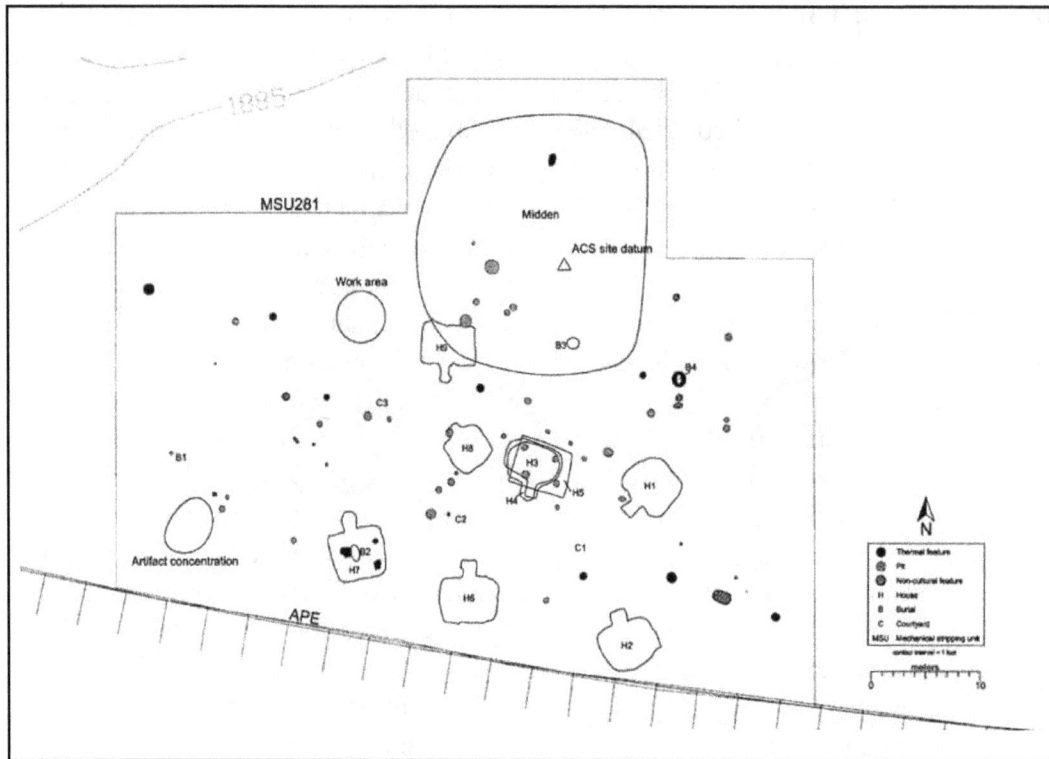

Figure 2.5. AZ U:11:252 (ASM) (after Wegener et al. 2002: Figure 7).

HOHOKAM MIDDENS AT AZ AA:12:251(ASM): THE CLASSIC PERIOD

At some point in the Preclassic to Classic transition, residential architecture shifted away from pithouses and towards above-ground adobe structures, often enclosed within walled residential compounds. Compound architecture appears at the Marana Platform Mound site (AZ AA:12:251), occupied during the Early Classic period (A.D. 1150-1300). As described by P. Fish and Fish (2000:250-252), the site covers an area of at least 1.5 by 0.5 km and has about 35 to 40 adobe compounds enclosing residential and other structures. Each compound may enclose about 20 rooms, based on size and melted adobe concentrations, and could have been occupied by 30 to 40 people. Subdivisions of each compound might reflect individual households comprised of multiple

buildings. At least 80 trash mounds are visible on the surface of the site (Bayman and Sanchez 1998:80).

Groups of structures have a more diffuse distribution at AZ AA:12:251(ASM) than in Dalupa. The residential area of the site is approximately 750,000 m² compared to Dalupa's 40,800 m², making it 18 times as large. The population estimate is only two or three times as large.

At the Marana Platform Mound site, the spacing of trash mounds suggests that each compound has its own mound or group of mounds (Figure 2.6). Richness values are similar between the 16 mounds with relevant data (Roos 2002), supporting the notion that the catchment zones may be similar. The mounds around a given compound might be defined as household or local middens, depending upon the economic and social integration of

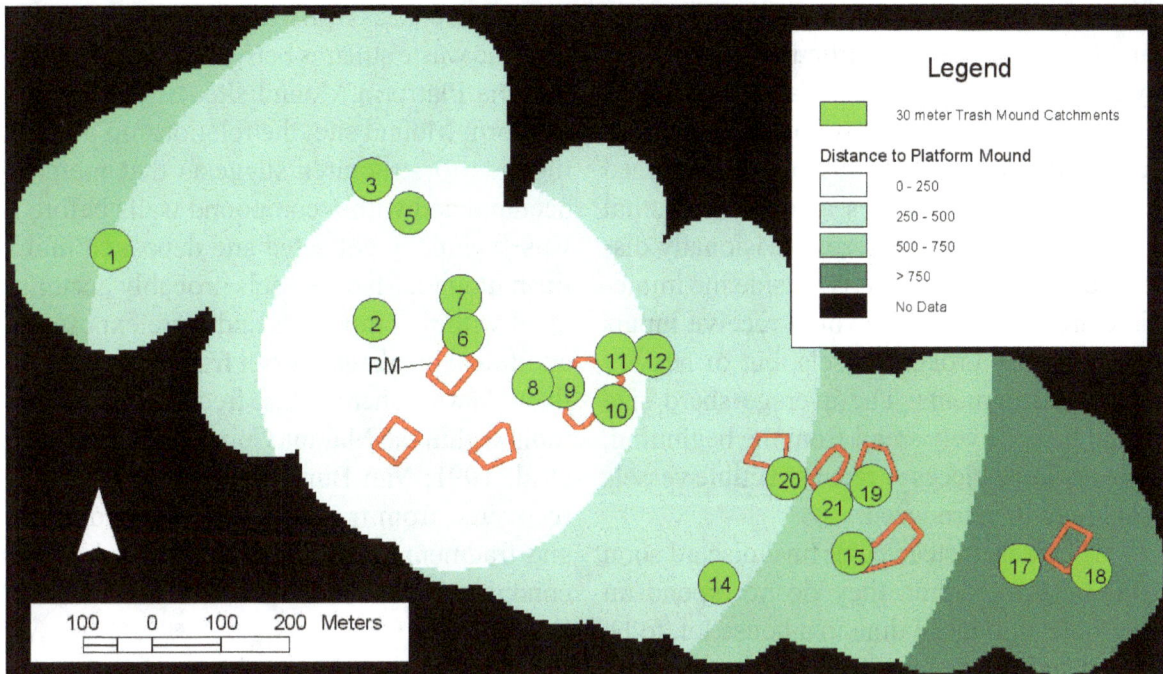

Figure 2.6. Placement of tested trash mounds at AZ AA:12:251 (ASM).

people and structures within the compound and whether different mounds for a given compound have different contributing households within the compound. At 40 people per compound, the number of people contributing to the compound midden or middens would be the equivalent of eight Dalupa households.

Because many trash mounds accumulate in borrow pits from compound construction, final discard location may be more determined by the history of construction activities than by preferred settlement layout and convenience for residents (Roos 2002). This probably serves to increase distances between these middens and activity areas. For example, one trash mound (TMA) within a borrow pit is located about 10 m from the wall of Compound 5. We do not know the path distance from TMA to structures and other activity areas within Compound 5, but it is probably farther than 10 m. If transport distance became too large, perhaps over 35 m, one would expect temporary refuse accumula-

tions within the compound that would be carried out periodically to the trash mound.

Differences in use of provisional discard would also produce visible differences in refuse accumulation between Dalupa and the Marana Platform Mound site. Ceramic reuse was more intense at Marana than Dalupa, as discussed below, so there may have been considerable numbers of vessels in provisional discard within the compound.

CERAMIC ACCUMULATION PATTERNS

Ceramic discard behavior affects the range of sherd sizes possible in various contexts at the time of deposition. There are two competing models for initial ceramic discard: (1) provisional discard of vessels and fragments in house lots with final discard after some period of time and (2) final discard of vessels at or near the time of breakage. While these models are not mutually exclusive, one mode of disposal might predominate in a particular site or activity area or with certain materials.

Provisional discard of ceramics is described by Deal (1985, 1998), who examined ceramic discard practices among the Txeltal Maya. If most vessels were provisionally discarded, then accumulations outside the immediate area of the house would receive inputs not of freshly broken vessels, but of heavily damaged fragments. The average sherd size would be relatively small from the beginning, and very large pieces or reconstructible vessels would not be introduced.

If vessels instead enter final discard soon after breakage, then they do not spend an indefinite amount of time in a house lot, to be kicked and stepped on. They are sent, in their complete or partial state, directly to a final secondary deposit. Trash accumulations therefore receive inputs of large sherds or even partial or whole vessels.

Rapid final ceramic discard predominated during 2001 in Dalupa (Beck 2003; Beck and Hill 2005). Unsystematic observation of cleanup after vessel breakage suggests that most small sherds from the breakage episode itself do not reach middens, particularly communal middens. Debris from sweeping activities is instead deposited nearby, off residential terraces and into surrounding vegetation. Most damaged vessels go directly to middens as large fragments or reconstructible vessels, and reconstructible vessels were occasionally observed on midden surfaces. The proportion of provisional discard to immediate final discard is probably related to overall vessel reuse patterns. In Dalupa, most completely broken vessels are not reused, but discarded at the time of breakage (see Beck and Hill 2005). Reuse rates of vessels with cracks or other damage are relatively modest. Only one-third of damaged vessels in 2001 were saved for potential reuse and placed in provisional discard.

There are significant differences in ceramic waste streams between Dalupa and the Marana Platform Mound site. At the Marana Platform Mound site, the relationship of trash mounds to structures suggests that material accumulated within compound walls before it was eventually collected and deposited into a trash mound. Many vessels probably accumulated within compounds and were exposed to additional breakage. Vessel fragments, primarily plain ware sherds, were frequently reused as tools within the Marana Community (Sullivan et al. 1991; Van Buren et al. 1992). Vessels recovered from trash mounds are incomplete and fragmented and may have arrived in that condition (Roos 2002; Sullivan et al. 1991; Van Buren et al. 1992).

Ideally, an archaeologist could distinguish between these two different modes of ceramic accumulation in middens. The resulting deposits do not look that different, unfortunately. In the following comparison of midden deposits between the two communities, we focus on one variable: artifact size. Significant provisional discard of ceramic vessels does not lead to smaller sherd sizes in midden deposits, contradicting authors who argue that small sherd size is an indication of secondary refuse (e.g., Ruscavage 1992a,b).

Artifact Size and Deposit Transformation

Site formation processes, including those disturbing deposited material, have been outlined and studied by Schiffer (1972, 1987; see also Wood and Johnson 1978). Considerable work has been devoted to individual postdepositional processes, including human and nonhuman trampling (Gifford-Gonzalez et al. 1985; Nielsen 1991), faunal turbation (Bocek 1986, 1992; Limbrey 1975:315 in Schiffer 1987:269), children's play (Hammond and Hammond 1981; Wilk and Schiffer 1979), and scavenging (Schlanger 1990). These studies have shown that disturbance is often linked with artifact damage and vertical and/or horizontal displacement, perhaps producing stratigraphic mixing and combining unrelated materials. The location of refitting pieces, sherd size, density, and abrasion or other damage have been used to determine the extent of deposit transformation, but sherd size appears to have a strong correlation with these other variables, and is the most easily recorded (Craig and Wallace 1992; Wallace et al. 1992). Artifact size is affected by a variety of formation processes (Schiffer 1987:267-269). In the approach used here, these processes are grouped as "transformation," and it is assumed that increasing levels of transformation or disturbance will reduce overall sherd size.

Sherd size was originally recorded as a way to distinguish between primary and secondary refuse (Bradley and Fulford 1980). Subsequent related applications include the evaluation of exposure and disturbance (Heidke 1995; Mills 1991; Nielsen 1993; Roos 2002; Wallace 1986a,b) and the identification of secondary refuse used as fill (Ruscavage 1992a, 1992b). Size has been measured as individual or mean weight (Bradley and Fulford 1980; Mills 1991; Nielsen 1993; Ruscavage 1992a,b), area as determined with a template (Heidke 1995; Wallace 1986a,b) or by screening (Roos 2002), or maximum length (Nielsen 1991). Sherd density is also frequently used as evidence of depositional history (Heidke 1995; Ruscavage 1992a,b; Seymour and Schiffer 1987:567; Wallace 1986a,b).

The template method groups sherds into one of four size classes: (1) < 5 cm^2, (2) 5-16 cm^2, (3) 16-49 cm^2, and (4) > 49 cm^2. These size classes have been used in previous studies (Heidke 1995; Wallace 1986a, 1986b). Size 1 sherds may be the most useful for identifying heavily transformed assemblages. After extended transformation, "[e]ventually a stable [sherd] size where no further breakage occurs would be reached. This value would be a function of the microstructure of the paste, sherd thickness and curvature, and the nature (weight and contact surface) of the trampling agent" (Nielsen 1991:493). For most non-industrial, open-fired ceramics, this stable sherd size is probably in the Size 1 range (< 5 cm^2). Trampled sherds should have a unimodal distribution "with the mode lower than 30 mm" (Nielsen 1991:495). The most heavily trampled (and transformed) assemblages will be weighted most heavily towards sherds < 5 cm^2, as indicated by Nielsen (1991: See Figures 2.3-2.6).

The 3,001 midden sherds recovered from surface collections and excavations in Dalupa and 4,290 sherds from the Preclassic Hohokam trash mound (Feature 19) at AZ U:11:252(ASM) were sorted into the above size classes using the template method (Beck 2003:217-219, 234). Sherds from 19 trash mounds at the Marana Platform Mound site were screened through a series of nested screens (Roos 2002). Sherds that passed through the smallest (quarter-inch) screen were not counted. The closest size class at Marana to Size 1 is actually 0.4 to 6.4 cm^2 and consists of sherds recovered between the quarter-inch to half-inch and half-inch to 1-inch screens. Sherds that passed through the 1-inch (2.5 cm) hole should be 6.4 cm^2 or smaller.

Figure 2.7 shows the percentages of very small sherds (sherds under 5 cm^2) in trash deposits at Dalupa, Marana, and AZ U:11:252(ASM). On the right side of the graph, towards 100 percent, deposits are dominated by very small sherds. Axel Nielsen argues this size distribution is characteristic of "intensively occupied midden areas, sheet trash, repeatedly redeposited trash, and surface material in general" (Nielsen 1993:163). Toward the left, there are increasing numbers of larger sherds, suggesting less disturbance.

Marana Platform Mound site middens, and at least some Dalupa middens, are domi-

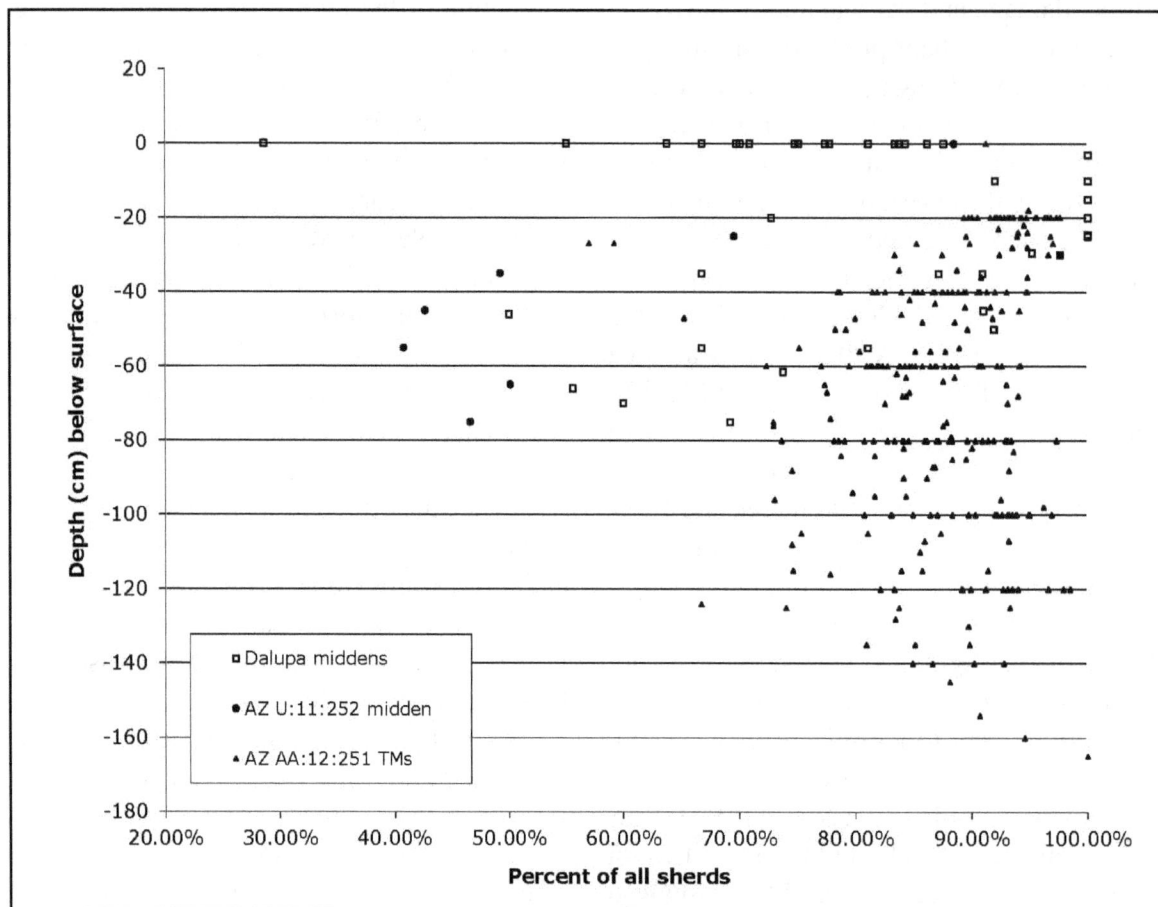

Figure 2.7. Very small sherds in three midden contexts.

nated by very small sherds. Post-depositional disturbance erases the difference one would expect between middens in the two communities on the basis of differences in ceramic reuse patterns and provisional discard. Dalupa middens accumulate slowly and are very heavily disturbed by domestic animals, which outnumber people in this community, and by children. Slow accumulation, possibly from periodic cleaning of shared compound space and provisional discard locales, and disturbance by children and adults may have characterized Marana midden accumulation, as well (Roos 2002). The sherd size data alone do not indicate whether breakage occurs within the midden, or if vessels are heavily damaged before reaching the midden.

The Preclassic midden from AZ U:11:252(ASM) has larger sherds, which suggests several possible differences in midden accumulation. First, in the absence of temporary refuse piles within compounds, ceramics might have reached the midden more quickly. Second, more people may have contributed to this midden, so burial would have been faster, protecting sherds from disturbance. Rapid accumulation is consistent with the hypothesis that this midden was the primary midden for the entire community.

CONCLUSIONS

We draw the following conclusions from our midden analyses:

1. Trash mounds at the Marana Platform Mound site appear to belong to individual compounds, as suggested in earlier studies (Bayman 1994:44; P. Fish and Fish 2000; Fish et al. 1992b). Spatial proximity can be used in a general way to link midden deposits with their sources.

On a cautionary note, a sampling problem may remain. Even household middens in Dalupa do not receive all of the trash from that household. The refuse deposited elsewhere is probably not a random sample but is weighted more heavily toward certain artifact classes. For example, in Dalupa, vessel types frequently transported away from the house, such as water jars and cooking jars that are washed frequently, are more likely to be broken and discarded away from the house and the household's primary midden (Beck and Hill 2005). Not all waste streams may terminate in middens; hazardous materials may never reach the midden but may be immediately deposited elsewhere for safety reasons, as seen in Mesoamerica with obsidian debris (Clark 1991; Hayden and Cannon 1983). The under-representation of certain materials or artifact types should be considered when interpreting artifact frequencies.

2. Small sherd size indicates heavy disturbance, but this disturbance could affect sherds before or after they reach final discard. Middens in village settings receive enough disturbance to be dominated by small sherds, even if reconstructible vessels are deposited directly into middens. The size of the contributing social unit, however, may be an important factor affecting the rate of refuse accumulation and, by extension,

opportunities for post-depositional transformation of midden deposits. Despite probable differences in reuse and provisional discard, sherd size from household and local middens from Dalupa and Marana suggest relatively slow rates of accumulation. In contrast, the communal middens of Preclassic Hohokam village segments have a greater "social" catchment and associated faster rates of accumulation, which reduce opportunities for post-depositional transformation.

3. Simple least-cost principles predict use of existing middens but may not always accurately predict midden placement, since historical factors of community development produce different spatial patterns of refuse disposal. However, midden placement may provide information about village layout, integration between structures, and the use of residential space. Additionally, spatial variation of Hohokam middens in borrow pits is contingent upon, but chronologically related to local construction histories. Coupled investigation of construction history and midden formation histories surrounding particular compounds may provide opportunities for chronological sub-divisions of occupation of the Marana Platform Mound village and elaboration on the existing political economic story (Bayman 1994, 1995, 1996b; P. Fish and Fish 2000; Harry and Bayman 2000).

The model of midden classification from the Dalupa case study sheds further light on the social changes associated with the Hohokam Preclassic to Classic period transition. The Classic period shift from communal to house-hold and local midden accumulation mirrors architectural shifts from multi-household court-yard groups and village segments to enclosed, household focused compound units. Although the assemblage contents of Marana Platform Mound village middens do not support substantial interhousehold economic differences (Bayman 1994, 1995, 1996b), the shift to more restricted architectural forms and smaller social units contributing to middens reinforces the suggestion that sweeping social changes accompanied the Preclassic to Classic period transition (Crown and Fish 1996).

Chapter 3

Analysis of Adobe Architecture at the Marana Platform Mound Site

R. Emerson Howell
Jeffrey A. Homburg

INTRODUCTION

Archaeological research conducted at the Marana Platform Mound site over the past several years provided a unique opportunity to investigate many architectural structures across the site. Numerous adobe structures were tested to measure several engineering properties, such as caliche content, strength, bulk density, and organic matter. The results of this study are reported here.

With a few noteworthy exceptions (Burton et al. 1972; Hovezak 1988; Littmann 1967; Wilcox and Shenk 1977), archaeologists in the Southwest rarely study the composition and engineering properties of adobe, and even fewer study adobe in the context of social implications. Most previous adobe studies have been done to aid in preserving, conserving, or restoring adobe. Only a few (Alder 2003; Spensley 2004) have identified recipes for differentiating adobe use in different contexts.

Our study aims to assess adobe compositional variability in terms of construction technology, architectural integrity, and possible social implications of differential labor investment requirements for processing adobe. This involves searching for archaeological evidence of "vertical differentiation in the Marana Community [that] could have been generated in more than one way" (Fish et al.

1992b:39). Vertical differentiation could have been manifested in competition and differential labor investment for different resources, such as caliche. To accomplish this, adobe composition at the Marana site was characterized to determine various engineering properties, focusing on $CaCO_3$, but also including tests of bulk density, organic matter content, and strength of adobe relative to on- and off-site soils. We will compare caliche content in public or communal contexts at Marana (i.e., the platform mound compound), the presumed center of social power, with that of residential compounds that may reflect lower status contexts. Inhabitants or organizers of construction efforts at the platform mound compound must have had greater access to labor resources and therefore might have used more $CaCO_3$ in constructing the adobe.

Secondary goals of our research are to: (1) analyze properties of the Marana adobe relative to other Hohokam sites in central and southern Arizona; and (2) compare the results of two commonly used methods (loss-on-ignition and Chittick) for quantifying $CaCO_3$ in soil samples. The loss-on-ignition and Chittick methods vary in how caliche is quantified, with the first based on dry combustion (loss-on-ignition, or LOI) of $CaCO_3$, and the latter based on dissolving $CaCO_3$ in hydrochloric acid (HCl) and then measuring the volume of carbon dioxide (CO_2) gas that evolves. The Chittick method is a gasometric test that is based on this chemical reaction (Allison and Moody 1965; Nelson 1982): $CaCO_3 + 2\,H^+ \rightarrow Ca^{2+} + 2\,CO_2 + H_2O$.

BACKGROUND DISCUSSION

There is considerable ambiguity in how the term "caliche" is used in different disciplines, so it is important to define it and provide some additional background information. Caliche, also known as desert hardpan, is a form of calcium carbonate ($CaCO_3$) that is especially common in the soils of arid and semiarid regions (Machette 1985; McFadden and Tinsly 1985; Nelson 1982). As defined by the Soil Science Society of America (1996:15), caliche is "a zone near the surface, more or less cemented by secondary carbonates of Ca or Mg precipitated from soil solution. It may occur as a soft thin soil horizon, as a hard thick bed, or as a surface layer exposed by erosion" (see Goudie 1973; Machette 1985; Watts 1980 for other, more inclusive definitions). The Hohokam quarried, ground, and added caliche to adobe to strengthen it, as well as to make plaster for coating adobe walls. Borrow pits where caliche was mined have been found at Pueblo Grande, Casa Grande, the Rock Ball Courts site northwest of Gila Bend, and at Snaketown (Burton et al. 1972; Gladwin et al. 1938; Wasley and Johnson 1965). No caliche borrow pits have been found at the Marana site, but they may be present to the east on older, Pleistocene fan terraces where caliche is widespread.

Field et al. (1993) mapped the geology and dated soils in the northern Tucson Basin, including the Marana area, based in part on the stages of carbonate development. Field et al. (1993) found that $CaCO_3$ occurs only as small filaments (or threads) in the Holocene soils at the Marana site. The concentration of $CaCO_3$ here is too low for collecting it for adobe, but it is readily available in calcic and petrocalcic horizons in soils formed in Pleistocene fan alluvium slope just off-site to the east (Field et al. 1993). Calcic horizons contain at least 15 percent $CaCO_3$ and are at least 15 cm thick, and petrocalcic horizons are indurated and contain at least 50 percent $CaCO_3$ (Soil Survey Staff 1999). The latter is much like limestone bedrock that has formed due to soil formation processes.

Caliche that is thick, soft, and relatively pure is best for use in adobe. Access to caliche was probably one of several factors that influenced settlement of the Marana Platform Mound community near the older alluvial fans. Caliche develops in several stages that can take hundreds to thousands of years to form (Gile et al. 1966; Watson 1989). McFadden and Tinsley (1985) found that $CaCO_3$ accumulates in the soil from calcareous dust in the atmosphere at a rate of 1 g/m^2 per year in southern California, while Gile et al. (1981:Table 27) found that $CaCO_3$ accumulated from dust in Holocene soils of southern New Mexico at rates ranging from 1 to 5 g/m^2 to 2 to 10 g/m^2 per year. Accumulation rates in the Tucson area are probably intermediate between these two states.

Chemical and physical properties of caliche make it a valuable addition to adobe architecture. As this study will show, caliche profoundly impacts the structural integrity of adobe. Caliche can be very difficult to mine and process. It must be procured from horizons that are soft and pure enough to balance energy inputs and outputs. Once a suitable caliche source is identified, it can be difficult to excavate and grind into a usable form. However, its properties as a cementing agent make it understandable why the Hohokam expended so much effort procuring and preparing it for architectural use.

FIELD AND LAB METHODS

In all, 193 bulk soil samples were analyzed, including 165 samples from the Marana site and 28 samples from several other Classic period Hohokam sites in the Tucson and Phoenix Basins (University Indian Ruin, Mesa Grande, Las Piedras, and Rawley sites). Of the 165 samples from the Marana site, 156 were from rooms and compound walls (Compounds 1, 3, 5, and 9) and non-architectural control samples from soils across the Marana site. Samples were taken from Rooms 1, 3, and 5 from Compound 5; Rooms 3, 5, and 9 in Compound 9 (platform mound); and Room 1 of Compound 1. The control samples were collected about 1 m outside of walls for comparison with the cultural features. Nine additional samples were collected from a variety of other contexts, including floors, wall plaster in Rooms 3 and 9 of Compound 9, extramural puddling pits, and off-site natural soils. To minimize sampling and experimental errors, two samples were normally analyzed from every test location to obtain a mean for each wall segment tested.

Figure 3.1 shows an example of a typical sampling strategy. Bulk samples were collected from the interior of room wall surfaces at 1 m intervals along the length of the wall at similar heights above the floor surface. Multiple samples per wall were taken and then averaged for each soil test by wall, then by house. Control samples were collected away from adobe melt, 1.5 m outside of walls at evenly spaced intervals. Additional control samples were collected over 50 m away from all adobe structures.

$CaCO_3$ content was measured by LOI using methods outlined by Heiri et al. (2001) and Kolb and Homburg (1991). About 1 g of soil, measured at a precision of 0.0001 g on an analytical balance, was used for measuring $CaCO_3$ content. Samples were analyzed using a muffle furnace and other laboratory equipment in the Soil Lab of Statistical Research, Inc. Air-dried samples were first weighed and then heated overnight in a drying oven at 105°C to remove free moisture. The oven-dried samples were placed in a desiccator, cooled to room temperature, and then weighed to determine the moisture content of air-dry samples. This same process was repeated two more times in successive heatings to 550°C for four hours and then to 950°C for two hours; the weight loss of organic matter and $CaCO_3$, respectively, was measured after each of these steps.

After LOI testing was completed, 67 samples (about one-third of the samples analyzed by LOI) were analyzed using the Chittick method of determining $CaCO_3$ content. This analysis was done in the Geoarchaeology Laboratory at the University of Arizona. The Chittick method is a modified version of the Van Slyke Manometric method, which is based on the principle that HCl will dissolve $CaCO_3$ and yield a volume of CO_2 gas proportionate to the carbonate (Dreimanis 1962; Martin and Reeve 1955; Rader and Grimaldi 1961; Van Slyke and Folch 1940). The amount of $CaCO_3$ in the sample is based on this formula: %$CaCO_3$ = (0.386 x CF x V)/W; where CF = a correction factor for temperature and pressure (correction factor values from AOAC 1945:Table 44.3) at the time of testing, V = volume of CO_2 gas produced, and W = weight of air-dried sample.

Penetrability was measured in situ using pocket or cone penetrometers. Penetrability is defined as, "the ease with which an object can be pushed or driven into the soil [and it] is a proxy measure of "relative density, shear strength, bearing capacity, and soil strength" (Bradford 1986:463). Penetrability relates to soil compressibility, a measure of the resistance to stress and weight capacity, based on the maximum weight that can be supported when stress is applied (Bradford and Gupta 1986:479; Lowery and Morrison 2002). Penetrometer

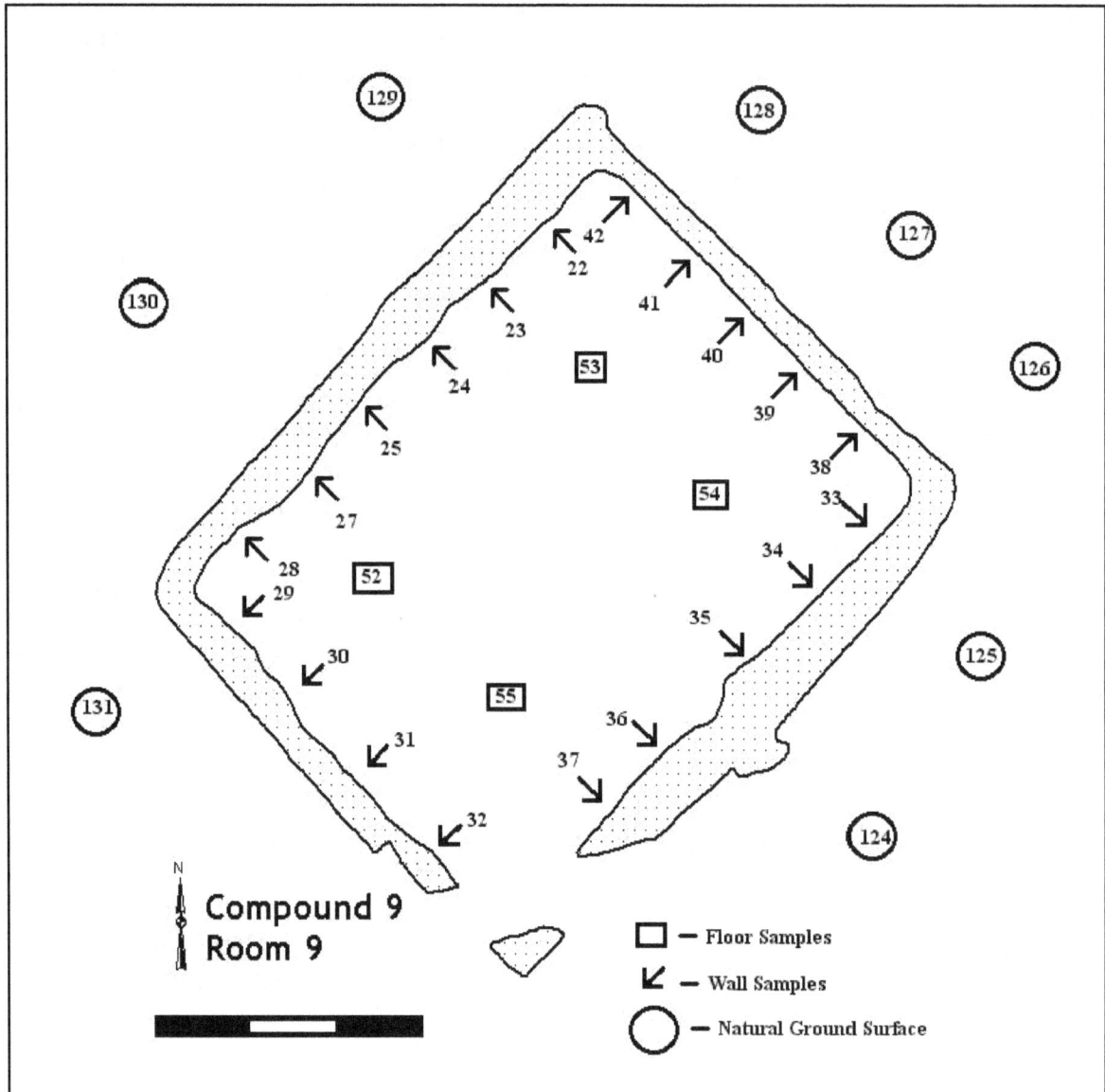

Figure 3.1. Example of room sampling strategy.

tests were used to compare the strength of the adobe walls relative to the adjacent natural soils that were used for constructing the adobe. The tests were repeated several times for each sampling point and then averaged in units of kg/cm². Soil strength and bearing capacity are moisture-dependent properties, so these tests were conducted under dry field conditions to model conditions expected in plastered adobe at the time the site was occupied.

The color of all samples was measured using a standard Munsell Soil Color Chart (1994). Bulk density was measured using the clod method (Grossman and Reinsch 2002). The clod method is based upon the Archimedes Principle, which states that an object submersed in water is buoyed up by a force equal to the weight of the displaced water. The density of the object relative to water can be determined because distilled water is the standard measure of density. Clods of soil were removed from the samples and weighed. They were then coated in paraffin and reweighed. The paraffin coating sealed the soil samples so that they would not soak up the water, thereby drastically altering the measured bulk density. Paraffin-coated clods were weighed in water and bulk density calculated, based on the weight of water that is displaced. Bulk density is a way to estimate and compare the porosity of soils in different contexts. Soil samples from walls were compared to soil samples from natural, undisturbed context to determine how much compaction of soil particles occurred when sediment was processed into adobe.

RESULTS

LOI results indicated that caliche levels at Marana were all surprisingly low. Previous studies of adobe (i.e., Burton et al. 1972; Hovezak 1988; Littmann 1967) suggest that caliche content would be higher at Marana, but $CaCO_3$ levels were similarly low in all architectural contexts, averaging about 1 percent in the Marana adobe. This suggests a high degree of uniformity in the adobe construction recipe. Caliche levels and Munsell soil colors were so uniform that $CaCO_3$ use and wall color must not reflect differential effort, and thus status differentiation, by the occupants.

One important finding is that carbonate levels are consistently higher in all architectural features than comparable natural soils, which indicates that at least small quantities of caliche were added to adobe (Figure 3.2 and Figure 3.3). The T-bars in the bar graphs represent standard deviations above the means for each room or other context. The slightly elevated $CaCO_3$ contents in each room indicate that caliche must have been harvested and transported from off-site areas to the site. Although the caliche is not far, it still requires additional labor for house construction. It is noteworthy that slightly elevated $CaCO_3$ levels were found in the walls of puddling pits as some of the carbonate coated the walls. The $CaCO_3$ levels in these pit walls are not significantly higher than the natural levels in the soil, and that suggests these features were used only briefly.

All cultural features were compacted relative to their respective control samples. Compaction levels, as measured in the bulk density tests, are inversely related to porosity; that is, bulk density increases correspond to decreases in porosity. As shown in Figure 3.3, the walls of puddling pits have the greatest bulk density, a finding that is not surprising considering that puddling pits are features used for mixing water, soil, and caliche to make adobe or plaster (probably the latter given the small size of these features). Room floors had the next highest bulk densities, which is obviously due to continual trampling by inhabitants. Compound and room walls had the next highest compaction levels. Even though there were only minor caliche additions in the Marana adobe, it still had a strengthening effect on the architecture, because caliche effectively binds and cements soil particles. The Hohokam clearly understood the importance of caliche for strengthening walls.

Preliminary tests with the pocket penetrometer failed to obtain readings because the strength of the walls exceeded the limit of the penetrometer. A cone penetrometer was then used, but again, readings could not be obtained in the dry adobe. The limit of measurement for the cone penetrometer was 7,590 kPa (kilopascals, or 1100 psi). We could obtain penetrability readings for the adjacent natural soils, however, and these averaged about 700 kPa (or ~100 psi). Although we were unable to quantify the strength of the adobe, we can conclude that the adobe was at least 11 times as strong as the natural soils, and it may be several orders of magnitude higher than that.

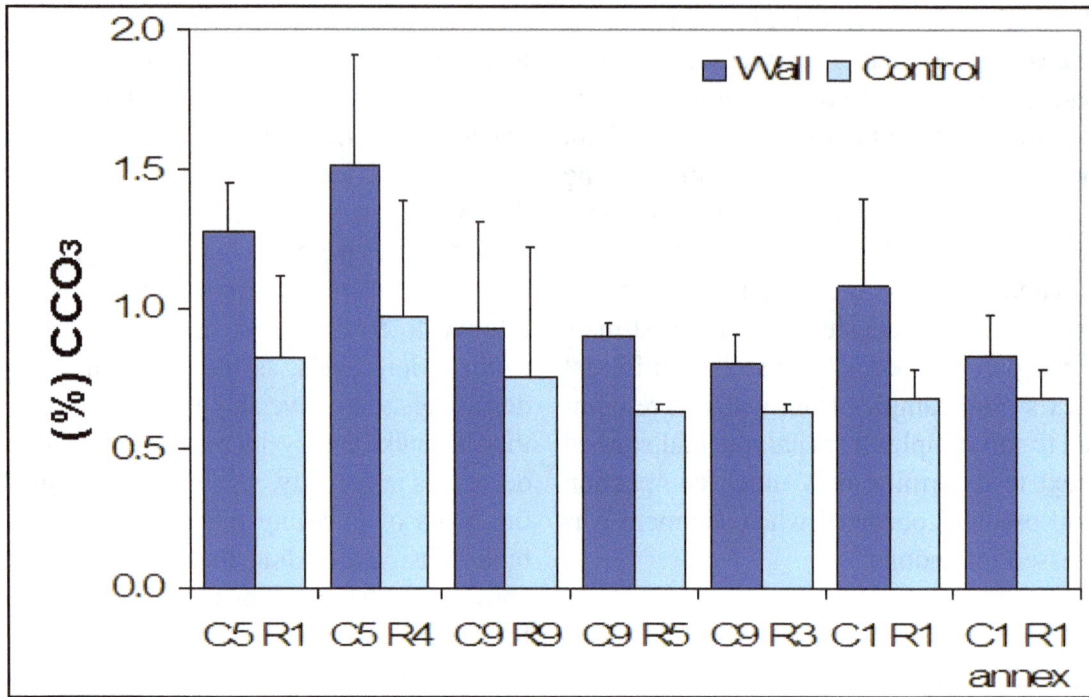

Figure 3.2. Caliche content - Marana rooms vs. controls.

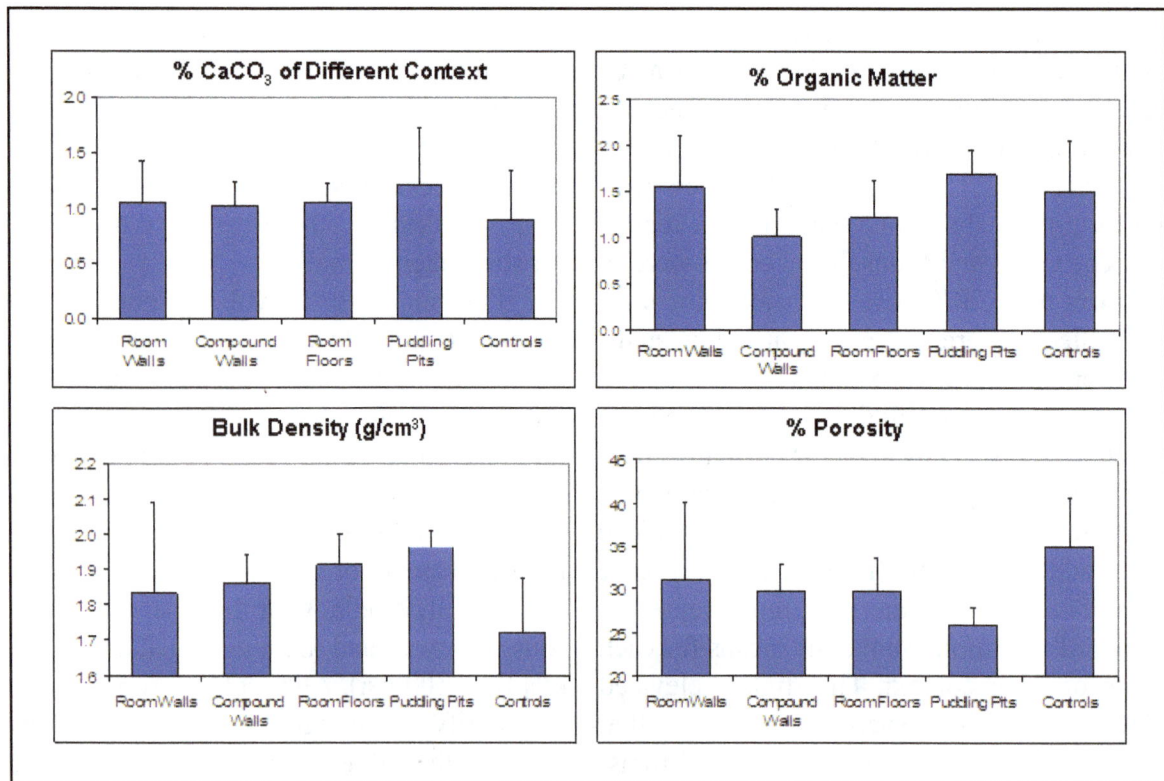

Figure 3.3. Caliche content, organic matter content, bulk density, porosity in different contexts at MPM.

Organic matter levels in the Marana adobe are similar to the controls, which indicate it was not added as a binding agent (Figure 3.3). Ethnographically, organic matter such as grass or animal dung was commonly added to adobe (Shemie 1995). Organic matter additions in adobe, similar to that of inorganic temper in ceramics, strengthens adobe and makes it less susceptible to cracking when dried.

DISCUSSION

A few other studies of caliche additions in adobe have been conducted in southern and central Arizona (Table 3.1). Although not the first such study, the Marana study is based on the largest sample analyzed to date in Arizona, and it is the first to explore caliche content and variability across an entire site to search for evidence of social differentiation. It is also the first to synthesize archaeological literature about $CaCO_3$ content in architecture across the Hohokam world for comparative purposes. In addition to Marana, Tucson Basin sites used in this comparison include University Indian Ruin, and the Brady Wash and McClellan Wash sites, and Phoenix Basin sites include Mesa Grande, Rowley, Las Piedras, Casa Grande, and Pueblo Grande (Table 3.1). Data on the Brady Wash and McClellan Wash sites, Casa Grande, and Pueblo Grande, rely on published and unpublished reports.

Caliche analysis at University Indian Ruin (see Hayden 1957 for information on archaeological excavations) included 12 samples taken from various contexts at the site, including eight samples from exposed walls and four control samples from soils at least 30 m away from architecture to ensure samples were collected outside of rooms and the adjacent adobe melt. Adobe walls averaged 6.5 percent $CaCO_3$ content, 2.3 percent organic matter, 1.8 g/cm^3 in bulk density, and 33 percent porosity. Control samples averaged 4.3 percent $CaCO_3$, 1.6 percent organic matter content, 1.8 g/cm^3 in bulk density, and 66 percent porosity. These findings indicate that caliche was added to strengthen the adobe. Organic matter content in the adobe and controls is too similar to conclude that it was added to adobe.

The McClellan Wash (NA18,031) and

Table 3.1. Number of Samples Analyzed for Caliche Content by Site

Site	Wall	Control	Other	Total
Marana	96	37	32	165
Univ. Indian Ruin	8	4	0	12
Brady Wash*	2	1	0	3
McClellan Wash*	12	3	0	3
Mesa Grande	8	2	1	11
Rowley	3	0	0	3
Las Piedras	1	0	1	2

*Data from Hovezak (1988)

Brady Wash (NA18,003) sites had $CaCO_3$ contents that averaged 3.2 percent in adobe and 1.3 percent in controls (Hovezak 1988:322), so caliche was added to adobe at slightly higher quantities than at Marana. Ceramics from the McClellan Wash Site indicate it was most intensively occupied during the Classic period, possibly during the Civano/Tucson phases (Downum and Madsen 1993). Hovezak speculated that the low quantities of $CaCO_3$ in the adobe might reflect the "difficulty in obtaining sufficient caliche suitable for adobe wall construction."

Wilcox and Shenk (1977) found caliche content in walls at Casa Grande averaged between 22 percent and 35 percent. At Pueblo Grande, the walls had caliche contents of between 26 percent and 38 percent (Burton et al. 1972:21). The methods for measuring $CaCO_3$ in the Casa Grande and Pueblo Grande studies was not reported and no control samples were analyzed, so we lack information on how much caliche was added to the adobe. Consequently, we could only compare the caliche in the Casa Grande and Pueblo Grande adobe with that of the other sites.

Jerry Howard, archaeologist at the Mesa Southwest Museum, provided wall samples from Mesa Grande, Rowley, and Las Piedras for analysis, along with information on the room number and wall location where samples were collected. LOI and bulk density tests were conducted on these samples using the same methods. Eight wall samples from Mesa Grande had an average $CaCO_3$ content of 16.2 percent, organic matter content of 5.1 percent, a bulk density of 1.70 g/cm³, and a porosity of 36.5 percent. Two control samples from the site had an average $CaCO_3$ content of 9.5 percent, organic matter content of 4.7 percent, a bulk density of 1.4 g/cm³ and a porosity of 45.5 percent. Three wall samples from the Rowley Site averaged 21.1 percent in $CaCO_3$ and 3.7 percent in organic content. Two samples from

Las Piedras had an average $CaCO_3$ content of 9.9 percent and organic matter content of 2.4 percent. The clod samples from the Rowley and Las Piedras sites were not large enough for measuring bulk density.

The most striking finding is that carbonate levels are similarly low in the Tucson Basin area sites, which contrasts sharply with Classic Period sites in the Phoenix Basin (Figure 3.4). High levels in the Phoenix Basin are in all likelihood a function of higher natural levels in the on-site soils used for making the adobe, while low levels in the Tucson Basin reflect much lower $CaCO_3$ contents in the natural soils of those sites. There is also a functional reason why several of the Phoenix Basin sites (especially Casa Grande, Mesa Grande, and Pueblo Grande) would require much higher caliche contents. The multi-story architecture in the Phoenix Basin sites would have required much greater load-bearing capacity to support the massive walls, so it is not surprising that much more effort was expended to process caliche for architectural use at these sites.

Bulk density and porosity values are similar between all sites in the Phoenix and Tucson Basins (Figure 3.5). Organic matter is significantly higher at Mesa Grande and other sites than at Marana, and that is probably due to the addition of midden soil with high humate levels (Figure 3.5). High organic matter levels at Mesa Grande, and possibly Rowley and Las Piedras, suggest that it functioned as a binding agent that further strengthened the adobe.

CHITTICK TESTING AT MARANA AND OTHER SITES

Overall, the Chittick testing results are strongly correlated to the LOI data for the Marana and other samples. Both methods yielded similar results but the standard deviations for the Chittick method are slightly higher. Although there

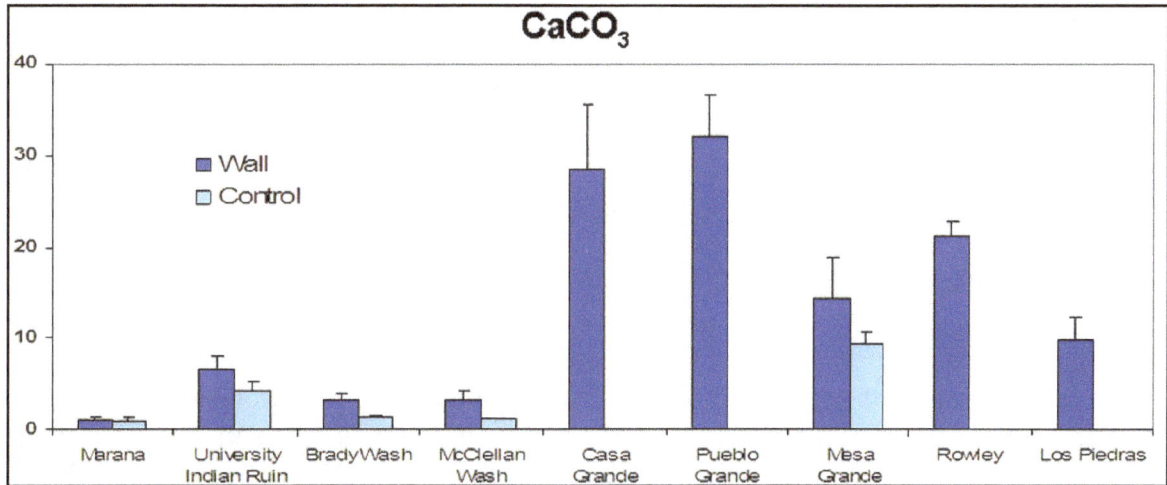

Figure 3.4. Caliche content at different sites.

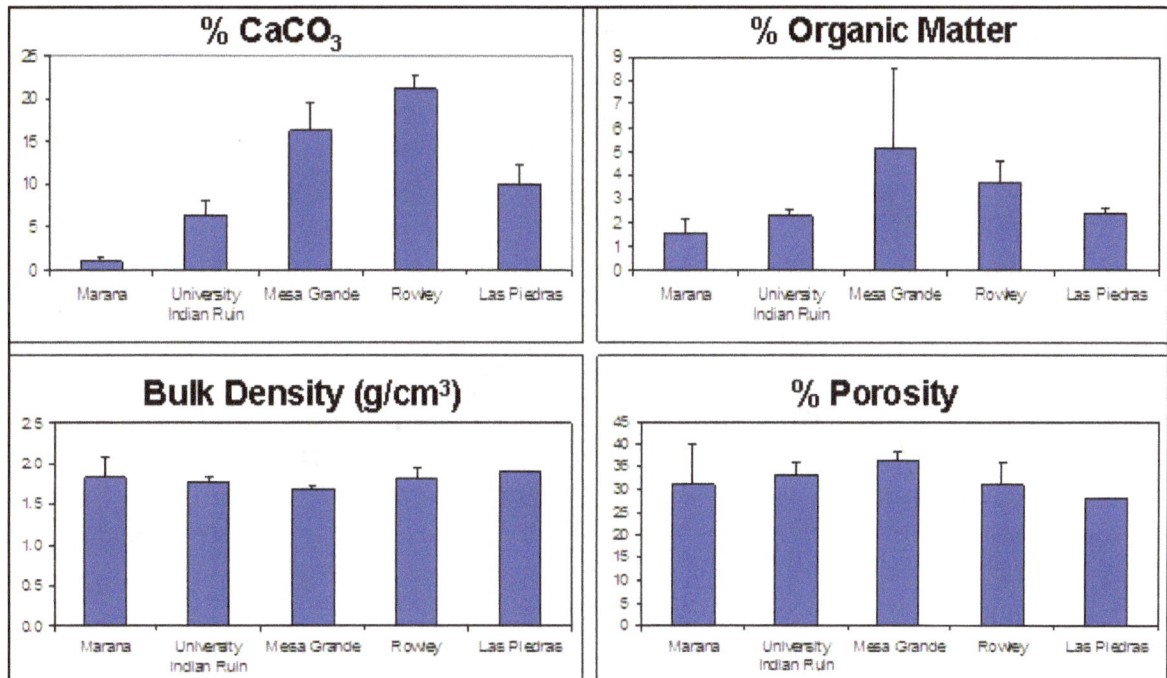

Figire 3.5. Caliche content, organic matter content, bulk density, and porosity at different sites.

is greater variability for the Chittick results, this method helped verify the LOI results. Regression analysis indicated a strong correlation between the LOI and Chittick method, with an R^2 of 0.964 (Figure 3.6).

In comparing the two methods by the individual rooms and their respective control samples, the correlation between the two methods is clearly illustrated. As Figure 3.7 indicates, the Chittick method yielded slightly higher percentages of $CaCO_3$ than did LOI, with the exception of two rooms. One interesting finding is that the Chittick testing yielded higher quantities of caliche in the room wall samples than LOI, but the control samples were notably lower. If this study had been based solely on the Chittick testing, then it would have indicated that slightly higher amounts of caliche were added to the walls. LOI indicated average additions of 0.34 percent, while the Chittick method indicated 0.43 percent. One-tenth of a percent is an insignificant difference until total amount of caliche is considered. For example, a Hohokam room at Marana in the very smallest range, measuring 2 m by 3 m, with 30-cm-thick walls standing 2.5 m high would require 7.5 m³ of soil for adobe construction. According to LOI testing, 25,500 cm³ (0.0255 m³) of caliche was added. According to the Chittick method, 32,250 cm³ (0.03225 m³) of caliche were added to the walls. If mass is calculated using the bulk density data for the walls, then the difference of caliche added between the methods is 12.8 kg (28.2 lbs). This difference is important in considering the implications for labor investment. It is arguable that processing an additional 6,750 cm³ (roughly the size of a loaf of bread weighing 30 lbs) of caliche would require greater labor investment. The two methods of testing yield different estimates of the labor investment requirements. Chittick testing of 15 samples from the other Hohokam sites varied from LOI testing results in most cases, and that is especially true for samples with high $CaCO_3$

contents (Figure 3.8). In comparing the overall results from the two methods, we consider LOI to be less accurate than the Chittick method for testing soils with high caliche contents, but LOI appears to be better for measuring $CaCO_3$ in soils low in carbonate.

The question remains as to why the results from LOI testing and Chittick testing vary so much in soils with naturally high carbonate contents. A study conducted by Holiday and Stein (1989) addressed this very issue through analysis of seven soil samples using both techniques. They found that the results from LOI testing were consistently 10 to 15 percent higher than the results produced by the Chittick method. By contrast, our study based on a much larger sample, suggests that LOI produces results 20 to 50 percent lower than Chittick testing. Of course there is a significant difference between the samples analyzed by Holiday and Stein and ours. The vast majority of our samples had low caliche contents, with about three-fourths of all samples having $CaCO_3$ contents less than 2 percent and about 45 percent of samples with $CaCO_3$ contents less than 1 percent. Consequently, percentage comparisons on a relative basis are not that meaningful except for samples with high amounts of caliche. As with previous studies (Dean 1974; Holliday and Stein 1989), the present study shows that different test methods of $CaCO_3$ can yield different results. Still, we found a high degree of correlation between the Chittick and LOI methods, with an R^2 over 0.96.

Conclusions

This research focused on determining if caliche was used to express social differentiation at the Marana Platform Mound site. We originally thought that higher status contexts, such as the platform mound, might have higher $CaCO_3$ contents because of greater access to labor

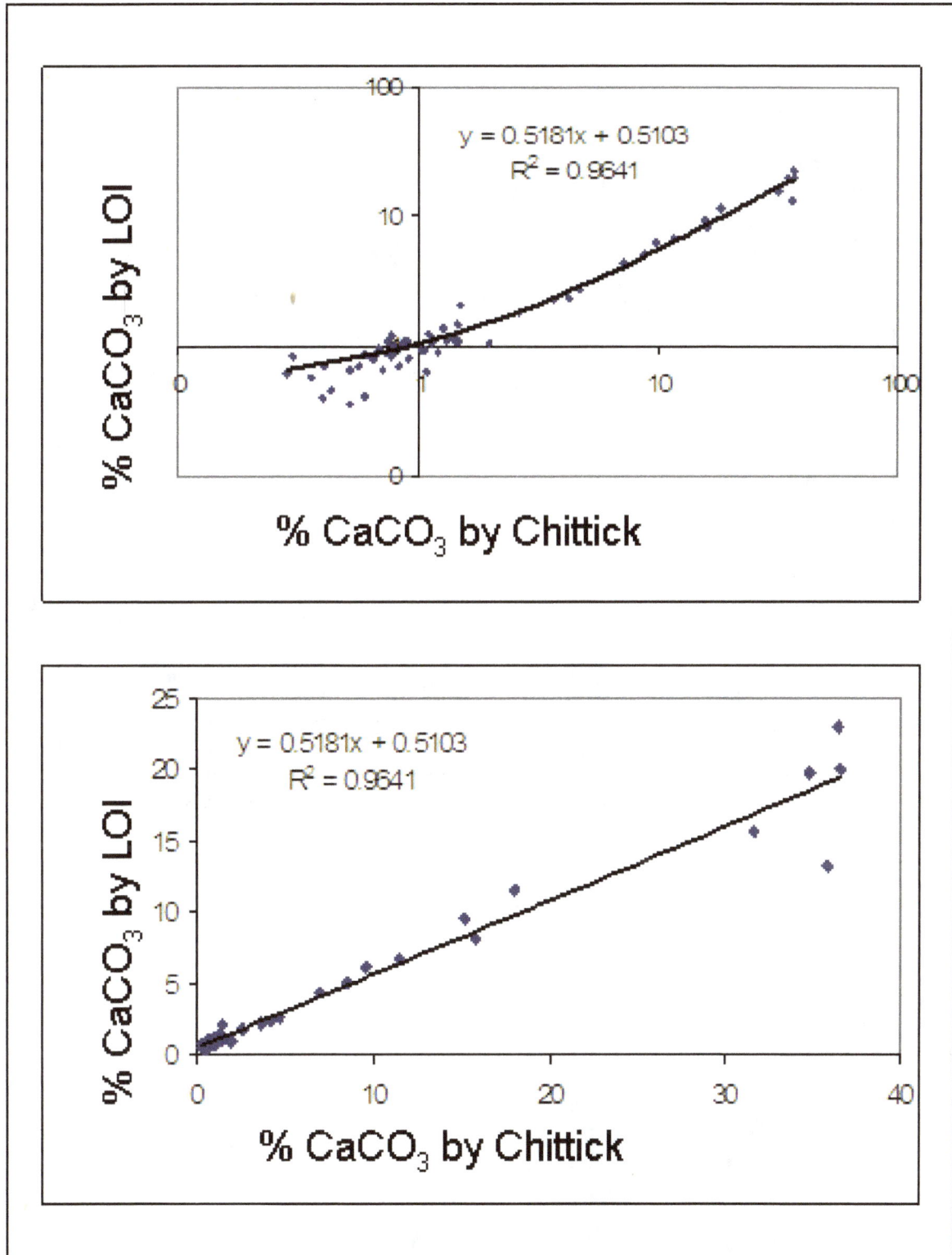

Figure 3.6. Loss-on-Ignition vs. Chittick - walls and controls.

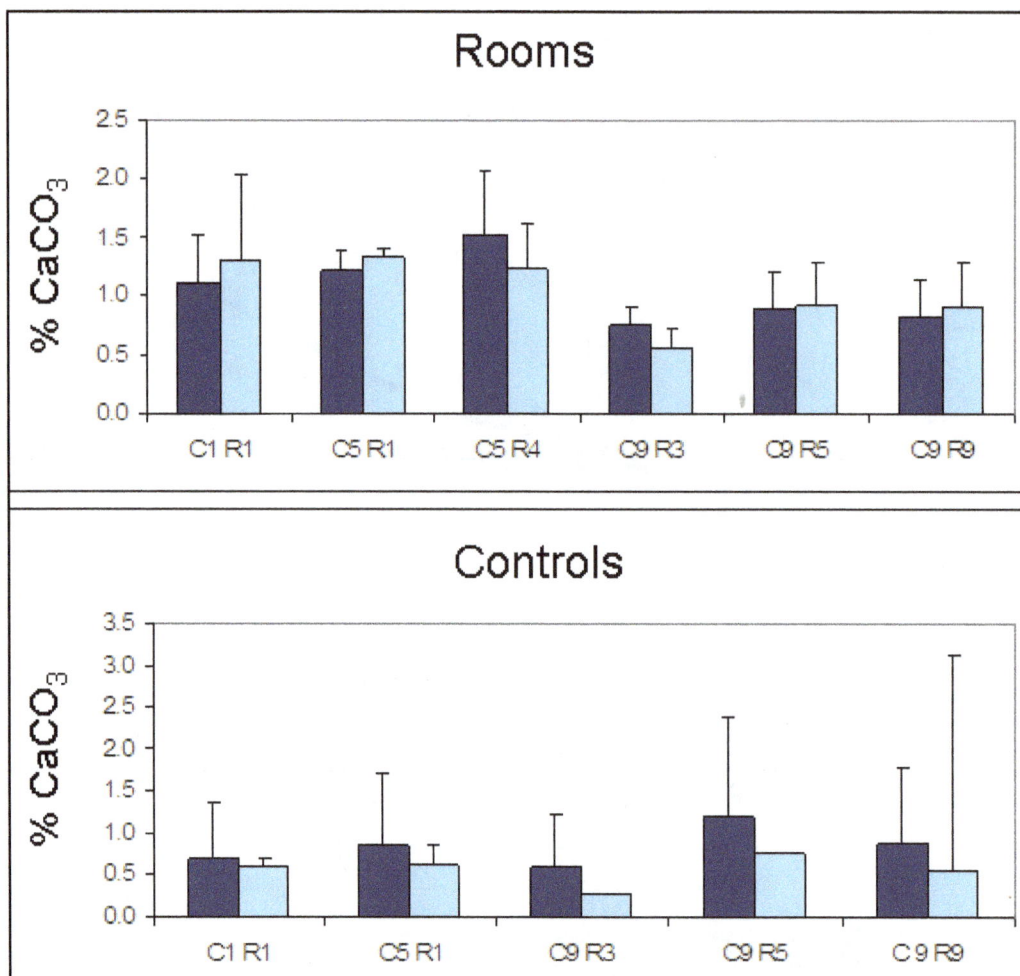

Figure 3.7. Loss-on-Ignition vs. Chittick - Marana rooms and controls.

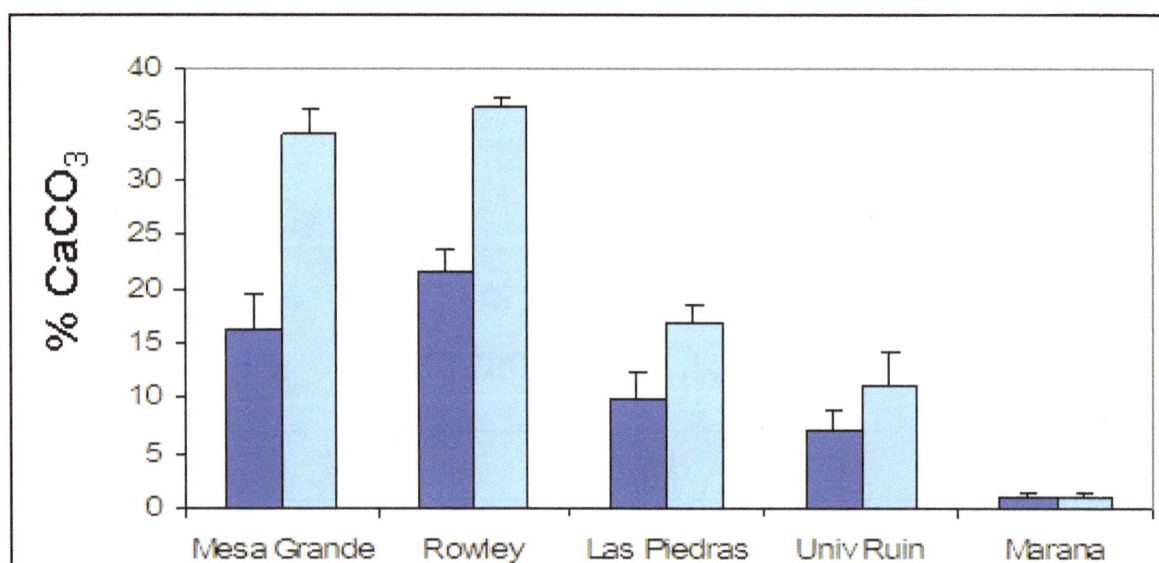

Figure 3.8. Loss-on-Ignition vs. Chittick - sites compared.

resources for construction of adobe architecture. Higher caliche content would result in more durable and weather-resistant walls, which might also symbolize a higher social status or designate an area of social power and significance. In comparing $CaCO_3$ content in different contexts at Marana, we found low variability among compounds, and similar contents between the platform mound and other compounds. This suggests that caliche content does not reflect social or economic inequality among site occupants.

This research did, however, find that some caliche was added to adobe in all contexts. Even minor $CaCO_3$ additions are important in their cementing effect on adobe, but at such low levels of caliche, compaction of natural soils is even more important in terms of strengthening the adobe. That is because compressive strength increases logarithmically with a linear bulk density (Ruhe 1967:55). Compaction in adobe increases the shear strength and load-bearing capacity relative to natural soils, because increased grain-to-grain contacts results in much greater interlocking friction. Penetrometer tests offer some quantitative support for this conclusion. Penetrometer tests indicated the Marana adobe is at least eleven times as strong as natural soils under dry conditions.

Comparison of the Marana and other Tucson Basin site results with results from sites in the Phoenix Basin indicated that the latter had significantly elevated caliche levels. This is one of the most interesting and surprising results of this study. Large sites in the Phoenix Basin, such as Casa Grande, Mesa Grande, and Pueblo Grande, were established in places with higher natural carbonate levels than the setting of Marana and other Tucson Basin sites. This must be a functional difference as well, because these large structures would require much greater strength to bear the weight of multi-story construction.

This research also highlighted methodological considerations between using LOI versus the Chittick method. Based on the results of our study, we recommend the Chittick method for testing samples high in $CaCO_3$, and LOI for testing those low in $CaCO_3$. Both methods are commonly used in soil and geological studies, but more work is needed to compare the results. Another technique being used increasingly today is the Leco Carbon-Carbonate Determinator method (Gross 1971). This method is both rapid and accurate, but the equipment is much more costly than equipment used by the Chittick and LOI tests.

We hope that our research will spur others to explore the archaeological implications of adobe wall construction and composition. Additional work is needed to compare carbonate content in adobe relative to available source areas at different Hohokam sites. This kind of study opens up a new research avenue for reconstructing labor requirements and studying technological changes in Hohokam adobe architecture. In addition to the techniques used here, future studies of Hohokam adobe architecture should take advantage of soil micromorphology as a way to characterize the composition and cultural use of adobe and plasters in different settings in southern and central Arizona.

Chapter 4
Compound Redefinition at the Marana Mound Site

Cory Harris

INTRODUCTION

The Marana Community was the scene of significant population growth at the dawn of the Classic period—one obvious result of this coalescence being the establishment of the platform mound site (Bayman 1995; Fish et al. 1992b; S. Fish and Fish 2000; Harry 1997). The mound site, a new mechanism of social integration and coordination for the expanding population, likely served as an important central node of communication and exchange at both intra- and inter-community levels. Because of this preeminent position, residence at the mound site may have bestowed certain advantages on its inhabitants.

Regionally, the Hohokam Classic period is characterized by a number of changing archaeological patterns, including ritual technology, public and domestic architecture, and mortuary behavior (Abbott 2003; Doyel 1974, 1981; S. Fish and Fish 2000; Gregory 1987; Wasley and Doyel 1980; Wilcox and Sternberg 1983). Evidence from the mound site demonstrates how some prehistoric residents of the Tucson Basin adapted locally to this dynamic situation and reconfigured social groupings during the early Classic period. In the introduction to this volume, Fish, Fish, and Bayman note that consistent remodeling and reconstruction of individual structures suggest a symbolic connection to place and continuity

in social groups through time. Evidence of this heightened connection to architectural space is present at both the level of the individual structure and the compound. This paper details the redefinition of compound space in one compound at the mound site and examines ties between people and space through the lens of an unusual mortuary feature associated with the compound.

COMPOUNDS

In addition to the platform mound, the other hallmark architectural features at the site are walled, adobe compounds. In the early years of Hohokam archaeology, compounds were interpreted as markers of social class distinction (Cushing 1890; Fewkes 1912) or ethnic identifiers of an immigrant group (Gladwin et al. 1965; Haury 1945; Schroeder 1953). More recently, most archaeologists would argue that the emergence of compounds was the result of internal cultural developments, stemming from the larger social reorganization of the Classic transition (Doyel 1980; Sires 1987; Wasley and Doyel 1980; Wilcox et al. 1981).

Classic period compounds represent continuity and elaboration of social and spatial organization through the Hohokam sequence. Preclassic precursors to the compound were unwalled courtyard groups, thought to represent individual households, consisting of contemporaneous pit structures opening onto a common extramural area (Wilcox et al. 1981). These spaces were intensively used for day-to-day social, economic, and ritual activities. Exterior to these spaces, in less intensely used areas, more specialized activities often occurred, such as refuse disposal, construction, and mortuary internment. This basic pattern persisted into the Classic period, though formalized with the addition of aboveground adobe structures and surrounding compound walls (Sires 1987). Also during the Preclassic, aggregates of courtyard groups are apparent at many sites and are thought to indicate suprahousehold social units (Doelle et al. 1987; Fish and Fish 1991; Henderson 1987b; Howard 1985; Rice 1987a,b; Wilcox 1987a,b). Such units seem to continue in the large compounds of the Classic period.

For the Marana Mound site, the volume editors argue that the crystallization of the compound, from its less formal antecedent, was one response to the social pressure coincident with increasing population aggregation. In this framework, the compound is the archaeological manifestation of a corporate group, organized around common activities over extended periods of time. While these social groups existed prior to the development of the Marana Community, their importance and need for obvious boundaries grew from the challenges posed by the Classic period.

The construction and maintenance of architectural features served to physically, socially and symbolically demarcate compounds, while reinforcing residents' membership within the corporate group. Assuming continuity in a specific social group's residence, compounds with substantial evidence of renovation indicate the resident group's longevity and successful management of social relationships in the community. Such groups would be better able to mobilize labor needed

for adobe construction, and subsequently, multiple episodes of remodeling indicate the persistence—continued success—of those groups. Additionally, consistent remodeling illustrates the value that was placed on living at the mound site. Despite being situated on floodwater land of secondary quality, the mound site is the obvious nexus of population and "elite" life in the community, as evidenced by the presence of the platform mound, differential access to decorated ceramics and other exotic artifacts, and the prevalence of adobe architecture (Bayman 1995, 1996a,b; P. Fish and Fish 2000; Harry 1997). Living at the mound site may have afforded social benefits to compound occupants and made alternative residential choices unattractive or impossible. The repeated investment into the same architectural spaces suggests that residents purposively chose mound site life over other alternatives, such as living in outlying villages.

COMPOUNDS AT THE MARANA MOUND SITE

Residential compounds at the Marana Mound site may be much larger (5,000 m², roughly the area of a football field) than similar Phoenix Basin features (mean 1,600 m² for Los Muertos and Pueblo Grande). Some scholars suggest that these larger compounds represent the aggregation of smaller social units that were usually housed separately in smaller compounds at other sites (see P. Fish and Fish 2000:252). Approximately 35 of these large compounds stretch 0.754 km in two directions—from the platform mound and enclose groupings of up to 30 individual structures.

Frequently, compounds exhibit spatial complexity beyond a wall surrounding groups of structures. Internal dividing walls partition domestic space within compounds, separating them into relatively distinct sections (P. Fish and Fish 2000:252), and these architectural divisions may reflect the boundaries of past social units. If so, untangling the sequences of construction and relationships to other compound walls could reveal important contours of the occupational histories of specific compounds and social dynamics and interrelations of life at the mound site. Were all walls built simultaneously? Were internal dividing walls built subsequent to the exterior compound walls? Did internal walls serve as exterior ones prior to the enlargement of a compound?

In the case detailed below, a single known internal wall roughly bisects a larger compound. Several scenarios of exterior and interior wall construction are possible: (1) If both the exterior and interior walls were built at once, at least two household units may have composed a larger corporate group at the compound's founding. This suggests some level of cooperation between households from initial occupation. (2) Dividing walls may have been built after exterior walls, suggesting internal growth and subdivision of the corporate unit, or the incorporation of immigrants newcomers into the compound. (3) In other cases, internal walls may serve to diminish the size of an original, larger compound, suggesting a contraction in modular social groups. (4) Conversely, a wall that appears "internal" may have originally served as an exterior boundary until a point when the compound was enlarged. This renovation could serve to accommodate a larger social group—the result of accretional growth—or simply a shift in occupation of the compound from an older section to a newer one. In the latter case, group size remains constant, but the social unit shifts its occupation to accommodate changing conditions.

Each of these scenarios has different implications for how space was utilized at the mound site in response to growth, contraction and change. This study was designed to explore the changing use of corporate space at a single compound, Compound 3, at the mound site.

COMPOUND 3

Compound 3 sits about 0.5 km east of the platform mound (Figure 4.1) and measures about 65 m by 35 m, consistent with the lower range of other compounds at the site. An internal wall articulates with both the eastern and western exterior walls, completely dividing the compound (Figure 4.2). This wall was found in the process of investigating other features, so the presence of additional internal walls in Compound 3 is unknown. Determination of construction sequence is notoriously difficult with most architectural elements at the mound site, and Compound 3 is no exception. Corners and wall junctures are often marked only by a break, with no apparent pattern of bonding or abutment. At both the eastern and western junctions of the bisecting wall and exterior wall, breaks in adobe separate all elements, as no portion of the exterior wall convincingly connects with the bisecting wall. Also, the exterior wall's northern and southern segments do not directly intersect. Subsequently, interpretations of sequence are all but impossible using patterns of bonding and abutment.

Other (less direct) indications suggest that the dividing wall originally composed an exterior side of the compound (Scenario 4). The width of the exterior wall is noticeably narrower in the northern section, ranging from 20 to 25 cm, while the southern section is 35 to 40 cm. The smaller width of the northern portion mirrors the size of the dividing wall, 20 to 25 cm. Based on the assumption that during a given construction episode, builders will attempt to standardize wall width, this observation suggests that the northern half of the compound was built in conjunction with the dividing wall. The thicker, southern half of the exterior wall would have been erected at a later time, utilizing a portion of the old compound wall in the creation of the new space.

If this limited evidence and sequence of

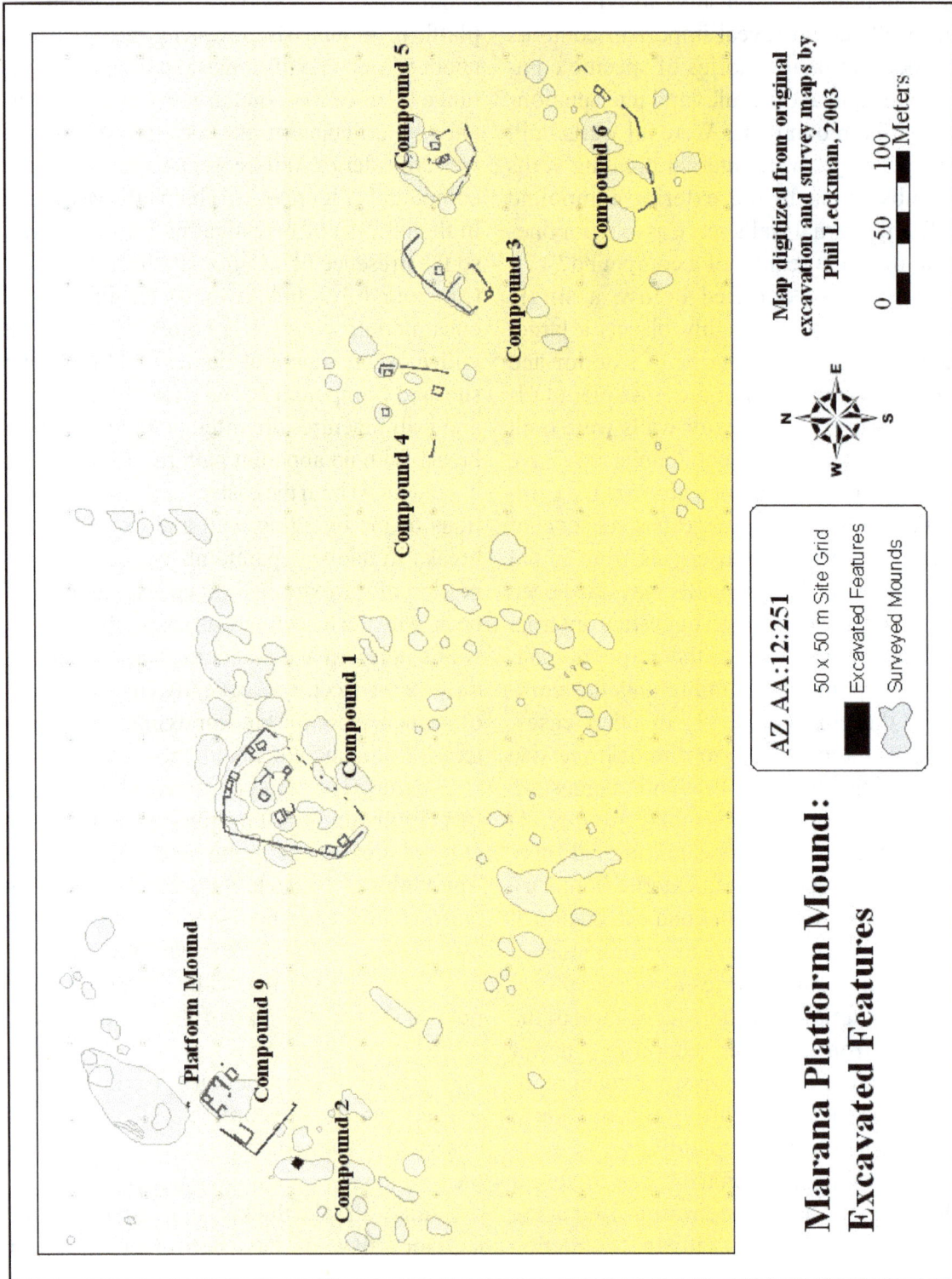

Figure 4.1. Platform Mound Compound relative to Compound 3.

Figure 4.2. Compound 3 (points near intersection of walls represent the corners of excavation units).

compound construction is correct, Compound 3 exhibits renovation and sequential change in compound use. The northern, small, thin-walled compound was later augmented with more compound space to the south, surrounded by a more labor-expensive wall. This construction sequence does not transparently produce a social group's occupation sequence, however. Was the construction of the new portion of the compound an enlargement of corporate space or a shift in occupation to the south? A borrow pit (Figure 4.3), positioned just north-east of the intersection of the western exterior and dividing walls, which contained an unusual collection of artifacts and an inhumation, offers some clues.

BORROW PIT

Borrow pits are identifiable by their large size and irregular shape (Mitchell 1988a:130), and this feature is no exception. A quarter of the pit was excavated, providing two profile axes, each depicting a radius of approximately 3 to 3.5 m (Figure 4.4). The pit's depth was about 1.5 m from modern ground surface to its low-est extent, which was marked by a distinct contact line between cultural fill and sterile, orange soil beneath. The feature was probably the result of mining for sediment used in the construction of adobe walls, possibly for sec-tions of Compound 3's walls. The borrow pit's contents included abundant artifacts, ash, bits

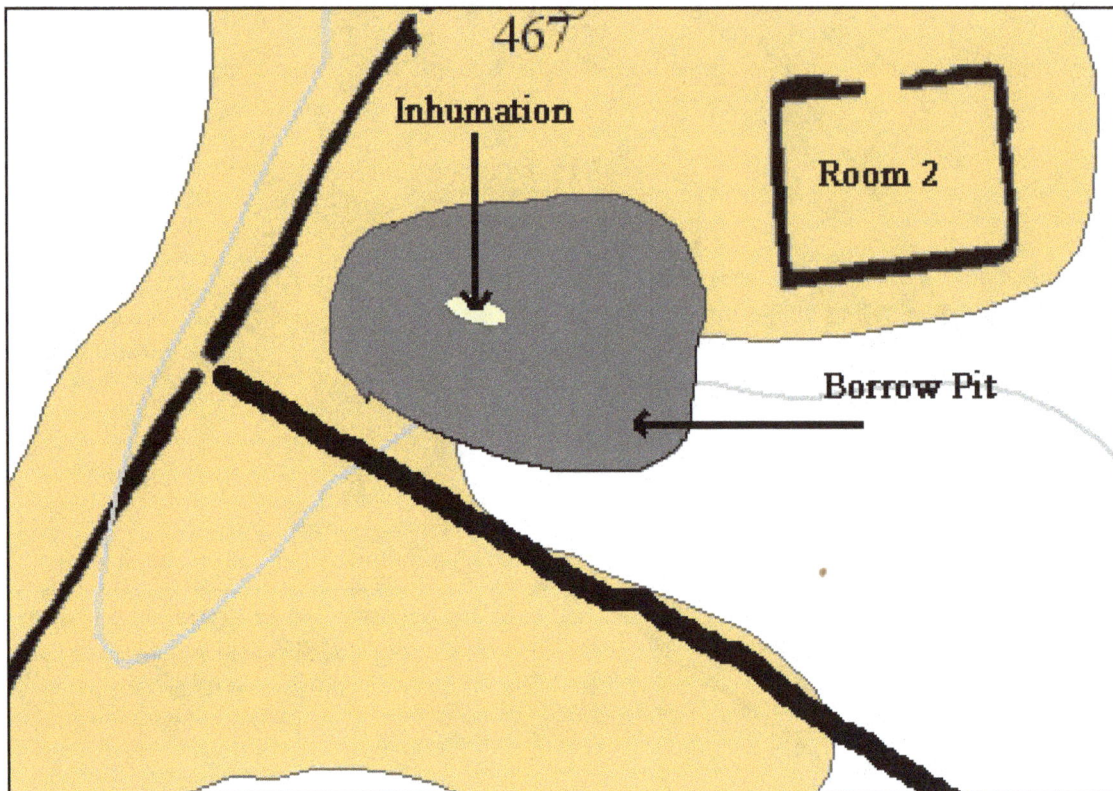

Figure 4.3. Borrow pit within Compound 3.

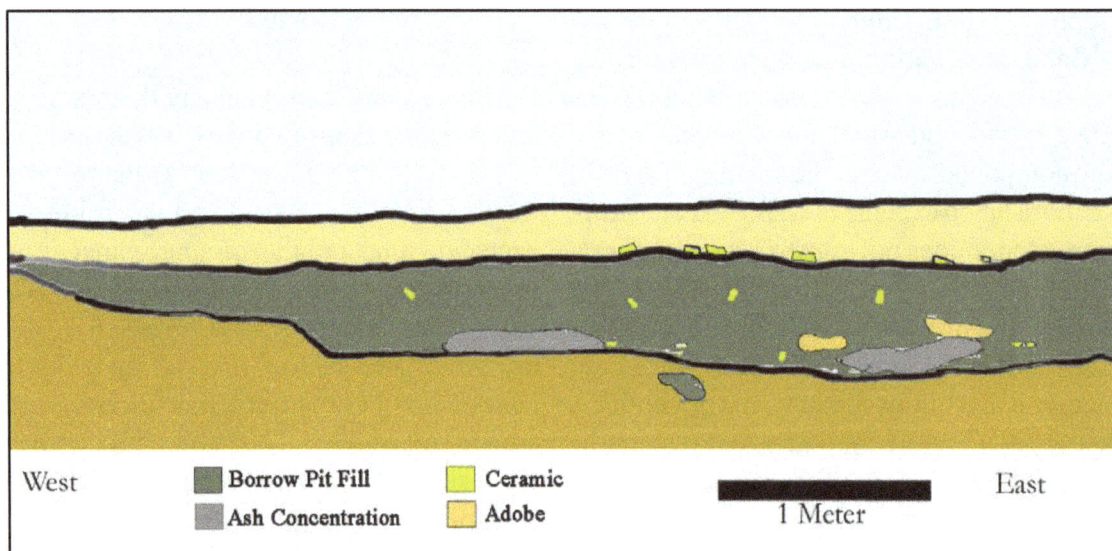

Figure 4.4. Profile of borrow pit's western radius.

of charcoal, and blocks of adobe, which seem consistent with trash deposition, though, as described below, the deposit differs from that of a typical trash pit.

Though adobe mixing pits were not found in association with this borrow pit, in other contexts—at the mound site and elsewhere—they are found nearby, suggesting the pit may have been involved in the construction of the compound walls (Doyel 1974; Hammack and Sullivan 1981; Howard 1988; Mitchell 1988a: 130; Wasley and Johnson 1965). Because the excavation of borrow pits creates uneven ground surfaces, they are often spatially segregated into discrete zones away from areas of regular use (Doelle et al. 1987:83; Mitchell 1988a:130)—such as outside compounds (Howard 1988)—in special use areas, similar to trash and cemetery areas (Gregory 1984:73; Mitchell 1988a,b). Because borrow pits are not typically located within compounds, the presence of such a pit within the boundaries of the compound argues that the two halves were occupied sequentially, a point further supported by the character of the deposit.

The pit's shape was similar to other borrow pits, but its fill was not. Often, Hohokam borrow pits serve as convenient receptacles for secondary refuse after their excavation (Howard 1988:846; Mitchell 1988a:130), and trash mounds are often contained by such features—an assertion supported by previous excavations at the mound site (Bayman 1994; Harry 1997). One consequence of the deposition of trash into borrow pits is that the fill ultimately serves to raise the level of the pit back to ground surface, eliminating the hole. Further, borrow pits and secondary refuse are typically deposited on the peripheries of activity areas (Elson 1986; Haury 1976; Henderson 1987a; Mitchell 1990). The borrow pit in Compound 3 contains an abundance of cultural material; however, several lines of evidence suggest that the subsequent use of this feature does not exclusively fit a model of routine deposition of secondary refuse. The deposit may have been produced ritually, rather than economically (Preucel 1996:127). Sherd size, weight, and density data, in addition to the qualitative nature of other contents in the pit, argue that such non-economic processes were responsible for the deposit's creation.

Sherd Data

The abundance of ceramic sherds at Hohokam sites makes these artifacts an excellent indicator of the operation of both natural and cultural formation processes. Specifically, sherd size can be used as a proxy measure for the degree of archaeological transformation of an artifact from the systemic context (Craig and Wallace 1992; Schiffer 1996). Many formation processes modify a village's material inventory into the many deposits encountered by archaeologists throughout a site. At a general level, larger ceramic pieces have been subject to fewer post-depositional formation processes than smaller ones (Craig and Wallace 1992:41). Subsequently, artifact size can reveal the intensity of transformative forces that have impacted a deposit—house floors generally being subject to less and secondary trash to more.

In laboratory processing, all excavated sherds for each provenience unit were passed through nested wire screens to divide the artifacts into three basic size categories—diameters larger than one inch, between one inch and 0.5 inches and less than 0.5 inches (for the remainder of this paper, "large" sherds refer to those larger than one inch). Each size category was counted and weighed. In particular, large sherds were weighed in order to better understand the deposits' character. Because the sherd sorting procedure did not discriminate sherd size larger than a one inch diameter, large sherds could potentially be of significantly differing sizes and weight measures were used as an efficient means to mitigate this problem.

Sherd size from the borrow pit was compared to several other proveniences at the mound site, including 16 trash deposits, and the floors of 11 house structures (Table 4.1). House floor assemblage percentages of large sherds range from 19 to 54 percent with a mean of 33 percent. Large sherd percentages from trash mounds range from 4 to 36 percent, though they cluster toward the lower end of that scale with a mean of 14 percent. The sherd size profile of the borrow pit fits between the trash and house floor patterns. All levels, except ground surface, exhibit large sherd percentages greater than 30 percent, falling comfortably into the lower range of house deposits. Based on sherd-size profiles, the borrow pit deposit does not fit clearly into the deposition patterns of houses or trash pits.

Average sherd weight by size class further underscores this alternative pattern. Large sherd weight measures are consistently greater in house floor contexts relative to trash. In other words, of sherds larger than one inch, those in houses tend to be larger than those in trash pits. House floors exhibit a range in large sherd weight from approximately 17 to 53 g per sherd with a mean of 39 g per sherd. Trash deposits have a smaller average large sherd weight with a range of 5 to 38 g per sherd and a mean of 23 g per sherd. While these ranges overlap, both deposit types have different centers of gravity. The borrow pit's range again occupies a middle ground with a spread of 24 to 44 g per sherd, and mean of 38 g/sherd, which closely matches the house floor pattern.

Sherd density can also help untangle the nature of a deposit's creation. Mound site trash deposits were found to have a mean density of approximately 1,500 sherds per cm³ and houses 482 sherds per cm³. Again, the borrow pit's profile fits between trash and houses with a mean density of 904 sherds per cm³.

Summarizing, the contents of the borrow pit suggest a different depositional history than typically found in trash pits or house floors. The borrow pit includes a higher percentage of sherds and heavier, large sherds than trash pits, but a lower percentage of lighter sherds than found on house floors. Additionally, the borrow pit contains a lower density of sherds than trash pits but a bit higher density than that of house floors. The borrow pit's deposit seems not to be *de facto* refuse, more often encountered on house floors, but also does not exhibit the degree of archaeological transformation that usually characterizes secondary refuse. Compared to a typical trash pit, these data suggest the fill of the borrow pit accumulated more rapidly and was subject to fewer post-depositional, transformative processes (Craig and Wallace 1992). While the character of this deposit may have simply been the result of rapid trash deposition, the presence of a few unusual inclusions in the pit and an inhumation underlying it—described below—suggest some kind of ritual behavior was at play.

Unusual Inclusions

In addition to sherd data, the borrow pit's deposit was distinct from trash pits and houses in other respects. Numerous chunks of adobe were distributed, somewhat randomly, throughout the feature's fill. The adobe pieces appear to be fragments of wall courses that seem to have separated when moved or pushed from their original location. The borrow pit also contained 15 Tularosa black-on-white sherds and one corrugated sherd, comprising a significant percentage of intrusive ceramics recovered throughout the entire site. Two complete modeled spindle whorls and several disc whorls were also found. A much larger archaeological sample, however,

Table 4.1. Sherd Data for Room, Trash and Borrow Pit Samples

Provenience	Percent of large sherds	Average Weight (g)	Sherd Density
Structures			
Compound 3, Room 1	24	17.73	304
Compound 3, Room 2	22	27.30	330
Compound 3, Room 3	26	24.20	62
Compound 4, Room 1	48	44.21	44
Compound 4, Room 2	35	50.74	878
Compound 4, Room 3	21		313
Compound 5, Room 1	43	53.58	198
Compound 5, Room 2	26	35.81	401
Compound 6, Room 1	54	29.61	104
Compound 6, Room 2	29	25.50	777
Compound 7, Room 1	33	43.77	576
Trash Deposits			
Trash Mound, Grid 73	13	24.94	945
Trash Mound, Grid 211	18	23.93	1051
Trash Mound, Grid 235	12	20.17	1434
Trash Mound, Grid 255	16	21.17	1650
Trash Mound, Grid 271	21	28.33	1324
Trash Mound, Grid 272	11	19.00	1126
Trash Mound, Grid 311	11	22.81	1242
Trash Mound, Grid 330	21	22.90	1007
Trash Mound, Grid 349	19	29.75	1745
Trash Mound, Grid 351	17	24.14	1473
Trash Mound, Grid 370	11	22.00	1330
Trash Mound, Grid 485	15	24.27	2201
Trash Mound, Grid 507	16	17.31	1580
Trash Mound, Grid 528	15	13.06	1730
Trash Mound, Grid 577	14	24.12	765
Trash Mound, Grid 600	13	19.70	1315
Borrow Pit			
3 levels	33-42	38	904

was recovered from this feature compared to other trash pits, which could explain the presence of these artifacts.

Additionally, the borrow pit contains some truly unusual pieces that may suggest a qualitative difference between this and other features at the site. A possible inference is that non-economic or ritual behavior led to the incorporation of these artifacts into the borrow pit's fill. Walker notes that "ritual behaviors create aggregates of objects whose lives within a society are distinguished from those of nonritual objects" (Walker 1995:72) and these inclusions may represent the archaeological signature of such ritual activities. Several pieces of shell were found throughout the pit, including a cluster of 22 drilled bivalves. Further, one larger bivalve with a drill hole was recovered nearby (Figure 4.5). This cluster of drilled shells suggests that a necklace may have been intentionally placed in this feature. Additionally, two apparently curated artifacts were recovered from this feature. A fragment of a late Archaic tray and an anthropomorphic ceramic figurine, similar to ones of earlier periods, such as the Early Agricultural and Colonial, were recovered from the bottom of the pit (Figure 4.6). Their inclusion in a deposit that otherwise dates exclusively to the Tanque Verde phase suggests an extended curation of the artifacts prior to the filling of the pit. Interestingly, at Pueblo Viejo, the only ceramic figurine and exotic sherd recovered were from a borrow pit that also included a cremation (Zyniecki 1993:35).

Inhumation

An extended inhumation was encountered at the termination of the borrow pit (Figure 4.7), a relatively unusual finding, because most other mortuary remains at the mound site have been cremations rather than inhumations. At its highest extent, the burial feature was an oblong pit, aligned with the long axis of the inhumation, and covering the lower three-quarters of the body, with the chest and head in an undercut niche extending east. The orientation of the remains is similar to inhumations at other sites in the Tucson Basin (Slaughter and Roberts 1996:437). Skeletal characteristics suggest the individual was a male between 14 and 16 years of age with no signs of pathology or trauma (McClelland 2003). Classic period inhumations have been found in compound courtyards or in structures (Brunson 1989; Crown and Fish 1996; Wilcox 1987), as well as in special use areas of sites (Effland 1988; Mitchell 1992:90; Mitchell et al. 1989). The placement of individuals within compounds has been thought to symbolize ties between the dead and individual households (Ciolek-Torrello et al. 1999:219; Huntington 1986).

The presence of the inhumation helps explain the unusual nature of the pit's deposit. The destruction of objects and even structures in mortuary ritual is relatively common in Southwestern ethnographic literature (Beals 1934:7; Drucker 1941; Gifford 1932:185; Kelly 1977; Spier 1928:234, 1933:303; Steward 1933:62). The burning of structures, found throughout the prehistoric Southwest and amongst the Hohokam (Craig and Walsh-Anduze 2001:98; Doelle 1985:195; Doelle and Wallace 1991:322; Elson 1986; Fish and Fish 1989:121; Greenleaf 1975:105; Seymour and Schiffer 1987) may be a component of the ritual closure of space associated with an individual after death. At the mound site, the burning and destruction of other structures is often thought to have been associated with mortuary or other ritual ceremony, rather than catastrophic abandonment (P. Fish and Fish 2000:254).

In the present case, the structure may not have been destroyed and left in place, but instead removed and deposited into the borrow pit, over the individual. The fill, described above, was deposited after the body was

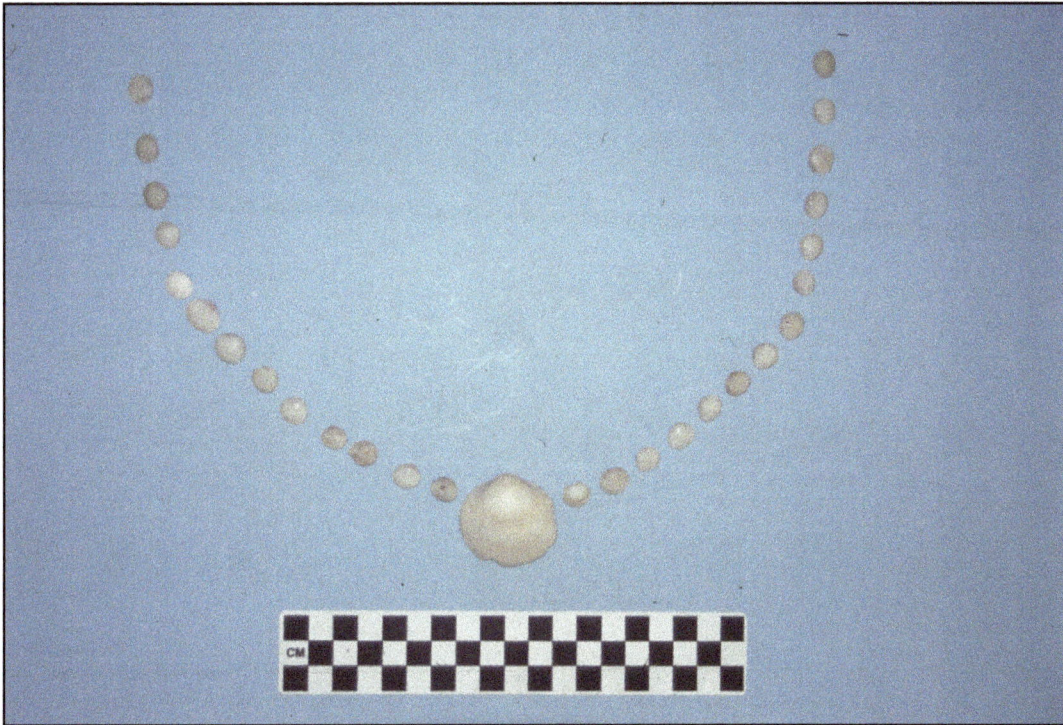

Figure 4.5. Cluster of 22 drilled bivalves.

Figure 4.6. Anthropomorphic ceramic figurine.

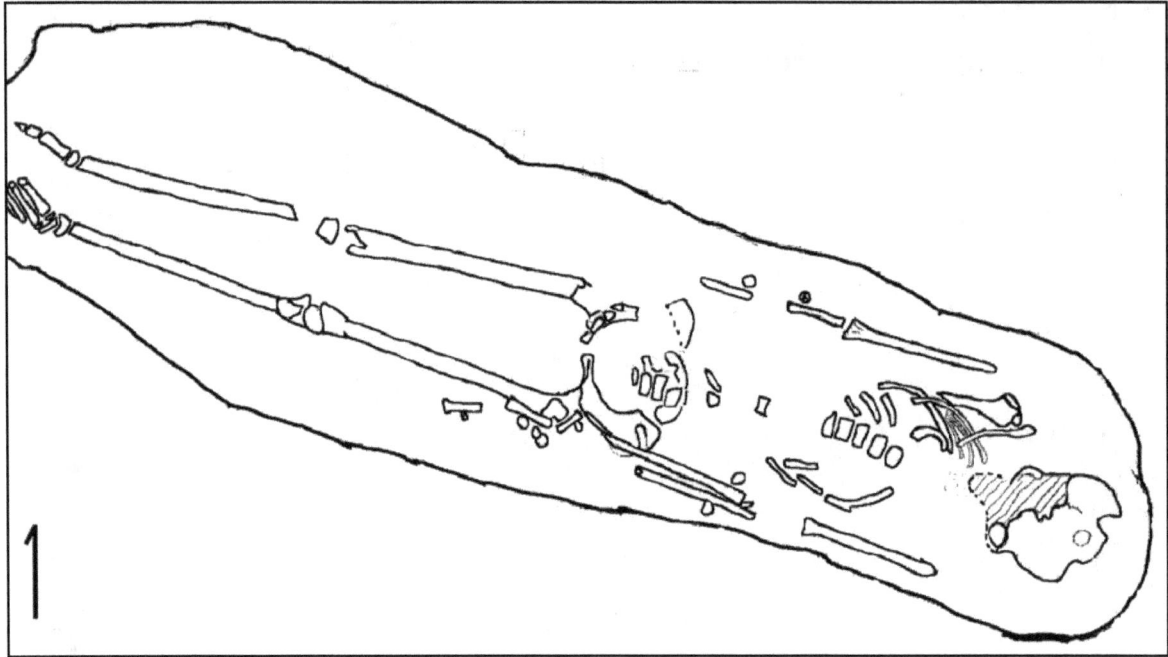

Figure 4.7. Inhumation at base of borrow pit.

interred as the burial pit only became apparent at the bottom of the borrow pit. This interpretation may account for unique character of the deposit. The sherd size profile and unusual contents could result from the inclusion of both a house's inventory and mortuary offerings (i.e., figurine, complete shell necklace, tray) within this deposit. The pit's high sherd density relative to structures could simply result from packing a house's assemblage into a smaller volume, plus the addition of mortuary offerings. The presence of adobe chunks and ash throughout the fill may represent segments of the actual house structure, destroyed and moved into the pit. The use of the borrow pit as the location of a mortuary feature may have conveyed special status to the space and prevented subsequent disturbance—seen at many other trash-filled borrow pits—and limited further transformation of the deposit. The deposit was surely visible to residents (as it was to the excavators) and may have served as a grave marker.

SUMMARY AND DISCUSSION

A possible interpretation of Compound 3's history unfolds in the following manner. Initially, the compound was small with a fairly thin adobe wall encircling it. This section of the compound would correspond to the northern half of the total compound that was encountered archaeologically. Based on evidence from other Hohokam sites, borrow pits are not typically found within compound—or courtyard group—boundaries, so Compound 3's borrow pit would not have existed during the early occupation. If this assumption is correct, the ancient excavation of the borrow pit would have corresponded with a cessation of occupation in the northern section. If compound residence ended, this raises the question of what activities created the borrow pit. One interpretation is that the borrow pit was, in part, the byproduct of the extension of Compound 3 to the south. What had been the southern boundary of the early compound became what I have discussed as the internal or dividing wall. According to this scenario, active occupation of Compound 3 shifted from the northern to the southern section. While technically in a compound, the borrow pit may not have been constructed until the northern section of the compound was abandoned for daily use and so the norms of Hohokam spatial behavior would not have been violated.

The inhumation and its possible mortuary deposit must have postdated the borrow pit, and if this inference is correct, the construction of the newer section of the compound. It is unclear if the individual's death motivated the shift in compound occupation. However, the deposit directly overlies the burial at the bottom of the borrow pit, suggesting that the internment happened relatively soon after the pit's excavation. In this case, the borrow pit/mortuary deposit would have been in place while the southern section of Compound 3 was actively occupied. Assuming continued residence of a corporate group, the death of the individual interred in the borrow pit may have inspired the shift in residence and the ritual consecration of the compound's southern half, and perhaps simultaneously, the closure of its northern half. Regardless of the actual sequence of events, the inclusion of this individual inside an area that was once occupied by, and still physically linked to compound residents may have had implications for their, and the deceased's, social membership and identity. While the burial would now be outside of actively occupied compound space, the older wall would still likely provide some concrete connection to Compound 3's residents, as well as a physical and visual barrier to members of other compounds.

This interpretation, specific to the history of one compound, supports the general importance of ties between compound space, and by extension the site, to the corporate group. The residents continued their occupation at the mound site and retained a spatial connection to their older residential incarnation. Rather than leave and settle elsewhere, the new addition utilized a component of the previous one. If the occupational shift to the south was the result of this individual's death and associated rituals, the residents of Compound 3 chose to remain in the same space, albeit with some modification. The decision to remain near the previous compound implies that space was at a premium at the mound site and that living at this central village conferred significant social advantages to its members. Living at the center of the Marana community may have offered political, social, religious and economic opportunities that were unavailable elsewhere. These conditions encouraged strategies that maintained corporate group residence at the site during the Early Classic, a time of dramatic changes in the Hohokam social environment.

Chapter 5
Analysis of Plant Remains from the Marana Mound Site

Karla Hansen-Speer

INTRODUCTION

This paper is an overview of carbonized plant remains found at the Marana Mound site (AZ AA:12:251) in southern Arizona and take a closer look at several specific contexts that give insight into how plants were used at the site. Plants have multiple uses, from food to craft to construction. Here, the focus is on plants as they relate to subsistence. Food, however, is more than a source of calories needed by the body to function. Food reinforces social bonds; the everyday act of preparing and sharing a meal establishes and maintains domestic traditions (Twiss 2004). Food is also "a prime political tool; it has a prominent role in social activity concerned with relations of power" (Dietler 1996:87).

By the Early Classic period (A.D. 1150-1300) in the Tucson Basin, the Hohokam of the Marana Mound site were a well established agricultural society (P. Fish and Fish 2000). In this paper, I refer to the specific mound compound as the "Platform Mound," the compounds surrounding the platform as the "Marana Mound site," and the larger community including Muchas Casas and Rancho Derrio as the "Marana Community." A complete survey of the Northern Tucson Basin by Fish, Fish, and Madsen (1992a) identified these sites, among others.

Much of Hohokam social organization must have been shaped by being agriculturalists; for example the need for labor scheduling, planting and harvesting, and the resolution of water and land disputes. Prominent features of the Hohokam culture, noted by the earliest archaeologists, such as Gladwin and Haury, are the irrigation canals (Haury 1976). The presence of large canal networks drew inevitable attention as a means for intensification sensu Wittfogel and accompanying social organization. The enduring fascination with canals led researchers to focus on studying agricultural techniques: canals, checkdams, *akchin* farming, and rockpile fields (e.g., Ackerly 1982; Crown 1987; Fish 1995; Woodbury 1961). Researchers know a fair amount about how the Hohokam grew crops and that they expended a lot of energy in this task. The compliment of paleoethnobotanical evidence to the database of agricultural techniques fills out the picture of plant use and provides information about which plants were actually brought into a household, how they were used, and in what proportion. Cultivated plants were obviously of great importance, but wild and weedy plants were also used.

Two basic questions are addressed. First, does the Marana Mound site (as a whole) show a difference in plants when compared to the Marana Community? Second, is there variation in the distribution of intra-site plant remains? That is, were Platform Mound residents using plants differently than residents in adjacent compounds, in terms of the type or abundance of various plants?

Several points about the Marana Mound site should be kept in mind during the following discussion. First, the Marana Mound site is centrally located within the larger Marana Community. It was the most important site in the community, as evidenced by its architecture and artifacts. Second, it is not located on prime irrigated land. This suggests that, even though it was part of an agricultural society, the site's importance did not come from control of the best land for growing maize or controlling access to irrigated fields which potentially should produce the most abundant harvests.

In the remainder of this paper, I will give an overview of the plant assemblage from the Marana Mound site, maintain that agave was a principle resource at the site, and discuss the value of small seeded wild grasses such as dropseed (*Sporobolus* spp.) and lovegrass (*Eragrostis* spp.) to Marana inhabitants. Finally, I'll examine several spaces in the Platform Mound compound that have abundant plant remains. Before turning to the results, I briefly describe my methods of plant analysis below.

METHODS

Soil samples of approximately four liters were taken systematically for flotation from 16 structures and eight trashmounds excavated at the Marana Mound site. The flotation samples were processed at the Arizona State Museum using a modified bucket method of flotation. The data set presented here consists of 164 samples, 137 of which were analyzed by me, and 27 of which were analyzed by Charles Miksicek (Table 5.1). One hundred forty-three flotation samples and five macrobotanical samples came from structures, while 17 flotation samples came from trashmounds. Because the majority of samples came from structures and the floors and features within them, they should relate to household use. I assumed that only carbonized plant material is preserved because this is an open site. It is also noted that these preservation conditions bias the type of plants and plant parts recovered (Gasser and Adams 1981). Laboratory analysis of the samples began by screening the samples through a series of size-graded geological sieves (3.35 mm, 2.00 mm, 1.00 mm, .5 mm, .335 mm). All material 2.00 mm and larger was fully sorted. Material between 2.00 and 1.00 mm was scanned for corn (*Zea mays* spp. mays), agave (*Agave* sp.), squash rind (*Cucurbita* spp.), and seeds. Material below 1.00 mm was scanned for seeds. Carbonized plant material was identified by comparison to the plant collection in the Paleoethnobotanical Laboratory at Washington University in St. Louis and to books such as Martin and Barkley (1961). Following identification, I quantified the plants and interpreted their uses, as discussed in the next section.

Table 5.1. Marana Plant Sample Size and Context

Analyst	Structures	Trashmounds	Total
KHS	128	9	137
CM	19	8	27
Total	147	17	164

KHS = Karla Hansen Speer

CM = Charles Miksicek

RESULTS AND DISCUSSION

Plant assemblage and inferred plant uses

A variety of both domestic and wild plants were found at the site (Table 5.2). Corn (*Zea mays* spp. *mays*), squash (*Cucurbita* spp.), agave (*Agave* spp.), and beans (*Phaseolus* spp.) are crops that would have been consumed as food. These plants were mainstays of the Hohokam diet (S. Fish 2004; K. Hansen-Speer 2006). Corn is represented by kernels, cupules, glumes, and cob fragments. Agave, squash, and cotton were also related to craft production: agave and cotton for fiber, and squash as a container. Fragments of agave fibers and tissue have been primarily identified on the basis of distinctive calcium oxalate crystals in the shape of raphides and styloids (Figure 5.1). I also identified a number of marginal teeth from the leaf edge of agave.

The processing steps of agave (see Parsons and Parsons 1990) lead me to believe that teeth are probably an indicator of its use as fiber rather than as a food, because most of the processing as food would happen near the roasting pits. Processing the leaves for fiber, however, is less likely to take place in the field, and teeth are more likely to be a by-product, although the marginal teeth may be stripped from the leaf edge during harvest in the field (Parsons and Parsons 1990:147). Ethnographic accounts of various southwestern groups such as the Apache (Buskirk 1986), and Yavapai (Gifford 1936) relate how agave was processed for food: the heart of the plant would be harvested, the leaves removed, and then it would be roasted in a large pit near the rockpile fields. Once roasted, it could be pounded into cakes and dried for storage (Hodgson 2001); however, much that is recognizable about the plant would no longer be preserved at this point. In contrast, the leaves are used for fiber, and the process of heating the leaves to loosen the fiber

from the rest of the leaf, removing the marginal teeth, and then scraping the fiber clean, may have taken place in a household rather than in the field (Parsons and Parsons 1990).

Pigweed or amaranth, (*Amaranthus* spp.), is a small grain with both wild and domestic forms. The cultivated variety is distinguished by a thin seed coat. Only a few amaranth seeds with thin seed coats that could be potential domesticates were found at the Marana Mound site. Many seeds were rather poorly preserved and missing seed coats, making it difficult to distinguish *Chenopodium* from *Amaranthus*, and even more difficult to distinguish domestic *Amaranthus* from wild. Most seeds of this type fell into the category of "cheno-am", an artificial group encompassing members of both the Chenopodiaceae and Amaranthaceae families whose seeds are similar to one another. Although *Amaranthus* can be cultivated and has been documented in Hohokam sites (Bohrer 1991; Fritz 2007; Miksicek 1983), *Chenopodium* and *Amaranthus* are more often considered wild or weedy plants in the American Southwest. Along with a variety of other small-seeded plants, they may have grown in fields along with the crops, along canals or washes, or in household areas.

Many of these types of plants grow preferentially in disturbed habitats and are often described as "weeds." Other plants of the small seeded wild and weedy type include tansy mustard (*Descurainia* spp.) and spiderling (*Boerhaavia* sp.) (see Table 5.1). Miksicek (1987:210) divided these small seeded types into "Encouraged Plants or Edible Seeds" and "Agricultural Weeds." The former category includes amaranth, tansy mustard, dropseed (*Sporobolus*), plantain (*Plantago* sp.), chia (*Salvia*), and panic grass (*Panicum*) while the latter category includes globemallow (*Sphaelracea* sp.), spurge (*Euphorbia*), spiderling, purslane (*Portulaca*), and Lupine (*Lupinus* sp.). These categories are not mutually exclusive,

Table 5.2. Marana Mound Site (AZ AA:12:251 ASM) Plant List		
Scientific Name	Common Name	Plant Part
Agave	Agave	heart, leaf, marginal teeth
Amaranthus	Pigweed	seed
Astragalus	Milk-vetch	seed
Atriplex type	Saltbush	seed
Boerhaavia	Spiderling	seed
Carnegia gigantea	Saguaro	seed, wood
Chenopodiaceae	Chenopod family	seed
Chenopodium	Goosefoot	seed
Cleome	Spider flower	seed
Cucurbita pepo	Squash/pumpkin	rind
Cucurbitaceae	Squash family	rind
Descurainia	Tansy mustard	seed
Echinocerus	Hedgehog cactus	seed
Euphorbiaceae	Spurge family	seed
Gossypium	Cotton	seed
Lepidium	Pepper grass	seed
Malvaceae	Mallow family	seed
Nicotiana	Tobacco	seed
Oenothera	Evening primrose	seed
Opuntia	Cholla/prickly pear	seed
Papavaraceae	Poppy family	seed
Phaseolus	Bean (common or tepary)	cotyledon
Plantago	Plantain, Indian wheat	seed
Poaceae	Grass family	seed, stem
Polansia	Clammy weed	seed
Prosopis	Mesquite	seed, pod, wood
Salvia	Chia	seed
Sphaeralcea	Globemallow	seed
Sporobolus/Eragrostis type	Dropseed/lovegrass	seed
Zea mays spp. *mays*	Maize	kernel, cupule, cob, embryo

Figure 5.1. Charred agave. Note the raphides (rod-like crystals) embedded throughout the material (Photograph by Karla Hansen-Speer).

however. Several plants such as *Chenopodium* may have grown in fields as an "encouraged agricultural weed." Categorizing plants as "weeds," however, may unintentionally imply that they were pests and had no utility even though some, such as globemallow, had medicinal benefits. These useful plants should not be dismissed as unwanted weeds. Instead, I have simply grouped these types of plants into a "small seeded" category as being analytically comparable (following Diehl 2001).

The Marana Mound site also contained evidence that the inhabitants gathered wild plants, such as the fruit of the saguaro (*Carnegia gigantea*) and other cacti, as well as mesquite beans (*Prosopis* spp.) (Table 5.3). These seeds were found in trace amounts and may suggest the use of specialized gathering camps away from the main village where collection and processing would have taken place. Such camps have been ethnographically documented (Castetter and Underhill 1935; Hodgson 2001).

I also identified two tobacco seeds (*Nicotiana* sp.), which are not a food crop, but used for other social/ceremonial purposes. Smoking of tobacco among the Pima, for example, usually took place in a ritual context and played an important role in creation stories (Rea 1997:316-320). Interestingly, the tobacco

Table 5.3. Marana Mound Site (AZ AA:12:251 ASM) Plant Data

Category	Counts	Ubiquity (n = 164)
Agave sp.	364	30.5
Amaranthus sp.	45	11.0
Cheno-am	151	24.4
Chenopodiaceae	72	5.5
Chenopodium sp.	23	4.3
Atriplex sp.	28	4.3
Astragalus sp. type	6	3.7
Boerhaavia sp.	5	2.4
Carnegia gigantea	3	1.8
Cleome sp.	2	0.6
Cucurbita sp. rind count	586	45.1
Descurania sp.	176	20.1
Lepidium sp.	7	3.0
Brassicaceae	4	0.6
Echinocerus sp.	9	3.0
Euphorbiaceae	2	1.2
Gossypium sp. total frag	41	9.1
Nicotiana sp.	2	1.2
Oenothera sp. type	1	0.6
Opuntia sp.	6	2.4
Phaseolus sp	108	4.9
Plantago sp.	12	2.4
Poaceae	72	14.6
Prosopis sp.	12	6.1
Salvia sp.	10	3.7
Sporabolus/Eragrastis type	1888	57.9
Sphaeralcea sp.	30	7.3
Zea mays	710	46.3
CCSC*	14	2.4
Wood	11536	78.0
Stem	1400	47.0
Rhizome	285	23.2
Unknown	607	38.4
Unidentified seeds	45	12.2
Unidentifiable seed frag	872	56.1

*Columnar Celled Seed Coat

seeds at Marana were not found on the platform mound where special ceremonies presumably took place, but in Compounds 1 and 5. This implies that those who used the platform mound did not have a monopoly on ceremonial behavior.

In general, the carbonized remains from the Marana Mound site are similar in content to other sites in the Tucson basin (see Gasser and Kwiatkowski 1991; Miksicek 1987). The major cultivated plants, herbaceous plants, and cacti are all present. Although plant diversity is quite high and over 23 different taxa have been identified, there are some plants, in fact, that were not found at the site. In the agricultural weed category (sensu Miksicek 1987), the Marana Mound site lacks lupine, *Trianthema*, and clammy weed (*Polanisia*). In addition, no little barley (*Hordeum pusillum*) was found at the site, although a few grains are reported from nearby Los Morteros (Gasser and Kwaitkowski 1991:435). However, little barley is most common in the Colonial and Sedentary periods in the Salt and Gila River Basins (Gasser and Kwaitkowski 1991:442), therefore, the absence at Marana may not be particularly significant. Going beyond a simple list of plants and analyzing the abundance and density of plants within the community reveals further insights concerning plant use in the Marana Community.

Intra-Community Comparison

The Marana Mound site had a substantial amount of corn, agave, and squash rind as measured by ubiquity or presence value (Table 5.3). Ubiquity is the percentage of samples containing a given taxon out of the total number of samples. The presence of squash (*Cucurbita* sp.) is based on the identification of rind (Figure 5.2); there were no seeds found in the samples. Its high ubiquity (45 percent) indicates widespread use at the site, but this number is not comparable to other sites, because most records are based on seeds rather than rind identification. That beans were present in only a few samples (5 percent ubiquity) is consistent with most Southwestern flotation samples. Beans are notoriously rare in archaeological sites because of their poor preservation potential rather than because of how much they were used by prehistoric inhabitants. Gasser and Kwaitkowski (1991:431) note that beans are usually abundant in the Tucson Basin sites; surprisingly, the Marana Mound flotation samples simply record that beans were used, but not that they were especially plentiful.

Thirty-one percent of flotation samples from the site contained agave. Fish, Fish, and Madsen (1992a) have presumed agave to be especially important at the site because of the association of rockpile fields and large roasting pits located on the bajada above. In comparison, Muchas Casas and Rancho Derrio (other sites in the community) had an average of about 15 percent comparable agave remains (excluding stalks used as construction material) (Gasser and Kwiatkowski 1991; Miksicek 1987). Given the Marana site's proximity to the rockpile fields, we might expect to find a lot of agave; but while the ubiquity of 31 percent is twice as much as at other sites in the community, it is not does not approach the 80 to 90 percent ubiquity sometimes recorded for sites in the Phoenix Basin (Gasser and Kwaitkowski 1991:423).

This discrepancy may be explained in several ways. First, roasting of agave hearts mainly took place in the large rockpile fields above of the Marana Mound instead of in domestic contexts at the site. In contrast, large roasting pits in fields are not common in the Phoenix basin, and processing of agave was probably done in habitation areas rather than in the fields; this would dramatically increase the amount of agave deposited in Phoenix basin sites relative to the Marana Mound site.

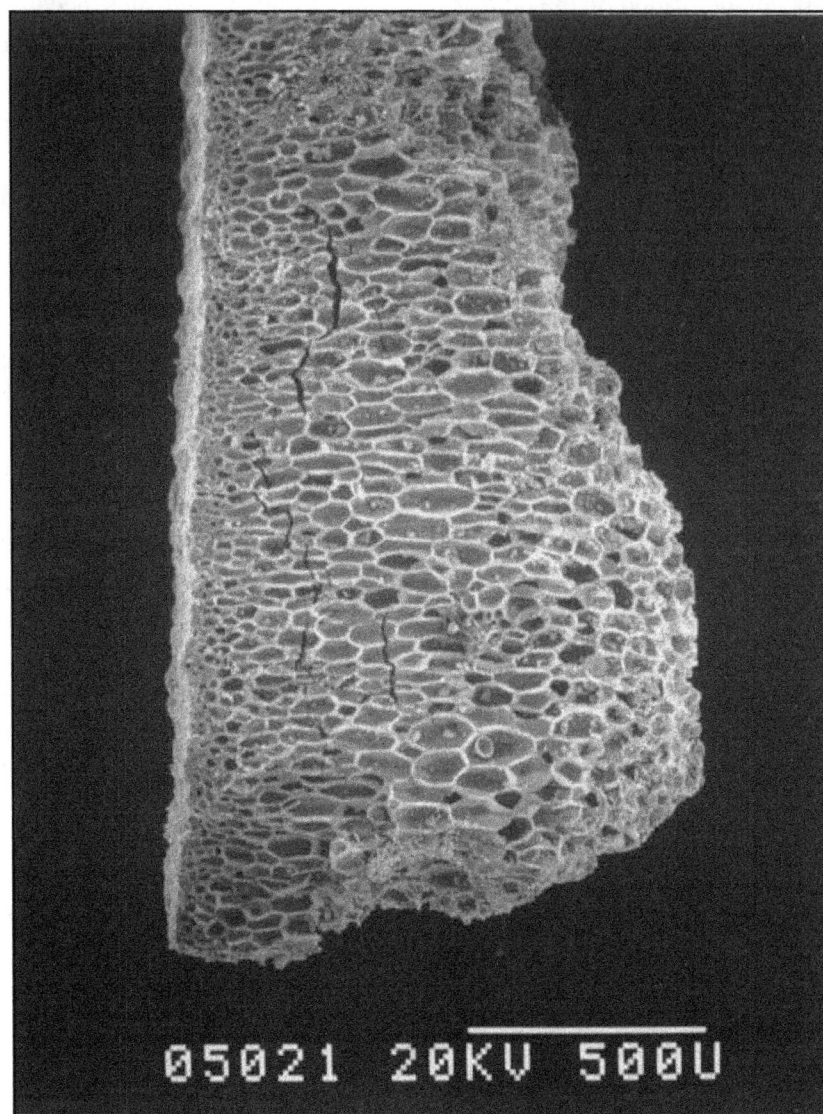

Figure 5.2. Scanning electron microscope (SEM) image of squash rind.

Second, agave stalks and leaves that were discarded as part of processing the plants for food or fiber may have been used as a source of fuel in the Phoenix area, but not at the Marana site. Fuel was probably scarce in the central Phoenix basin due to a landscape of irrigation fields set in desert scrub vegetation. Dense populations and limited wood would have made agave an attractive fuel source, which would increase the amount of agave preserved at the site through carbonization. In comparison, the only type of plant material that approaches 80 percent ubiquity (the amount of agave at some Phoenix sites) at the Marana Mound site is wood at 78 percent. Further evidence of the importance of agave at the Marana Mound site comes from the disproportionate number of tabular "agave" knives found there in comparison to the rest of the community (Bayman 1994), suggesting the residents' regular processing of agave. Finally, if the residents of the Marana Mound site were trading agave for other products, presumably some portion of it was taken away from the site and would be preserved elsewhere, if at all. Although agave was not as ubiquitious as at some other Hohokam sites, it was one of the more prominent plants at the Marana Mound site and was surely a principal resource.

Almost half (46 percent) of samples from the Marana Mound site had corn in them. Muchas Casas and Rancho Derrio, however, contained an average of about 30 percent corn. This is an exciting (yet unexpected) finding, considering the Marana Mound site's distance from irrigated fields and its location on agricultural land of secondary quality. But because of its role as a community center, we might expect that corn, an important staple, was provided by other parts of the community more suited to maize agriculture. Geographically, the Marana Mound site was the center of the community. It may also have been the center of the cultural and economic community.

The Mound site did not have high numbers of agricultural weed seeds (e.g., globemallow (6 percent), spiderling (*Boerhaavia*) (2 percent), and lupine (*Lupinus*) (0 percent)). Moreover, it did not have unusually high numbers of chenopodium or amaranth, which also may have grown in and around fields and canals. The low presence of plants that would grow in and around fields is another strong indicator that the Marana Mound inhabitants did not frequent agricultural fields.

One type of wild plant that the Marana Mound site had in abundance was grass (*Poaceae* or *Gramineae*). The grass was probably of one or two small seeded types: dropseed (*Sporobolus*) and lovegrass (*Eragrastis*). Like the cheno-ams, the grass seeds were often in a rather poor state of preservation, and identification to genus is problematic. At 58 percent ubiquity (Table 5.3), this small seeded *Sporobolus/Eragrostis* grass type had the highest percentage presence of all plant taxa, even higher than corn at 46 percent. Other sites in

the Marana Community also report a strong presence of dropseed, though not as much as the Marana Mound site. Miksicek (1987:210) records a low of 17.5 percent ubiquity for dropseed at Rancho Derrio, to a high of 47.8 percent ubiquity at Muchas Casas Locus A. Clearly, this was a widely used plant in the region.

Grass seeds not only had the highest ubiquity in the samples from the Marana Mound site, they were present in every single room. Dropseed and lovegrass vary from other small seeded plants, such as tansy mustard, in that they are not usually found in agricultural fields as a weed. Dropseed in particular is easily gathered and processed because it has a naked grain, that is, the seed is easily freed from glumes and bracts (Kearney and Peebles 1969). Although dropseed and lovegrass have very small grains, they are prolific in number. The grain could be parched and ground into a meal. Ethnographic accounts in the Southwest and elsewhere in North America document the importance of dropseed and lovegrass as a food source (Castetter and Bell 1951; Doebley 1984).

Although small grass seeds were used as a food resource, they may have had other purposes, too. The seeds could be related to thatching or construction of houses, or could simply be a prehistoric seed rain in which the grass blew into a room and was subsequently swept into a hearth. These alternative explanations cannot be completely discarded, but I think the grass is much more likely to be a source of food. Several contextual clues support this view. First, the flotation samples with abundant roof material in them do not have high numbers of dropseed or lovegrass, therefore it was not primarily a construction material. Dropseed was found in floor samples, and the largest concentration was from several storage pits. Some hearths also have dropseed. Parching the seeds was probably a step in their processing, and so it is likely that some would have been carbonized and preserved in the archaeological record. Seed rain tends to include a wide range of plants with little or no economic value, and yet the Marana assemblage does not reflect this pattern. Furthermore, small grass seeds were found only in samples from (enclosed) structures, whereas none were found in samples from open trash mounds that would have been most prone to seed rain. Finally, we have strong ethnographic evidence that dropseed in particular was used as a food source by many Southwestern groups (see Castetter and Opler 1936; Castetter and Bell 1951; Doebley 1984; Vestal 1952).

In summary, the plant remains from the Mound site are strikingly different from the larger community in a number of ways—there is a greater presence of corn, agave, and small grass seeds, and fewer weeds and cacti. The fact that corn was present in so many samples, despite the Marana Mound site's lesser agricultural potential, may be especially significant when looking at questions of power and economy at the site. Perhaps residents acquired this valuable staple by other means than producing it themselves. The low level of agricultural weeds supports an interpretation that Marana Mound residents did not primarily get their corn by growing it in irrigated fields. A relatively high level of agave is consistent with the presence of agave fields nearby. While the plant assemblage from the Marana Mound site differed from that of the larger community, plant use in the Platform Mound precinct appears to parallel the rest of the site.

Plant Use at the Platform Mound

The Platform Mound precinct is distinguished from other adobe compounds at the site by the presence of the mound itself as well as exclusive association with datura effigy vessels (P. Fish and Fish 2000:270). Other artifact classes,

however, including exotic goods, such as shell and obsidian, were found in all compounds at the site. Residents of the entire site appear to have had access to such craft items (Bayman 1994). Plants follow this pattern of similar assemblages among compounds. Type or abundance of certain plants does not distinguish the Platform Mound precinct, although plant assemblages vary from room to room at the Marana Mound site, which suggests discrete activity areas. Based on the similarity of plant remains in certain contexts of the Platform Mound precinct to other contexts in the site, I argue that activities occurring in the Platform Mound precinct probably paralleled activities taking place in other compounds.

The plant assemblage from a poorly understood context within the compound mound (Compound 9 Room 4, hereafter called C9R4) closely resembles that of an extramural food preparation area in Compound 5 Room 4 (C5R4). A correspondence analysis clustered these two contexts together because both had an abundance of maize, beans, agave, and small starchy seeds (Figure 5.3). These two contexts also exhibited the two highest species diversity indexes at the Marana Mound site (Table 5.4). I used the Shannon Index to calculate the diversity of plants for each room at the Marana Mound site. Low diversity means that there are few taxa present, or that the assemblage is dominated by a few species. High diversity means that many taxa are evenly distributed (Pearsall 1989:211). Although C9R4 had the highest species richness at the site with 15 different plant taxa represented, the assemblage was dominated by corn, so the diversity (1.55) was slightly lower than C5R4's (1.81) where the plants were more evenly distributed. Fifty-four percent of C9R4's plant assemblage was composed of maize, more than that of any other room. It also had a fair amount of agave (9 percent frequency) and cheno-am (12 percent frequency), but very little small grass (2 percent

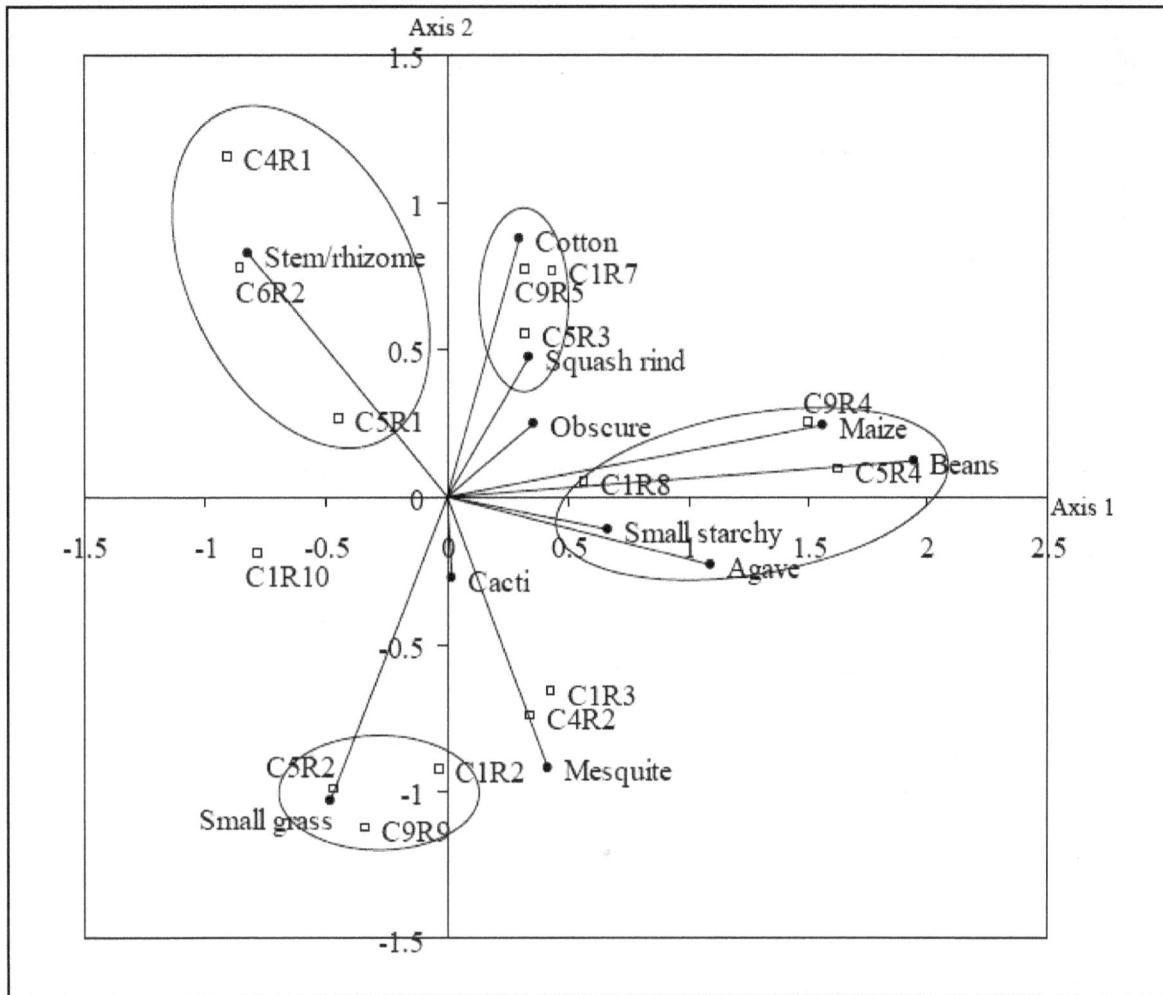

Figure 5.3. Correspondence Analysis map of plants and 15 rooms at the Marana Mound site. The first axis accounts for 40.1 percent of the variation while the second axis accounts for 23.2 percent, for a cumulative percent of 63.3 percent. Circles highlight rooms whose plant assemblages are dominated by a particular plant category (Hansen-Speer 2006: Figure 6.13).

frequency), which was widely present in flotation samples from the site as a whole. Based on the importance that corn plays in the traditions of the Pima (Rea 1997) and Papago (Castetter and Bell 1942), maize may be considered a more important food culturally and economically than a small seeded wild grass, such as dropseed. The presence of a large amount of maize at the Platform Mound points to this location as a significant center for the Marana Mound site, but the general pattern of plant

distribution is similar to comparable contexts in other compounds.

Similarly, a room on the mound summit (Compound 9 Room 5) shares an association between cotton seed fragments and craft tools, such as spindle whorls, with several other rooms (Compound 1 Room 10 and Compound 4 Room 1) outside the Platform Mound precinct. Interestingly, these are all distinctive from ordinary rooms. Compound 1 Room 10 had "ceremonial" evidence, Compound 4

Table 5.4. Interpreted Room Function, Species Diversity, and Species Richness (Hansen-Speer 2006: Table 6.4)

Room	Function	Species diversity	Species richness
C1R2	Storage	n.a.	14
C1R3	Habitation	1.30	7
C1R7	Habitation	1.31	11
C1R8	?	n.a.	5
C1R10	Ceremonial room	0.42	8
C4R1	Residence of compound head	1.43	12
C4R2	Habitation	1.30	9
C4R3	Extra mural work space, roasting pit	1.03	11
C5R1	Craft production	1.31	12
C5R2	Storage	0.67	12
C5R3	Habitation	1.15	12
C5R4	Extramural work space	1.81	10
C6R2	Craft production/ Habitation	0.75	3
C9R4sub	?	1.55	15
C9R5	Craft production?	1.28	4
C9R9	Ceremonial room	0.77	12
Average		1.15	9.8

Room 1 appears to have been the residence of a compound head, and Compound 9 Room 5 was located on the mound summit. The interpretation of room function is based on size, features, and artifact assemblage. Other rooms at the site have been interpreted as storage structures, for example, based on presence numerous large storage vessels.

One area of the platform compound that did not have an analogous plant assemblage elsewhere at the site was Compound 9 Room 9, a large room adjacent to the mound that had two hearths, thick walls, numerous tiny post-holes, and pieces of a *Datura* effigy pot. It had relatively low plant diversity (.77), but the highest seed density of any room. Almost all of the seeds in the house were small grass seeds; there was only one fragment of corn. A great deal of the diversity in plant remains came from the larger of the two hearths found in the room. In contrast, the small hearth had almost nothing in it. This suggests that the hearths were used for very different purposes; perhaps the small hearth burned so hot and that its only contents were ash.

Different rooms of the platform mound compound appear to have been areas of discrete activity. The plant remains from Compound 9 Room 9 are distinct from both Compound 9 Room 5 and Compound 9 Room 4. Some parallels in the plant assemblage between mound and non-mound contexts at the site elucidate activities, such as food preparation and craft production, that were apparently practiced across the site. There is still much to be discovered, however. Were the residents feasting at the mound? Did they hold festivals and ceremonies there? Were activities held community-wide or restricted to a particular segment of the population? It is difficult to use plant evidence to make a case for feasting, except in rare cases like Submound 51 at Cahokia (see Pauketat et al. 2002). Animal evidence can sometimes be more enlightening on this point (see Bayham and Grimstead, this volume). Other artifactual evidence will no doubt help clarify the economic and social roles of different areas within the Marana Mound site.

CONCLUSIONS

Analysis of the carbonized plant assemblages from the Marana Mound site leads to several conclusions. (1) In addition to crops, such as corn and agave, small grass seeds, such as dropseed or lovegrass, were a valuable and widespread resource in the Marana Community as evidenced in their high ubiquity in flotation samples. (2) The platform mound precinct had discrete activity areas that paralleled the site as a whole. One area on the platform mound contained high plant diversity as well as the largest amount of corn found in a room at the Marana Mound site, and is interpreted as a food preparation area, comparable to others found at the site. Other similarities in the plant assemblage are found with the association of cotton seed and craft tools in distinctive rooms across the site. Moreover, the presence of tobacco seeds in rooms away from the platform mound indicates that ceremonial activities were not restricted to the platform mound alone. (3) The Marana Mound site contains more cultivated crops and less agricultural weeds than other parts of the Marana Community. The residents did not occupy irrigated land that could supply all their needs and may not have grown all their own corn. The platform mound may have facilitated the circulation of subsistence staple goods within the community's economic system.

The nearby agave fields may have provided a resource that was less susceptible to fluctuation in climate and rainfall regimes, and so might have filled a niche as a stable crop with multiple uses of both food and fiber. The presence of agave at the Marana Mound site is greater than at other sites in the community and is prominent in the flotation samples. Although agave does not dominate the plant assemblages as it does in some Phoenix Basin sites, the lower ubiquity is no doubt explained in part by the fact that much of the initial agave processing at the Marana Mound site appears to have taken place in the fields where extensive roasting pits containing carbonized agave remains are associated with rockpile fields on the bajada (S. Fish, Fish, and Madsen 1992a). Rather than relying on one or two particular types of plants, the Hohokam residents of the Marana Mound site made use of a wide variety of wild and cultivated plants. Maintaining a diversity of plant resources offered an effective means to manage risk in an uncertain environment.

Chapter 6
Feasting at the Marana Platform Mound

Deanna Grimstead
Frank E. Bayham

Take the fattened calf and slaughter it. Then let us celebrate with a feast, because this son of mine was dead, and has come to life again; he was lost, and has been found (Luke 15:23-24).

INTRODUCTION

The consumption of food often serves purposes far beyond immediate sustenance and nutrition. The manner in which food is consumed can be culturally prescribed and imbued with personal, social, and political implications. "Feasting" is widely acknowledged as an event of this type, and its anthropological significance as well as its archaeological relevance has been addressed by a number of researchers in recent years (Bray 2003; Cameron 1995, 1998; Dietler and Hayden 2001; Szuter 1989; Wiessner and Schiefenhovel 1995). Feasting, as defined here and by others, involves the social consumption of food, can be accompanied by ceremony or ritual, and often may well be associated with the commemoration of an event (Dietler and Hayden 2001). Apart from these general observations, however, there remains a wide range of social food consumptive behaviors that might qualify an event as a feast. Perhaps most pertinent for this study, there are few unambiguous correlates for the phenomenon that can be identified from archaeologically derived material culture.

Reviews of the ethnographic and ethnohistoric literature from varied theoretical perspectives have resulted in a much broader appreciation of the myriad contexts and inherent variability linked to the widespread practice of feasting (e.g., Hayden 1995, Potter 1997). Elite feasting, for instance, can be undertaken with the intent of obtaining a variety of goals and will accordingly be manifest differently. Elites from one group may feast amongst themselves or they may invite elites from other groups to join. How might the intentions, purposes, and subtleties of this difference be detected or understood in the absence of direct observations? Additionally, archaeological efforts to outline specific criteria for the delineation of past feasts have grappled with its inherent variability in space and time, lack of visibility, and social variations. Despite these problems, detailed investigations of specific regions, time periods, cultures, and environments associated with feasting have begun to illuminate the social and political dynamics that underlie the prehistoric record; it would also seem that many of these recent efforts have relied on archaeofaunal data to strengthen their inferences (e.g., Hockett 1998, Kelly 2001, Pauketat et al. 2002).

The development of social complexity among the Hohokam of southern Arizona has been explored through archaeological study (Doyel et al. 2000; Reid and Whittlesey 1997), one aspect of which focuses on an impressive aggregate of archaeofauna (e.g., Cameron 1995, 1998; Szuter 1989, 1991). Recently, extensive survey and excavation of numerous middens, structures, compounds and pithouses associated with the Marana Community (Fish et al. 1992a) has resulted in an almost unparalleled opportunity to address the importance of feasting as a mechanism of power consolidation among Hohokam elites. In this paper, we comparatively examine the faunal record from selected contexts of the Marana Platform Mound and surrounding community in an effort to identify our hypothesized locus of elite feasting. Particularly, we want to assess whether or not a relatively high concentration of animal bone derived from a burned room adjacent to the Marana Platform Mound, known as Compound 9, Room 9 (hereafter referred to as Room 9), represented the remnants of prehistoric elite feasting. The integrity of this buried deposit coupled with its direct proximity to the main platform mound may well provide the degree of resolution needed to unequivocally identify the dynamic properties of a Classic period Hohokam feast.

Initially, we review some recent anthropological and archaeological studies to derive relevant archaeological signatures of feasting potentially applicable to the Marana faunal assemblage. General expectations are derived from Brian Hayden's (1995, 1996) extensive research of feasting within prehistoric and traditional societies and more specific archaeofaunal implications from a study of feasting at Cahokia (Kelly 2001; Pauketat et al. 2002). A discussion of the faunal analytical procedures is provided, followed by a synopsis of the comparative methodology employed. We show that in many ways the faunal material from this unique archaeological deposit is not unlike the archaeofaunal record from much of the surrounding community with one major exception: there is an inordinate amount of faunal material dominated by lagomorphs concentrated near the platform mound. We find support for a type of feasting not associated with elite aggrandizement, but much more akin to what Hayden (1995) has described as communal work party feasting. Ultimately, we speculate on the significance of this type of feasting and its meaning in the social and political context of the Classic period Hohokam.

FEASTING AND ANIMAL CONSUMPTION

Feasting is a cultural phenomena deeply embedded in the sociopolitical nature of cultural interaction. Brian Hayden (1995, 1996) has explored numerous ethnographic examples of feasting and has identified three distinct categories of feasting, with a total of eight sub-categories. The three major types of feasts include alliance and cooperation feasts, economic feasts, and diacritical feasts, which are not necessarily mutually exclusive (Hayden 1996). Hayden categorizes solidarity feasts, promotional feasts, reciprocal feasts, and political support feasts within the broader category of alliance and cooperation feasts. Economic feasts include competitive feasting and work party feasts, while diacritical feasts are best explained as exclusive elite activities designed to establish a division between the lower and upper classes (Hayden 1995:129). Work party feasting as defined by Hayden (1995:128) is a socially communal event occurring after large scale labor as been invested, such as clearing land or planting and harvesting crops.

Hayden (1995) focused his research on the archaeological indicators of competitive feasts, and identified six different categories of archaeological remains that can be used to detect the presence of elite competitive feasting. He suggests the availability of surplus producing food items, the presence of unique food items, the presence of special or elite serving vessels and features, the conversion of food surplus into prestigious items, the identification of special localities where feasting may have potentially occurred, and the presence of elites could be used to identify competitive feasting archaeologically (Hayden 1995). Hayden correctly notes that not all these criteria will always manifest themselves, especially given inherent problems with the archaeological record. After making this acknowledgement he suggests that when all these indicators are present it would certainly be a strong indicator that such sociopolitical activities did exist (Hayden 1995:141).

Yet animals, particularly large game, often have a pre-eminent role among the foods that constitute a feast. Additionally, we note there is a rather robust tendency among foragers and horticulturalists to preferentially select large prey items when there is a choice (Grayson 2001; Winterhalder and Smith 2000). Consistently, in a corroborative vein, researchers have demonstrated higher return rates on large prey items (Broughton and Bayham 2003; Ugan 2004). Meat is perhaps the highest quality source of protein, so consequently this is not surprising. When coupled with a relatively high amount of fat, there are few food items, which can match the high caloric content and palatability of meat (Speth and Spielmann 1983), which directly affects its utility as a symbol of power and prestige. The strength of these patterns is so compelling that it may well be possible to use the presence or absence of large or small taxa to discern the sociopolitical nature of a feast. This linkage between animals and social dynamics provides one of the more critical avenues to appreciating the ritual or sociopolitical meanings of prehistoric feasting.

Hayden's work clearly speaks to the underlying social complexity behind feasting behavior, and foreordains the type of problems that will be faced by archaeologists attempt-

ing to identify feasting. Essentially, with this degree of variability in the nature of feasting events, we would expect a commensurate degree of variability in the archaeological expression of feasting. That researchers such as Brian Hockett (1998) in the Great Basin and Christine Szuter (1989, 1991) and Judith Cameron (1995) in the American Southwest have found unequivocal faunal signatures of feasting to be elusive underscores this problem.

ARCHAEOFAUNAL EXPECTATIONS OF FEASTING

Archaeofaunal remains have been used to detect feasting events throughout the Southwest (e.g., Cameron 1995; Potter 1997; Szuter 1989), but a recent analysis of a unique context at the prehistoric metropolis of Cahokia in the Eastern Woodlands establishes a model for examining the faunal correlates of elite feasting (Pauketat et al. 2002). The case study from Cahokia will be used as a clear example of archaeologically identifiable elite feasting behavior and material correlates to which the Marana Platform Mound will be compared. The proposed archaeological evidence of a feast at Cahokia is compelling due to the stratigraphic isolation of a single event within a refuse pit that was potentially only in use for a single season (Pauketat et al. 2002:262). Archaeobotanical and paleoentomological evidence in conjunction with intermittent deposition of sterile soil enabled archaeologists to narrow down the season of this specific feasting event to late summer or early fall (Kelly 2001:343; Pauketat et al. 2002). While Room 9 at Marana does not have the fine-grained temporal parameters detailed in the Cahokia example, the archaeological evaluation of feasting at Cahokia provides strong empirical indicators of a feast that can be used to evaluate Hohokam feasting. The large quantity of artiodactyl remains (99.7 percent of the identified mammal remains) and artifacts associated with both elite and non-elite activities at Cahokia led Pauketat et al. (2002) and Kelly (2001) to the conclusion that this was a communal feasting event where both elite and non-elites were in attendance. The large quantity of artiodactyl remains may be representative of aggrandizing behavior by the elites that were believed to be in attendance (Kelly 2001:354). To summarize, the results of archaeofaunal analysis at Cahokia show: low taxonomic diversity, a prevalence of high meat yielding species, and a relatively large quantity of deposited bone (Kelly 2001; Pauketat et al. 2002). These results, as well as non-archaeofaunal evidence at Cahokia, are consistent with Hayden's (1995) expectations of elite feasting events.

If the faunal remains recovered from Room 9 at Marana do in fact represent an elite feasting event consistent with that found at Cahokia, then we would expect to find: (1) low taxonomic diversity (2) a large quantity of bone deposited, and (3) a high frequency of preferentially ranked taxa. We will examine each of these expectations in turn after further discussion is provided for the comparative material. We are primarily concerned with what occurred in Room 9, so in the remainder of the paper the fauna from Room 9 is compared with that from Compound 1, Room 1 (hereafter referred to as Room 1), and Pithouse 496 in a smaller village (James 1987); each of these loci are part of the greater Marana Community. This will allow us to comparatively assess how each of our expectations varies across Marana proveniences.

THE MARANA ARCHAEOFAUNAL DATA SET

Archaeofaunal studies in southern Arizona by Szuter (1989, 1991), Cameron (1995, 1998), Bayham (1982, 1990), Bayham and Hatch (1985a, 1985b) and Szuter and Bayham (1989,

1997) have documented the numerous ways that animal populations have been affected by the prehistoric sedentary horticulturalists known as the Hohokam. Additionally, these studies and others have also shown how animals have been fully integrated into the complex social fabric of Hohokam society. Faunal studies at the Marana Platform Mound site (Kendall 2002; Colwell 1995) and in the surrounding community (James 1987) have also addressed issues of social complexity and the ritual use of animals. These studies collectively provide the foundation and a departure point to explore the causes and significance of variation in a unique faunal assemblage derived from a burned room adjacent to the Platform Mound itself: Room 9. As mentioned earlier, it is this room that may well have been associated with elite social and political activities in this Classic period Hohokam community. To determine whether or not this was the case, we will comparatively assess the faunal contents of Room 9, those from a decidedly more mundane, domestic structure in Compound 1 (Room 1), and those from Pithouse 496, a unique elite or ritual context in another village within the Marana Community that James (1987) found to be associated with elite food consumption. Most of the archaeofaunal remains that are used in this study were recovered during the spring of 2003. A brief description of these contexts is followed by a discussion of their faunal contents.

Selected Sample Contexts

Compound 9, Room 9

Room 9 is perhaps the most important context in this study in that it was located adjacent to the Platform Mound within Compound 9. Excavations divided the room into four quadrants, which were excavated using both natural and arbitrary levels. Figure 6.1 shows the quad-

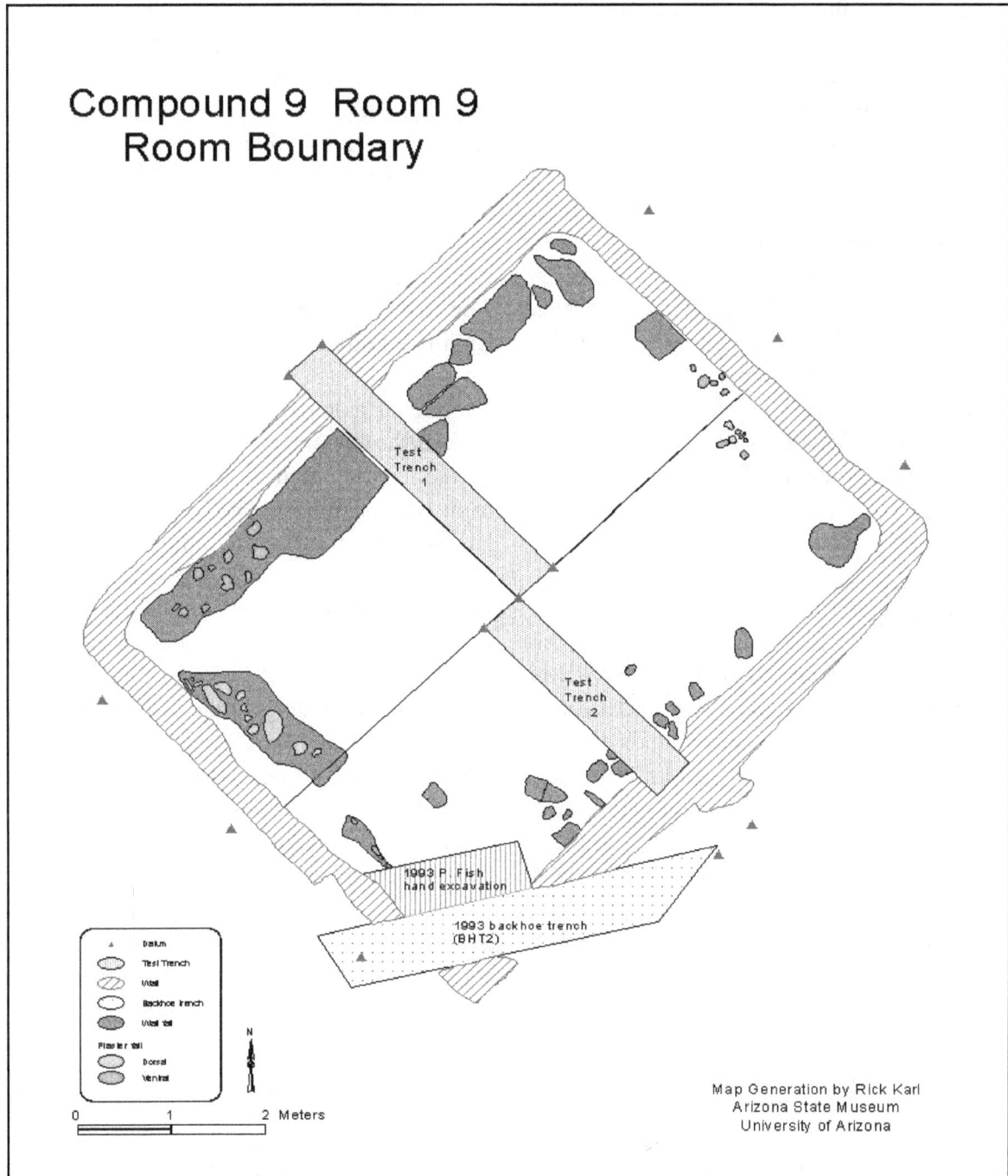

Compound 9 Room 9
Room Boundary

Test
Trench
1

Test
Trench
2

1993 P. Fish
hand excavation

1993 backhoe trench
(BHT2)

Datum

Test Trench

Wall

Backhoe Trench

Wall fall

Plaster fall

Dorsal

Ventral

N

0   1   2 Meters

Map Generation by Rick Karl
Arizona State Museum
University of Arizona

Figure 6.1. Compound 9 Room 9. Features, artifacts, and room boundary.

rants, artifact distribution, trenches, and wall boundaries of Room 9. The trenching revealed roof fall and wall fall that had encapsulated the burned archaeological deposits beneath. The method of recovery from the room included a backhoe to expose the room, followed by removal of the fall and sandy stratum from the fall to approximately 10 to 15 cm. From here the room was generally excavated using quarter-inch screens in arbitrary 10 cm levels. Two hearth features and 170 postholes were excavated. One hearth appeared typical in size and structure for the Marana Platform Mound site, while the other was abnormally large. This double hearth feature seems to be rather unique in the whole of the Marana Community. The large number of small postholes was interpreted to be associated with built-in furniture.

Compound 1, Room 1

Standing in contrast to this locus is Room 1, which is located 215 m due east of Room 9 in Compound 1. Room 1 is thought to have been associated with day-to-day household activities and represents the more mundane social activities surrounding the Platform Mound. It is dated to the Early Classic period, and appears to have functioned as a domestic residence. Figure 6.2 shows a map of floor features, artifacts, and soil samples recovered from Room 1. This room was excavated in a similar fashion to Room 9, where trenching, quartering, and exploratory excavations occurred.

Pithouse 496

Pithouse 496, Locus H is an Early Classic period structure (Rice 1987a) with a high density of artiodactyl bone (Rice 1987a). This locus was excavated as part of a larger complex of structures referred to as Muchas Casas, a smaller site near Marana Mound site. We wanted to include the faunal data

from this locality in our sample because of the abnormally high amount of artiodactyl bone recovered, although it may be somewhat biased in that it was recovered manually and not via standard screening (James 1987:173). Despite this recovery bias, this site could well be important for the purpose of evaluating elite feasting given that James (1987) has argued that the faunal contents represented high utility consumption practices that might be associated with elites.

The Archaeofaunal Data from Rooms 9 and 1

The faunal material discussed in this section anchors the remainder of this study and is based on the identification of 3,143 pieces of bone from two localities of the Marana site (Compound 9, Room 9 and Compound 1, Room 1) that were excavated in the spring of 2003. The identification of archaeofaunal remains recovered from both rooms was conducted at the California State University, Chico, Zooarchaeology Laboratory. Students from the summer 2003 'Zooarchaeology and Field Ecology' field school at the Eagle Lake Field Station, and fall 2003 'Zooarchaeology' laboratory class assisted in the faunal identifications under the supervision of Dr. Frank Bayham. All bone recovered from Rooms 9 and 1 was examined and identified to the most specific taxonomic level possible. Apart from recording provenience and taxonomic information, attributes recorded on each bone included anatomical part and portion, side, relative size, age/fusion, and various types of cultural and natural modifications. All specimens were examined visually, under 10x magnification. Taxonomic and systematic nomenclature follows that of Whitaker (1996) for mammals, the National Geographic Society Field Guide for birds (2002), and Stebbins (2000) for reptiles.

Room 9 within the Platform Mound

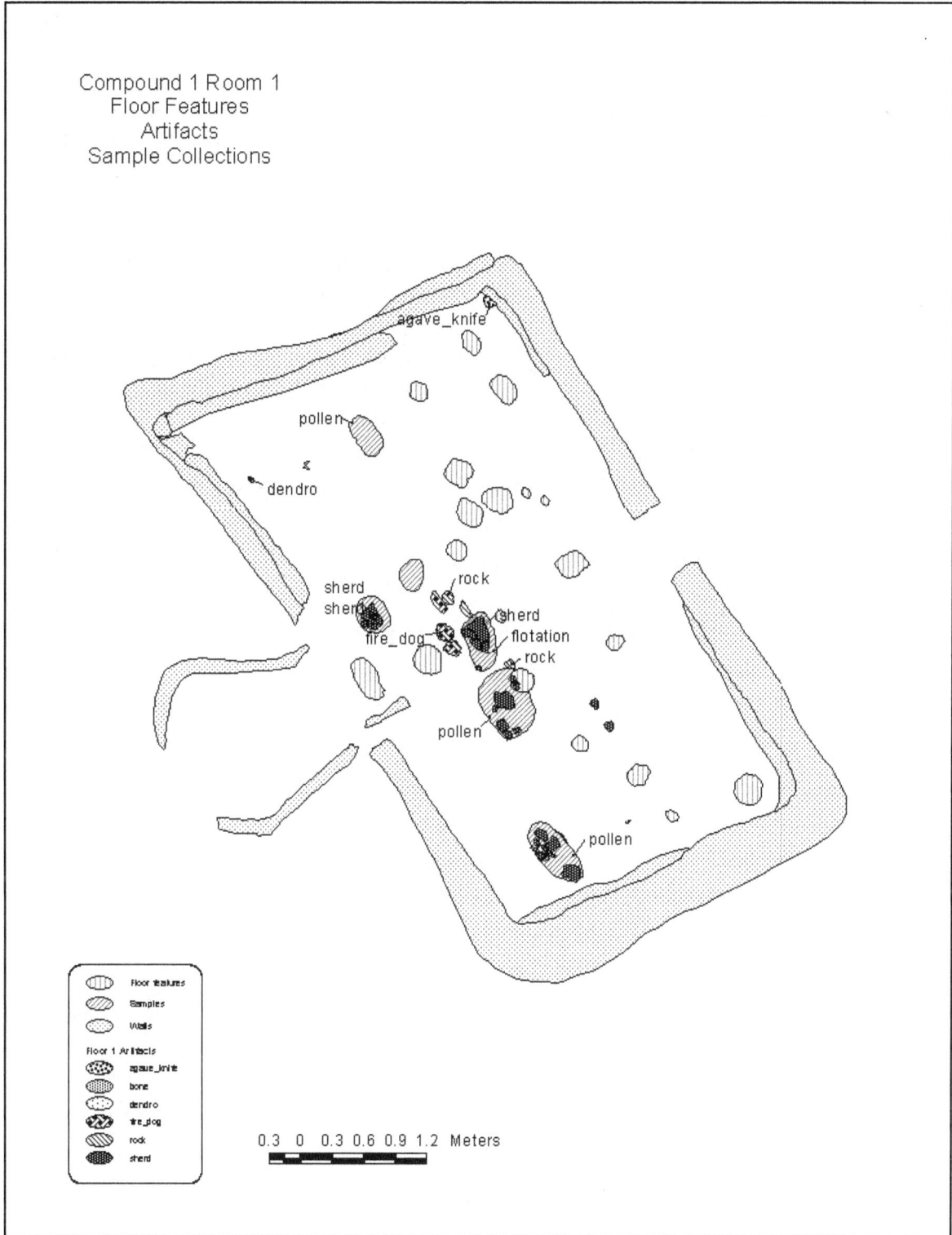

Figure 6.2. Compound 1 Room 1. Floor features, artifacts, and soil samples.

Compound produced 2,822 pieces of bone of which 1,084 (or 38 percent) were identifiable to at least the ordinal level; these numbers are distributed among 21 different species. Room 1 in Compound 1 produced far less bone fragments at 321, of which 156 (or 48 percent) were identifiable to the ordinal level; this represented at least 9 different species. Tabulations of the number of identified specimens (NISP) and unidentifiable bone from each of these localities by taxon may be found in Tables 6.1 and 6.2. A perusal of the taxa represented in these tables indicates a variety of species were recovered including reptiles, birds, and mammals. Both rooms are clearly dominated by lagomorphs, the taxonomic order that includes jackrabbits and cottontails, and constitute approximately 90 percent of the identifiable taxa in both cases. Interestingly, no reptiles or bird remains were recovered from Room 1, but this may be an artifact of small absolute numbers. Table 6.3 shows the distribution of major taxonomic classifications within Room 9 and Room 1, including: Reptilia, Aves, Lagomorpha, Rodentia, Carnivora, and Artiodactyla. Steve James' faunal study of Pithouse 496 totaled 551 identifiable specimens, almost exclusively dominated by the order Artiodactyla. Using these data the feasting expectations can now be evaluated.

COMPARATIVE ANALYSIS OF ROOM 9, ROOM 1, AND PITHOUSE 496

The unique location, contexts, and associations of Room 9 led to our hypothesis that this room represented the remains of an elite feasting event. Given the central role of food during any feasting event the archaeofaunal remains play an important role in testing this hypothesis. Three expectations for archaeological signatures of elite feasting were outlined previously, and can now be restated as three parts of the hypothesis. First, if Room 9 is associated with elite feasting, then we should detect low taxonomic diversity. Second, there should be a large density of archaeofaunal material deposited within the contexts of Room 9. The final expectation calls for a relatively high proportion of high meat yielding species deposited in Room 9. Room 1 and Pithouse 496 will be used to comparatively assess the hypothesis that Room 9 represents a locus of elite feasting. To test this hypothesis several different methods were used for each expectation. A tandem discussion of the methods and results for each expectation are presented below.

Diversity Expectation

In order to evaluate the degree of diversity represented in the identifiable faunal remains, the inverse of the Simpson's index was applied, following Grayson (1984). This form of diversity indices typically ranges between 1 and 18. A greater result from the reciprocal of the Simpson's index shows that individuals are more evenly distributed across taxa; conversely, lower values indicate a greater disparity in the representation of individual taxa (Grayson 1984:165). Results with lower numbers are consistent with low taxonomic diversity, as would be expected with rooms heavily dominated by one or a few taxa. Grayson (1984) cautioned that this index could be reflective of sample size and suggested using Spearman's rho and the reciprocal of the Simpson's index in tandem to detect any correlation with sample size. Both calculations were applied in this analysis.

Diversity indices are not the only way of assessing the taxonomic composition of an assemblage. In an evaluation of communal feasting from the Dolores Anasazi Project, Potter (1997) argued that there should be a higher diversity of species present if feasting was occurring. If feasting occurred we would expect

Table 6.1. Number of Identified and Non-Identified Taxa per Excavated Quadrant from Room 9

Compound 9 Room 9					
Identifiable	NE Quad	SE Quad	NW Quad	SW Quad	Total
Reptilia					
Testudinidae		2			2
Squamata			1		1
Aves					
Callipepla sp.		1	6		7
Accipitridae		1			1
Buteo sp.			2	1	3
Mammalia					
Lagamorpha				2	2
Leporidae	3	6	4		13
Lepus spp.	80	113	372	116	681
Lepus californicus	23	19	85	13	140
Lepus alleni	3	12	38	11	64
Sylvilagus spp.	10	19	32	24	85
Rodentia	2	3	3	1	9
Sciuridae	1			1	2
Ammospermophilus spp.		2			2
Spermophilus spp.			2	1	3
Geomyidae					
Thomomys bottae		2			2
Circetidae		1	2		3
Dipodomys spp.	1	3	2		6
Neotoma spp.	4	2	2	1	9
Perognathus spp.			1		1
Peromyscus spp.			2		2
Chaetodipus spp.		7			7
Mustelidae					
Taxidae taxus				1	1
Carnivora					
Canidae	1	1	1	2	5
Canis latrans				1	1
c.f. *Urocyon cinereoargenteus*					
Urocyon cinereoargenteus			1		1
Artiodactyla		4	16	3	23
c.f. *Antilocapra americana*	1	1			2
Antilocapra americana			1	1	2
c.f. *Ovis canadensis*	1				1
Ovis canadensis		1	2		3
Odocoileus spp.	1		5		6
Odocoileus hemionus				1	1
Sub-total	131	200	574	179	1084
Non-Identifiable	NE Quad	SE Quad	NW Quad	SW Quad	Total
Aves			1		1
Mammal/Indet	68	93	143	39	343
Sm mammal	114	133	490	128	865
Med mammal					
M/L mammal	11	20	41	35	107
Indet/Unid	39	27	62	32	
Sub-total	495	273	737	234	1738
Total	625	473	1317	413	2822

Table 6.2. Number of Identified and Non-Identified Taxa per Excavated Quadrant from Room 1

Identifiable	NE Quad	SE Quad	NW Quad	SW Quad	Total
		Compound 1 Room 1			
Reptilia					
Testudinidae					
Aves					
Callipepla sp.					
Accipitridae					
Buteo spp.					
Mammalia					
Lagamorpha		1			1
Leporidae	1		1	2	4
Lepus spp.	12	14	24	50	100
Lepus californicus		1		10	11
Lepus alleni				12	12
Sylvilagus spp.	2	3	2	8	14
Rodentia	1				1
Sciuridae				1	1
Ammospermophilus spp.					
Spermophilus spp.		1			1
Geomyidae					
Thomomys bottae					
Cricetidae					
Dipodomys spp.					
Neotoma spp.				2	2
Perognathus spp.					
Peromyscus spp.			1		1
Chaetodipus spp.					
Mustelidae		1			1
c.f. *Taxidae taxus*					
Carnivora					
Canidae	3				3
c.f. *Urocyon cinereoargenteus*			1		1
Urycyon cinereoargenteus					
Artiodactyla		1		1	2
c.f. *Antilocapra americana*					
Antilocapra americana					
c.f. *Ovis canadensis*					
Ovis canadensis					
Odocoileus spp.					
Odocoileus hermonius					
Sub-total	19	22	29	86	156

Non-Identifiable	NE Quad	SE Quad	NW Quad	SW Quad	Total
Aves					
Mammal/indet	19	18	6	14	57
Sm mammal	12	6	7	35	60
Med mammal					
M/L mammal			3	2	5
Indet/Unid	2		10	33	45
Sub-total	33	24	26	84	165
Total	52	46	55	168	321

Room 9 to exhibit low taxonomic diversity in comparison to other features at the site. The derived value for Room 9 is 1.37, for Room 1 it is 1.45, and for Pithouse 496 the value is 1.74. These values are rather low and rather uniform. Further, there was no statistically significant correlation with sample size, as tested via Spearman's rho. All results are consistent with low taxonomic diversity, as would be expected with rooms heavily dominated by Lagomorpha, or artiodactyls in the case of Pithouse 496. At face value, these results tend to support the diversity expectation, but implications for the hypothesis result from the observation that all loci produced uniformly low values.

Density Expectation

Our second expectation was that feasting should result in a large amount of faunal material. The hypothesis to be tested then becomes: the density of archaeofaunal remains recovered from Room 9 is greater than the archaeofaunal remains recovered from other loci. In order to provide support for this hypothesis, this difference must be statistically significant and not associated with sample size. To accomplish this task we must first tabulate the density of archaeofaunal remains per unit volume of sediment from each room. Then the observed archaeofaunal densities may be statistically evaluated via the chi-squared test. For the purpose of this paper statistical significance was achieved when $p \leq 0.05$. As can be seen in Table 6.3 there is a greater proportion of unidentifiable specimens to identifiable specimens within Room 9, when compared to Room 1. This disparity may be due to a greater amount of fragmentation within the context of Room 9. The evaluation of depositional density is the primary goal, not the degree of fragmentation; therefore density was evaluated using NISP rather than total recovered specimens.

Volumetric sediment excavation data and total number of bones recovered was used to derive the density of bone deposited. The research methods and diligence of the excavation crew at the Marana Mound site allowed us to make fine-grained evaluations of the bone density at Room 9 and Room 1, but no such data was available for Pithouse 496 at Muchas Casas. For this reason Pithouse 496 was excluded from this part of the analysis. For both Room 9 and Room 1 the total number of recovered bone specimens was divided by the total amount of excavated soil in cubic meters. This equation yielded the total number of identifiable and non-identifiable bone per cubic meter from each room, respectively (Table 6.1 and 6.2).

As seen in Table 6.4, Room 9 contained a total of 13.49 m³ of excavated sediment, while Room 1 yielded 8.31 m³ of sediment. Tables 6.1 and 6.2 shows Room 9 with a total of 209 identifiable specimens per m³, but Room 1 only has 39 identifiable specimens per cubic meter. These results show Room 9 had over 5 times the NISP per cubic meter when compared to Room 1. The difference in NISP per cubic meter between Room 9 and Room 1 was found to be statistically significant (x^2 116.532; $p < 0.001$). These results tend to support the hypothesis that Room 9 had a greater quantity of deposited faunal remains per cubic meter than other loci. It should be noted here that including the unidentifiable remains would not have changed these highly significant results, as this trend is upheld within both identifiable and unidentifiable categories.

High Utility Expectation

In order to evaluate the quantity of high meat yielding taxa, a few assumptions were made. The assumption was made that high meat yielding taxa are synonymous with highly ranked species and highly valued in social capital. This assumption has been productively used

Table 6.3. Distribution of Class and Order Level Identification in both Room 9 and Room 1

	Reptilia	*Aves*	*Lagomorpha*	*Rodentia*	*Carnivora*	*Artiodactyl*
C:9 R:9	0.22	0.82	73.01	3.49	0.52	2.81
C:1 R:1	0.00	0.00	16.98	0.84	0.48	0.24

Table 6.4. The Volume of Excavated Sediment for both Room 9 (top) and Room 1 (bottom)

C9:R9	NE Quad	SE Quad	NE Quad	SW Quad	Total volume per level
Level 1	1.29375	0.81675		0.55925	2.66975
Level 2	0.7425	0.7425	0.50275	0.55925	2.547
Level 3	0.7425	0.7425	0.902625	0.615175	3.0028
Level 4	0.7425	0.51975	0.9045	0.391475	2.558225
Level 5			0.9045		0.9045
Level 6			0.9045		0.9045
Level 7			0.9045		0.9045
Total volume per quad	3.52125	2.8215	5.023375	2.12515	13.491275

C1:R1	NE Quad	SE Quad	NE Quad	SW Quad	Total volume per level
Level 1	0.40095	0.40205	0.6657	0.1782	1.6469
Level 2	0.4455	0.3655	0.317	0.4455	1.5735
Level 3	0.4455	0.3655	0.317	0.4455	1.5735
Level 4	0.4455	0.3655	0.2536	0.4455	1.5101
Level 5			0.2219		0.2219
Level 6					
Level 7	0.4455	0.3655	0.5244	0.4455	1.7809
Total volume per quad	2.18295	1.86405	2.2996	1.9602	8.3068

in many archaeological applications where high ranked prey items correlate with large body size (Bayham 1979, 1982; Broughton 1994; Cannon 2000; Ugan 2004). Given that artiodactyls represent the highest ranked taxa available to the Hohokam, we opted to use the Artiodactyl Index as an indicator of the ratio of high ranked taxa to low ranked taxa or low meat yielding species.

The Artiodactyl Index is a value from 0 to 1, with low values representing an assemblage dominated by lagomorphs and a high value representing a much greater proportion of artiodactyls (Bayham 1979, 1990; Bayham and Hatch 1985a, 1985b). The artiodactyl index is derived by summing the total number of identified artiodactyl specimens, then dividing by the sum of the total number of identified artiodactyl and lagomorph specimens. In order to reduce the confounding effects of small sample sizes during statistical analysis the Cochran's statistic was chosen. The Cochran's statistic has been shown to reduce the risk of committing a Type I or Type II error where small sample sizes are an issue (Cannon 2001).

Thus our final expectation anticipates a high frequency of high meat yielding species within Room 9, as measured via the Artiodactyl Index. The results show Pithouse 496 with the highest value, at 0.99, while Room 9 is 0.04, and 0.01 for Room 1. In Tables 6.1 and 6.2 we can see there is a very small difference in the ratio of artiodactyls to lagomorphs within Room 9 and Room 1, but the difference between Pithouse 496 and the other two rooms is striking. The Cochran's statistic found statistically significant differences among the proportion of artiodactyls to lagomorphs within Pithouse 496 compared to Room 9 and Room 1 at Marana, which supports this visually observable trend (x^2 1405.616; $p < 0.001$ and x^2 660.491; $p < 0.001$). There was no statistically significant difference between Room 9 and Room 1.

DISCUSSION

In the remaining portion of our paper, we pose the question: Do the archaeofaunal remains recovered from the floor of Room 9, adjacent to the Marana Platform Mound, provide evidence of elite feasting? Our test results of Pauketat et al.'s (2001) indicators of elite feasting were mixed: first, the faunal material had a low diversity of species and was dominated by jackrabbits; second, the abundance of faunal remains from Room 9 was five times greater than is found in midden or other domestic contexts at the Marana site; and third, there was an extremely low proportion of artiodactyls such as deer and bighorn represented in the assemblage.

While there was a low degree of taxonomic diversity supporting our hypothesized expectation, we would note that the relative sparseness of meat resources in the desert Southwest might be influencing this to a high degree. Essentially, most Classic period Hohokam faunal assemblages from a variety of contexts show a low degree of taxonomic diversity. So we are not overly compelled to infer or interpret this as evidence of feasting by the fact that this prediction was upheld. In a similar vein, the near absence of artiodactyls in the assemblage is directly counter to what would be expected if the contents of Room 9 represented feasting by higher status elites. Elite status individuals should be consuming the most prestigious fauna, which should be deer and bighorn sheep in these contexts. The near lack of these highly prestigious animals is highly suggestive of a non-elite consumption event.

Perhaps the strongest evidence that the contents of Room 9 represented the results of a feast or feasts is found in the large quantity of faunal remains deposited. Room 9 had more bone per cubic meter by a significant order of magnitude than all other deposits at the site. While we cannot exclude use-related or functionally different activities contributing to this difference, such as the sweeping and habitual cleaning of room floors (Cameron 1995), the evidence at Room 9 does seem to represent an activity that is fundamentally different from day-to-day household consumption.

Szuter (1989) has observed, in a comprehensive review of the ethnographic literature, in the desert Southwest that more mundane feasting activities are often associated with post-communal agricultural activities like planting and harvesting. The selected animal of choice in these more mundane feasts appears to be jackrabbits. (The jackrabbits would also be collected communally in the context of a rabbit drive). Szuter's observations in the Southwest are consistent with a type of feasting that Hayden characterizes as 'work party' feasting which falls under his broader category of economic feasting.

James (1987) interpreted Pithouse 496 to be a non-domestic context. Pithouse 496 was dominated by artiodactyls as was evident from an Artiodactyl Index of 0.99. This observation provides support for using the frequency of high meat yielding species as an indicator for elite consumption. The Cahokia example (Pauketat et al. 2002; Kelly 2001), Szuter's (1989) observation's and the results of our analysis support the use of this expectation in detecting the presence of elites within a feasting context.

Returning to Hayden's expectations of competitive feasting we find that there may have been sufficient resources to provide surpluses as evident from archaeobotanical remains and the large quantity of lagomorphs, but prestigious food items were not prolific, comparatively. Both special features (e.g., the dual hearth feature and the high frequency of post holes) and the size and locality of Room 9 are suggestive of a feasting locality, but prestige items were not abundant (The results of any ceramic analysis are not included in this statement). The platform mound itself certainly suggests the presence of elite individuals, but it doesn't seem abundantly clear that these elites directly participated in the deposition of artifacts in Room 9.

The results of our study suggest that a type of food consumption occurred in Room 9 that is different from day-to-day household animal consumption, but it is not consistent with elite food consumption where high proportions of high-quality prey items would predominate. It doesn't seem to be consistent with Hayden's expectation of a competitive feast, but certainly Room 9 has distinctive attributes that are suggestive of such a preliminary categorization. Given our results and a review of research conducted by others, Room 9 potentially represents a non-elite communal feasting event that may have been the remnants of a work party feast.

It is important at this juncture to review problems associated with the archaeological identification of any type of feasting. Feasting can be elusive due to its dynamically changing patterns as previously alluded to in Hayden's work. Cameron (1995) also broaches this dilemma by explaining how a feast may celebrate the success of a rabbit drive, but be deposited in the individual homes of the hunters where it resembles day-to-day household consumption. If it is the large congregational feasting that archaeologists are interested in discovering, then most certainly there are indicators that are more telling than others. If it is any and all type of feasts that archaeologists want to identify, then potentially any refuse pit or midden is the result of both large and small feasting events. Essentially, food consumption at its extreme may be considered feasting at all times. Certainly, the authors do not wish to suggest that research into the signatures of feasting are fruitless, but they certainly want to project the complexity of feasting both in prehistory and modern society. This projection comes with the suggestion of the need for a clearly defined case-by-case definition of the type of feasting a researcher is attempting to detect, and archaeological assemblages with appropriate depositional contexts and temporal control.

CONCLUSION

The goal of this paper was to determine if the large faunal deposition within Room 9 represented our hypothesized locus of elite feasting. A review of relevant literature and previous archaeological investigations of feasting produced three criteria to detect elite feasting. These were: (1) low taxonomic diversity (2) a large quantity of bone deposited, and (3) a high frequency of preferentially ranked taxa. Including Room 9, Room 1 and Pithouse 496 in the analysis we comparatively evaluated these criteria. Comparatively, Room 9 had low faunal diversity, but so did the other samples. There was indeed a statistically significant density of deposition in Room 9, but there was a very low frequency of preferentially ranked taxa.

These results led us to the preliminary conclusion that Room 9 is representative of a communal non-elite consumption event, such as the kind of 'work party' feasting described above. While this conclusion does not support the original hypothesis, it is important to emphasize the importance of these results in interpreting how elites at Marana may have manipulated power within their economy. This study does not provide evidence of overt power displays, rather it suggests that the mechanism of power remained subtle during this period in Hohokam society. Further delineation of archaeological indicators of distinct feasting situations will provide an incredible opportunity to extract the subtleties of sociopolitical interactions between elites and non-elites.

The phenomenon of feasting is a highly variable and complex social event, and we do not expect that the archaeological indices of the phenomenon would be any less complex. Environmental factors undoubtedly have a significant effect on the manifestation of empirical indicators of specific feasting events, and therefore, environment must also be understood if archaeofaunal and archaeobotanical remains are to be used as indicators of feasting events. Continued study of the empirical signatures of different types of feasting, and their archaeological and faunal correlates, will enhance our understanding of prehistoric social and political complexity.

ENDNOTE

Potter (1997) implemented a richness index to evaluate the degree of taxonomic diversity represented between several assemblages. The empirical and statistical complexity of his expectation and associated choice of a richness index deserves a lengthy discussion, but it will not receive such a discussion here. For now it will suffice to explain that richness and diversity are fundamentally different. Richness measures the number of taxa represented in an assemblage or set of assemblages, while diversity measures the abundance within those taxa (Grayson 1984:131). Given this difference, Potter's expectation is not necessarily in contradiction to our own; rather it is something that we did not evaluate. The relative utility of richness indices versus diversity indices in evaluating feasting certainly should be evaluated in the future.

Chapter 7

Polishing Stones and Their Story: A Look at Production at the Marana Platform Mound Site

Abigail L. Holeman

The Early Classic period era of A.D.1150-1300 was a time of fairly rapid and widespread change not only in the Hohokam region of the Tucson Basin, but across much of the South-west. Among the Tucson Basin Hohokam, these changes encompass every level of society from the household to the broader landscape. One avenue useful for exploring both changes and continuities during the Classic period in the Tucson Basin is the organization of production. I focus here on one line of direct evidence, the spatial distribution of polishing pebbles and the use wear that is macroscopically visible on the pebbles. Direct evidence of production echoes findings from earlier trash midden (Bayman 1994) and sourcing studies (P. Fish et al. 1992; Harry et al. 2002). Polishing pebbles are most often associated with ceramic production, but can also be used in the production of other craft items, thus I use evidence from the polishing pebbles to discuss production in a general sense. While the evidence at this point is not entirely conclusive, distributions of ratios and use-wear do indicate a degree of variability in production at the Marana Platform Mound site. I argue that, at the household level, there are three distinctions in the degree of specialization at the mound site.

The Marana Platform Mound site provides a unique opportunity to look at specialization during the Classic period. Occupation at the

platform mound site at Marana was limited to the Classic period, about A.D. 1150-1300, with initial formation happening during the Early Classic period (Fish et al. 1989; Fish et al. 1992b). The single component occupation of the site provides a glimpse of social processes that took place during the transition to the Classic period. In addition to being a single component site, many of the houses were burned upon abandonment, which, along with minimal historic and modern disturbance, provides secure floor assemblages.

Long-term research at the Marana Platform Mound site and the surrounding community in the Tucson basin has demonstrated that the platform mound site developed in a central location in relation to earlier occupation areas (P. Fish and Fish 2000; Fish et al. 1989). The mound site was built between two earlier occupation locations on previously unoccupied and agriculturally secondary land (Fish et al. 1992b). Earlier occupation areas were located along the Santa Cruz River floodplain and at the base of the Tortolita Mountains.

Excavations at the mound site during all field seasons uncovered 19 rooms from 7 compounds across the site (Figure 7.1). Data from these excavations have been used to look at craft production through ceramic sourcing projects (Harry et al. 2002), as well as comparison of the trash midden deposits (Bayman

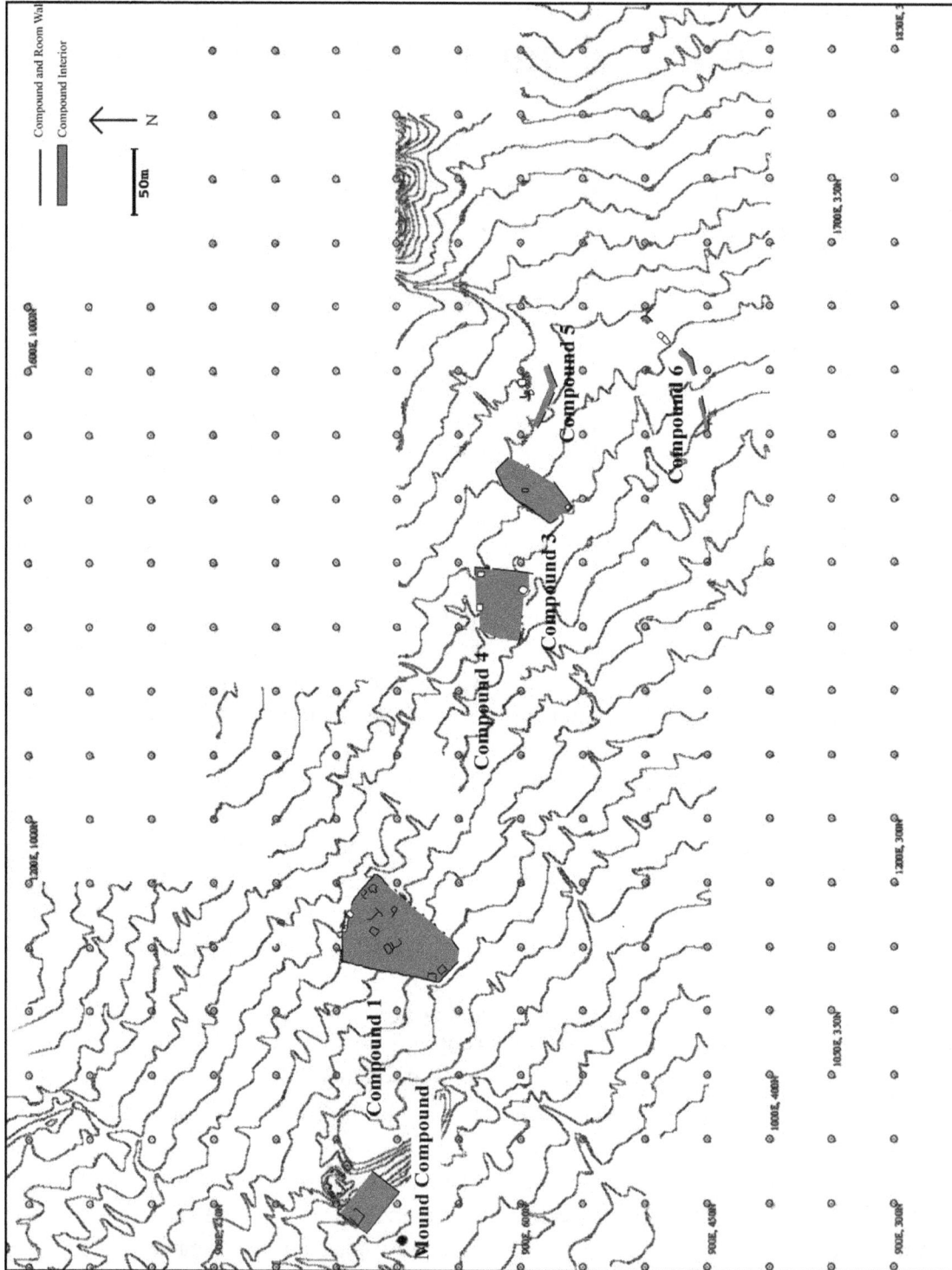

Figure 7.1. Compounds and rooms excavated at the Marana Platform Mound site.

1994). Ceramic sourcing projects indicate that production of Tanque Verde Red-on-brown ceramics at the Marana Mound site may have taken place on a small scale (Harry et al. 2002). Additionally, ceramic sourcing studies have suggested minor trade between the Marana Community and areas to the north (P. Fish et al. 1992:251).

Studies on the midden deposits within the Marana Mound site have shown that non-local trade goods and prestige goods are evenly distributed throughout the site rather than concentrated around the platform mound. This pattern indicates that trade and access to these items were not directly controlled by an elite class within the site (Bayman 1994). However, at an intra-community level there does appear to be specialization of production on the site level (Bayman 1996a; Fish et al. 1989; Harry 2000; Rice 1987a). Sites within the Marana Community appear to have specialized in different subsistence production. For example, the Marana Platform Mound site shows evidence of more flat stone knives or 'agave knives' used in the processing of agave, than other sites in the Marana Community (P. Fish and Fish 2000; Fish et al. 1989; Fish et al. 1992a; Rice 1987a). In order to examine another dimension of production, this study analyzes the spatial distribution of direct production evidence in the form of polishing pebbles.

First, I start with a brief discussion of how researchers approach the organization of production. Organization of production is often discussed in terms of the relation of laborers to non-laborers, or the degree to which certain groups of people may have specialized in non-subsistence production. Terms such as attached or independent specialists are often used to characterize these relations of production (Brumfiel and Earle 1987; Costin 1991). Attached specialists are defined as a social group which produces prestige items strictly for consumption by an elite class (Brumfiel

and Earle 1987; Costin 1991; Earle 1997). Within this definition, attached specialists produce prestige items in lieu of subsistence items and are supported by the elite class who consumes the goods. Attached specialists may be identified by spatially discreet workshops in proximity to elite architecture (Brumfiel and Earle 1987; Costin 1991). Independent specialists produce utilitarian items independent of elite control. Independent specialists are either part- or full-time, and are often removed from subsistence production and involved in a market or semi-market economy (Costin 1991; Earle 1997, 2002). Independent specialists are identified by concentrations of production tools and debris separate from elite structures, usually in the residential structures of non-elites.

In this model, labor is usually construed as a commodity, either owned and/or controlled by an elite class or by the individual laborer. Rather than construe labor as another commodity to produce more efficiently through specialization, specialization may be viewed as a particular form of knowledge that in and of itself demonstrates high status (Ames 1995; Helms 1993; Hendon 1999; Spielmann 2002). Constructing labor in this way puts the producers of craft goods in a different position within society, and opens the possibility that producers themselves may function as an elite class (Hendon 1999). Additionally, this moves the items produced by this labor out of the commodity class. Also, this conception of labor simply opens more possibilities for the roles producers of goods can play in a society. Studies on Hohokam material have shown that while there was some degree of specialization, few, if any households were completely removed from the tasks of subsistence production. Production may be more fruitfully conceptualized as a process of transformation bound up with this knowledge, which may have ramifications beyond just economic effects.

Spielmann's discussion (2002) of the

ritual mode of production helps move interpretations of craft production away from commodity and market economy assumptions, and is an approach that I find useful for bringing together the ritual, economic and political domains of society (Carsten and Hugh-Jones 1995; McKinnon 2000; Preucel 1996). This approach suggests that the need for food and goods for ritual feasting and ceremonies was a major impetus for periodic specialization (Spielmann 2002). The ritual and organizational requirements of large-scale feasts created a situation in which specialized knowledge was necessary for feasts to succeed. Large feasts are usually embedded in ritual occasions, such as bride wealth prestations or mortuary rituals that require a periodic increase in the production of important items.

Evidence for independent specialization thus may not automatically imply that specialization developed to improve efficiency in a competitive market environment. Ethnographic evidence from many parts of the world, including the Southwest, give examples of the need to anticipate and increase production for ritual purposes (McKinnon 1995; Talayesva and Simmons 1942). Increases in production are usually done on a small scale, by individual households (Spielmann 2002). What may be called 'ritual production' applies not only to food production, but also to items needed for rituals to be efficacious, such as paint (Stephen 1898, 1936), masks or head dresses, jewelry, and ceramic vessels among other things. Production of these items necessitates not only the technical and esoteric knowledge (Helms 1993), but also the social networks and knowledge of how to acquire the material needed to produce them. A ritual mode of production re-integrates the economy into a ritual system, and posits the household, or domestic space, as the main economic unit (Feinman 1999; Feinman and Nicholas 2004; Spielmann 2002). Thus by conceptualizing craft production in small scale societies as a ritual mode of production, we

can look at how ritual, political, and economic power are intertwined (McKinnon 2000).

Whether there is evidence for either attached or independent specialists at a site, it is also important to look for variability both within and between these categories (Costin 1991). Within the concepts of attached and independent specialization is the assumption of two distinct, bounded social classes of elites and non-elites. While the scale at which archaeological interpretation must be done often prohibits finer distinctions, recent work has shown that this clear cut distinction is problematic (Lesure and Blake 2002; Saitta 1999). Similar to studies done in Formative Period Mesoamerica (Lesure and Blake 2002), evidence at Marana suggests that status may not have been a clear-cut division of two segments of society resulting from a prestige goods economy. The architecture at the mound site suggests some social hierarchy through differentiated space in the form of habitation rooms on top of the mound platform. While artifacts usually labeled prestige goods, such as obsidian, shell, and imported pottery, were evenly distributed across the site, which would suggest equal access to these goods within the mound site (Bayman 1994, 1996a,b). Therefore it would appear that either these items are not prestige goods as traditionally defined by archaeologists, or there is more variability in these social positions. By looking at variability in production, we can perhaps move away from mutually exclusive categories such as egalitarian versus hierarchy and look at these as concurrent tensions within society.

POLISHING PEBBLE DISTRIBUTIONS

To assess variability in the organization of production at the Marana Mound site, I focus on the use wear and spatial distribution of polishing pebbles among houses and compounds. My analysis included 9 houses from 5 compounds, with a total of 72 polishing pebbles (Table 7.1). Due to a small sample size, the strongest pattern is evident at the household level, as some compounds are represented by only one house. However, the data suggest the possibility of some variation at the compound level.

Only the distribution of polishing pebbles will be considered here, however it is important to keep in mind the larger room assemblage, as this can speak to the variability in items produced. Data is available on the number of stone and sherd disk spindle whorls, modeled spindle whorls, tabular knives (used in processing agave), shell bracelet reamers, donut stones, and pottery anvils, but this material will not be analyzed in this study (Table 7.2). General room assemblages suggest that most of the households in this study were involved, to varying degrees, in production activities.

First, specialization is indicated by differential distribution of polishing pebbles in floor context. The counts of polishing pebbles per structure were standardized as ratios to plain sherds to make the data comparable to those used in trash mound studies. The distribution of standardized counts along with the raw frequencies indicates that there are noticeable distinctions in production activities among the houses at the mound site.

Assuming that the number of used polishing pebbles is indicative of the degree of specialization, then the groups shown in Table 7.3 indicate the degree of specialization present in the structures. Combined, the frequencies and standardized counts suggest that there are three groups or levels of distinction (Table 7.3). The level indicating the least amount of production comes from Compound 4, Room 3; Compound 6, Room 1; and the only room tested in Compound 7. The data indicate small-scale production, probably for household use. At the middle range are two structures, including Compound 4, Room 1, and Compound 3,

Room 1, that have 6 to 7 polishing pebbles per structure. Three structures indicate a higher level of specialization—two from Compound 5, Rooms 1 and 2, and one from Compound 6, Room 2, with between 16 and 19 polishing pebbles per structure.

The compounds and rooms that indicate a medium to high level of specialization of production are variable distances from the mound compound (Table 7.1). This suggests that production at these households was not under direct control of the mound residents. In fact, Compounds 5 and 6, which display the greatest evidence for specialization, are the farthest from the platform mound compound.

Distance from elite residences is often used as a measure of elite control over production. If residential occupation on top of the platform mound signified social difference in the form of hierarchy, then it appears that elite social capital did not come from direct control over production. The structures indicating the highest degree of specialization are located in compounds farthest from the platform mound.

Additionally, some degree of production is present in every compound tested, indicating that production may have been organized at the household level, nested within a larger social unit that was demarcated by compound walls. For example, Compound 6 contains one structure that indicated the least amount of production and another structure that indicated the highest level of production. This suggests that some households were more involved in the production of craft items than others. Compound 5 has two structures that fall within the group that revealed the highest level of production. This variability may be indicative of two social units involved in production: the household and the compound.

There is no evidence at this time to determine whether Hohokam households were synonymous with nuclear families or that

Table 7.1. Frequencies of Polishing Pebbles, Plain Ware Ceramics, and Standardized Counts

Compound/Room	Counts of Polishing Pebbles	Counts of Plain Sherds	Standardized Counts (Number of Polishing Pebbles/Plain Sherds x 1000)
Compound 4/Room 3	1	1441	0.7
Compound 7/Room 1	1	1450	0.7
Compound 6/Room 1	4	3551	1.1
Compound 4/Room 1	7	1229	5.7
Compound 3/Room 1	6	765	7.8
Compound 5/Room 1	17	1836	9.2
Compound 6/Room 2	16	1538	10.4
Compound 5/Room 2	19	1615	11.8
Compound 3/Room 3	1	74	13.5

Table 7.2. Craft Production Items in General Room Assemblages

Compound/Room	Stone Disk Spindle Whorl	Sherd Disk Spindle Whorl	Modeled Spindle Whorl	Tabular knives	Shell Bracelet Reamer	Donut Stone	Pottery Anvil
Compound 3/Room 1		3		12	2	1	
Compound 3/Room 3		1	2	2		1	
Compound 4/Room 1		2	2	1	2		1
Compound 4/Room 3							
Compound 5/Room 1	1	1		1	2		
Compound 5/Room 2	3	3	1	9	4		
Compound 6/Room 1				4	1		
Compound 6/Room 2		2	1	1			
Compound 7/Room 1		4	1	14	1		

Table 7.3. Frequencies and Ratios of
Polishing Pebbles

Compound/ Room	Frequencies of Polishing Pebbles	Ratio (# of polishing pebbles/# of plain sherds x 1000)
Compound 5/Room 2	19	11.8
Compound 5/Room 1	17	9.2
Compound 6/Room 2	16	10.4
Compound 4/Room 1	7	5.7
Compound 3/Room 1	6	7.8
Compound 6/Room 1	4	1.1
Compound 3/Room 3	1	13.5
Compound 4/Room 3	1	0.7
Compound 7/Room 1	1	0.7

the compounds were synonymous with traditional anthropological conceptions of lineage. I use the terms of household and compound in reference to the physical space these units demarcate on the ground. These spaces are likely to be spatial referents of social units that were active in the Marana Community. However, re-analyses of traditional anthropological concepts of kinship, such as lineage, have shown that even in the most classic of cases, these categories are awkward fits at best (Bloch 1995; Carsten and Hugh-Jones 1995; Fox 1993; Gillespie 2000; McKinnon 1995, 2000; Waterson 1990). Therefore, I am using household and compound as social units that most likely include persons beyond normative conceptions of kinship.

Rather than suggest a strict division between producers and non-producers or consumers, the spatial evidence at Marana suggests that there was continuous variability in the level of involvement in non-subsistence production. Producers at Marana may have been more able to create debt relationships with other groups through giving, thus allowing them to gain status (Mauss 1990[1925]). In this view, specialized producers do not commodify their labor to be sold either to an elite class or a free market economy. Rather, knowledge of production can lead to status in and of itself, and specialization may be a key dimension of this status (Ames 1995; Helms 1993, 1998).

USE WEAR PATTERNS

Use-wear evidence confirms the patterns that were detected in the spatial distributions of polishing pebbles. I compiled the frequencies of polishing pebbles with macroscopically visible striations and polishing facets (Table 7.4). The patterning of use wear overwhelmingly coincides with the structures that have the highest ratios of polishing pebbles, with Room 2 in Compound 6 having the largest number of faceted pebbles.

Those at the low end of the frequency chart show little to no visible use wear. While lower frequencies would automatically indicate fewer pebbles with use wear, the pebbles that were present in structures with low frequencies of pebbles showed almost no use wear at all. Use wear evidence suggests that there were not only houses that used more pebbles, but also that residents of these houses used their stones more heavily.

Thus the use wear distribution parallels evidence from the spatial distribution, and suggests there was household level specialization on a small scale with an emphasis on production in Compounds 5 and 6. The three-level

Compound/Room	Number of Striations (present/absent-without facets)	Number of Facets (without striations)	Number with striations and facets (both present)
Table 7.4. Types of Use Wear by Room			
Compound 3/Room 1	1	1	2
Compound 3/Room 3			
Compound 4/Room 1			
Compound 4/Room 3			
Compound 5/Room 1	5	3	4
Compound 5/Room 2	4	5	3
Compound 6/Room 1	2		
Compound 6/Room 2	1	10	1
Compound 7/Room 1			

distinction apparent in the spatial distribution of frequencies is not reinforced by the use-wear patterns, but there is an indication of a two level distinction that corresponds to the upper and middle levels of production.

DISCUSSION

With the seemingly most specialized structures being the greatest distance from the platform mound, the variable scales of specialization witnessed at the mound site, and the evidence for continued involvement in subsistence production, the production at the mound site appears to fit the category of part-time independent specialization. However, we cannot say that the groups in the more highly specialized structures were producing only utilitarian goods. The variability that is visible in the level of specialization and the relatively evenly distributed patterns of consumption suggest that there is not a clear-cut distinction between the production of utilitarian and prestige goods.

Spatial distributions indicate that there

were at least three levels of differentiation in the degree of specialization at the household level. The highest levels of use wear correspond to the pebbles found in structures in the middle and high range indicated by the spatial patterning of the ratios and frequencies. This pattern of production suggests that there was not a single, undifferentiated class of craft producers at the mound site, but that specialization varied, perhaps as ritual occasions called for it.

Organization of production at the mound site does not make identification of a separate elite class any more clear. Use-wear and spatial distributions of polishing pebbles show that specialization occurs regardless of the distance from the platform mound. Additionally, there are possibly three degrees of variability in the intensity of specialization. The variability in the degree of specialization indicates that, (1) production does not appear to be centrally controlled, (2) there may not have been an institutionalized class of undifferentiated specialists, rather specialized production involved multiple groups, and was possibly temporally variable, (3) there are at least two nested social groups demarcated by the house structure and compound walls, and (4) activities labeled economic cross-cut other social boundaries, such as compound walls, and do not appear to be a source of prestige in the sense of a prestige goods economy (Brumfiel and Earle 1987; Earle 1997, 2002).

When production is compared with other aspects of the mound site, such as the residences on the platform mound and distributions of non-local goods, the evidence for social status may appear contradictory in that there is differentiated space, but not pronounced material or artifactual differentiation (Bayman 1994; Fish et al. 1992a). I suggest that these are not contradictory forms of evidence, but speak to a differential construction of prestige or status, one that is more difficult to see archaeologically, such as ritual abilities or knowledge. Production may then be a pathway to prestige, not in the sense of wealth accumulation, but in the knowledge of transformation and the ability to create debt by giving. Production would then be bound up with ritual and politics, and specialization may be variable based on temporal and social necessity. These various aspects of the mound site also indicate that there may not have been a clear-cut distinction between elite and non-elite, but that these were negotiated positions that fluctuated through time.

CONCLUSION

This study is not meant to be all-inclusive, but simply adds a small piece to the puzzle of the Hohokam Preclassic to Classic period transition. Spatial distributions and use wear patterns supports findings in previous studies of the Early Classic period Hohokam (Bayman 1994, 1996; P. Fish and Fish 2000; Fish et al. 1992a; Fish et al. 1989; Harry et al. 2002; Rice 1987), indicating a degree of specialized production during this time period. The scope

of this study was purposefully limited to one site, the Marana Platform Mound site, in order to assess intra-site variability in production patterns. Additional comparative analysis would add to the degrees of variability noted here.

In Costin's (1991) definitive work on craft production, she demonstrates the importance of looking at craft production as a continuum. Not only can a continuum exist between different societies, such as societies labeled as having independent versus attached specialists, but a continuum can exist within a society and within a single occupation site as well. Additionally, the labor involved in craft production may not necessarily be a commodity, but an important form of knowledge that is a form of status (Ames 1995; Feinman 1999; Feinman and Nicholas 2004; Helms 1993, 1998). This status may come from the knowledge involved in the transformation of material, or the ability to create debt by giving, rather than accumulating (Gregory 1982; Mauss 1990[1925]), or both.

Much like the different sites within the Marana Community suggest site-level specialization (Fish et al. 1989; P. Fish and Fish 2000; Fish et al. 1992a; Harry et al. 2002; Rice 1987a), the houses within the platform mound site suggest different degrees of specialization. Direct production evidence at the Marana Platform Mound site suggests three degrees of specialization within the site. Three structures, two from Compound 5 and one from Compound 6, suggest a fairly high degree of specialization. An additional room from Compound 6 and rooms from Compounds 7, 4, and 3 suggest two separate groups that were specialized to a lesser degree or not at all.

Direct evidence of production, such as the polishing pebbles, indicates that the differential status suggested by architecture does not play out in terms of the organization of production taking place in the houses. The architectural patterns and patterns from direct evidence of production are not necessarily contradictory, but suggest that social status was not constituted through economic means, or that ritual practices could have been taking place that cross-cut compound boundaries. As more structures are excavated at the Marana Mound site these patterns of direct production can be further tested and combined with other forms of evidence to get a fuller picture of the inter-connections suggested here.

Chapter 8

Production and Exchange of Plain Ware Ceramics in the Marana Community

Karen G. Harry, Robert J. Speakman, Elizabeth Miksa,
Sergio F. Castro-Reino, Christopher Descantes, Paul R. Fish,
Suzanne K. Fish, Michael D. Glascock

INTRODUCTION

Previous studies of Early Classic period ceramic production in the Marana Community have focused on decorated ceramics, specifically Tanque Verde Red-on-brown ceramics (P. Fish et al. 1992; Harry 1997, 2003; Harry et al. 2002). The results of those studies indicate that during this period, not all villages produced these decorated wares. Instead, substantial quantities of vessels were obtained through trade from as yet unidentified production villages. Some type of centralized distribution system appears to have existed, though only settlements in the top tier of the settlement hierarchy participated in this system. Other settlements received lesser quantities of decorated vessels, apparently obtained from independently maintained trade networks.

In this paper, we report upon the sourcing results of plain ware ceramics from this same time period. The ceramic sample derives from sites located both within and adjacent to the Marana Community, and was generated to provide complementary information to that available from the previous studies. By comparing data obtained from these two pottery types, we hope to be able to more fully understand ceramic economic organization within and adjacent to the Marana Community during the Early Classic period. Our results indicate that, compared to the red-on-brown vessels, plain ware ceramics were produced at a larger number of settlements. In fact, most, if not all, of the settlements appear to have made plain pottery. This patterning contrasts to that which characterizes the red-on-brown pottery, which was produced at only a limited number of settlements. The data also suggest that plain ware vessels circulated in different exchange spheres than did the red-on-brown vessels. Whereas the exchange of plain ware ceramics was conditioned largely by settlement proximity, the circulation of Tanque Verde Red-on-brown ceramics appears to have been governed largely by political or economic factors. We interpret these different patterns as suggesting that plain ware ceramics were exchanged primarily among socially close individuals, whereas red-on-brown pottery was exchanged through more socially distant networks.

METHODS

To investigate issues of ceramic production and exchange we have focused on two types of analyses: the chemical analyses of ceramic pastes and the petrographic analyses of the sand inclusions found within the clay bodies. Three hundred thirty-three plain ware sherds were chemically analyzed, 180 of which come from sites within the Marana Community and the remainder of which come from sites in the surrounding area (Table 8.1; Figure 8.1). The chemical analyses were undertaken with the goal of identifying groups of chemically similar sherds; once these compositional groups were obtained, a sample of sherds from the different groups were submitted for petrographic analyses. The goal of the latter study was to determine the geographical source of the aplastic inclusions, in order to aid in the identification of probable production zones. Because the Hohokam generally tempered their sherds with locally-collected sands (see Heidke 1996, 2000), mineralogical analyses can potentially inform on where tempering materials were collected.

The chemical analyses were conducted using instrumental neutron activation analysis (INAA) by researchers at the University of Missouri Research Reactor Facility. Elemental concentrations were obtained for 33 elements, of which 31 were used in the data analysis.[1] The data were analyzed using standard MURR procedures described in previous reports (Glascock 1992; Neff 2002). Multivariate statistical techniques were used to derive chemically similar compositional groups.

Once the chemical compositional groups were identified, a sample of twenty plain ware sherds was submitted for mineralogical study. This study was conducted by researchers Elizabeth Miksa and Sergio Castro-Reino of the Center for Desert Archaeology using general techniques described elsewhere (Heidke et al. 2002; Miksa and Heidke 2001). Consistent with these techniques, the sherds were thin sectioned and point counted using established parameters for the Tucson Basin. Sherds

1. *Nickel was excluded from the data reduction analysis because of the large numbers of missing values among the specimens. Additionally, calcium was excluded because of results obtained from this and previous studies, which suggest that Hohokam potters intentionally added calcium to some ceramic pastes to lighten the vessel color.*

containing at least partial sand temper were then submitted as unknowns for classification by the discriminant analysis model recently developed for the Tucson Basin (Miksa 2006). The discriminant model assigned each sherd to a petrofacies (Figure 8.2) in the Tucson Basin, and each classification was then evaluated using qualitative analyses to assess whether it was reasonable and correct. More detailed descriptions of the methods and results of the mineralogical analyses can be found in Castro-Reino and Miksa (2005).

COMPOSITIONAL FINDINGS

Six compositional groups were identified in the plain ware collection (Table 8.2), none of which were identified in the previous studies of Tanque Verde Red-on-brown ceramics. Figure 8.3 illustrates the spatial separation of these groups in compositional space. Each of these groups is discussed below.

Group H

Group H comprises 120 plain ware sherds, most of which were recovered from sites north of, or in the northern portion of, the Tucson Basin (see Table 8.2 and Figure 8.1). This group occurs in the highest proportion (90 percent) at the Cake Ranch site, located north of the Marana Community, and at the Marana Mound site, where it comprises 62 percent of the collection. Sherds in this chemical group contain sands from a variety of sources east of the Santa Cruz River, including the Western Tortolita, Eastern Tortolita, Catalina, and Catalina Volcanic petrofacies (Table 8.3; Figure 8.2). Perhaps significantly, most of the Group H sherds in the petrographic sample were recovered from sites within or adjacent to the petrofacies from which their sands derived. Both of the sherds containing Western Tortolita sands were recovered

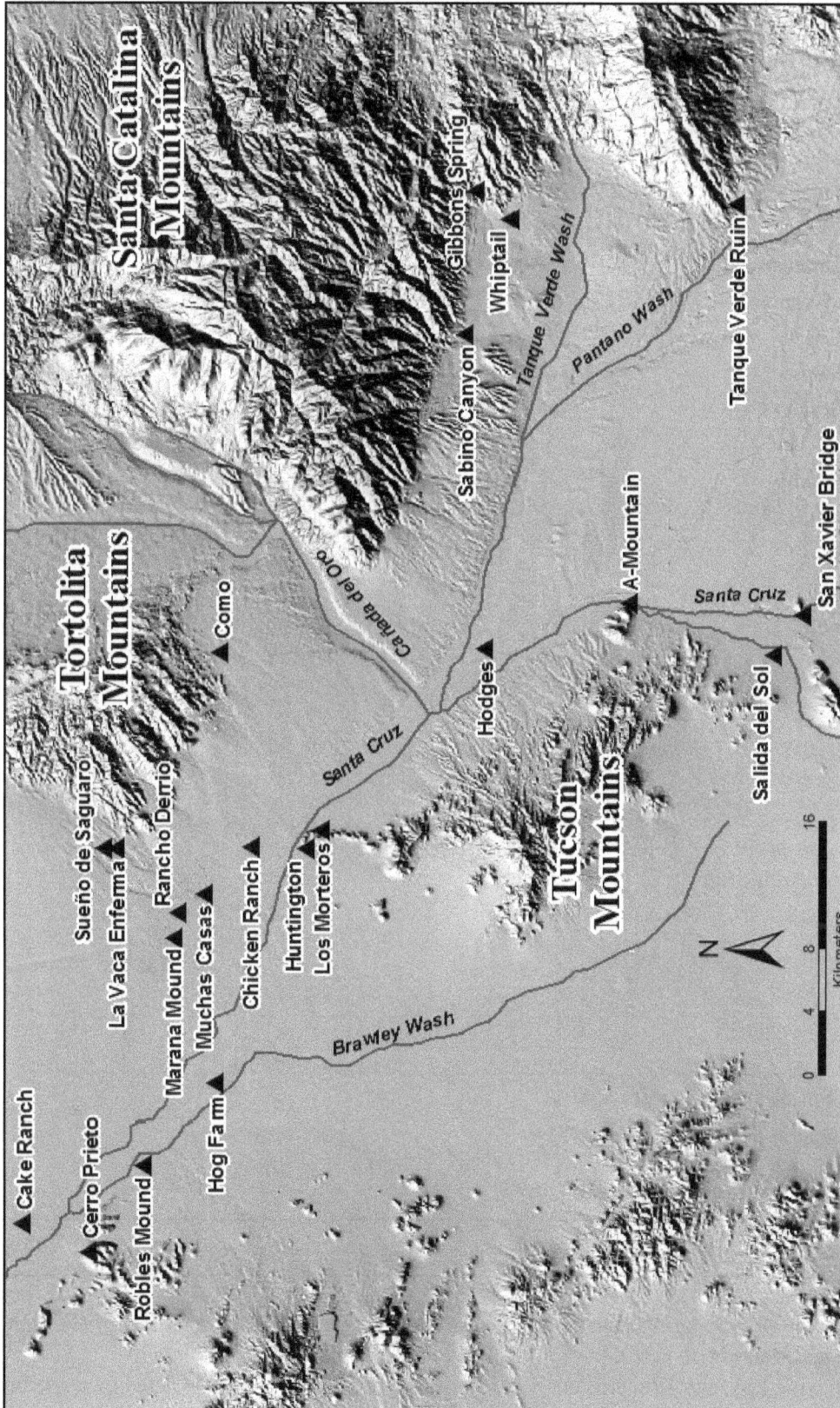

Figure 8.1. Location of sites discussed in text.

Table 8.1. Number of Chemically Analyzed Ceramics from the Marana Community and Surrounding Areas

Site	Ware		Total
	Plain	Tanque Verde Red-on-brown[1]	
Marana Community			
Marana Mound Site	81	210	291
Los Morteros	38	35	73
Huntington	-	29	29
La Vaca Enferma	-	19	19
Sueño de Sagurao	-	19	19
Muchas Casas	30	31	61
Rancho Derrio	31	10	41
Chicken Ranch	-	32	32
Other[2]	-	31	31
Robles Community			
Robles Mound	-	27	27
Cerro Prieto	-	24	24
Hog Farm	-	30	30
Cake Ranch	30	30	60
Other	-	31	31
Northern Tucson Basin			
Hodges	-	14	4
Como	-	33	33
Other	-	3	3
Southern Tucson Basin			
San Xavier Bridge Site	25	-	25
Salida del Sol	-	12	12
A-Mountain	-	10	10
Other	-	8	8
Eastern Tucson Basin			
Whiptail	31	10	41
Gibbons Spring	30	-	30
Sabino Canyon	37	-	37
Tanque Verde Ruin	-	10	10
Other	-	4	4
Total	333	662	995

Notes:

[1] The Tanque Verde Red-on-brown data have been previously reported in P. Fish et al. (1992), Harry (1997; 2003), and Harry et al. (200).

[2] Those sites having less than 10 sherds analyzed in either ware category are not listed by name but are included in the "other" category.

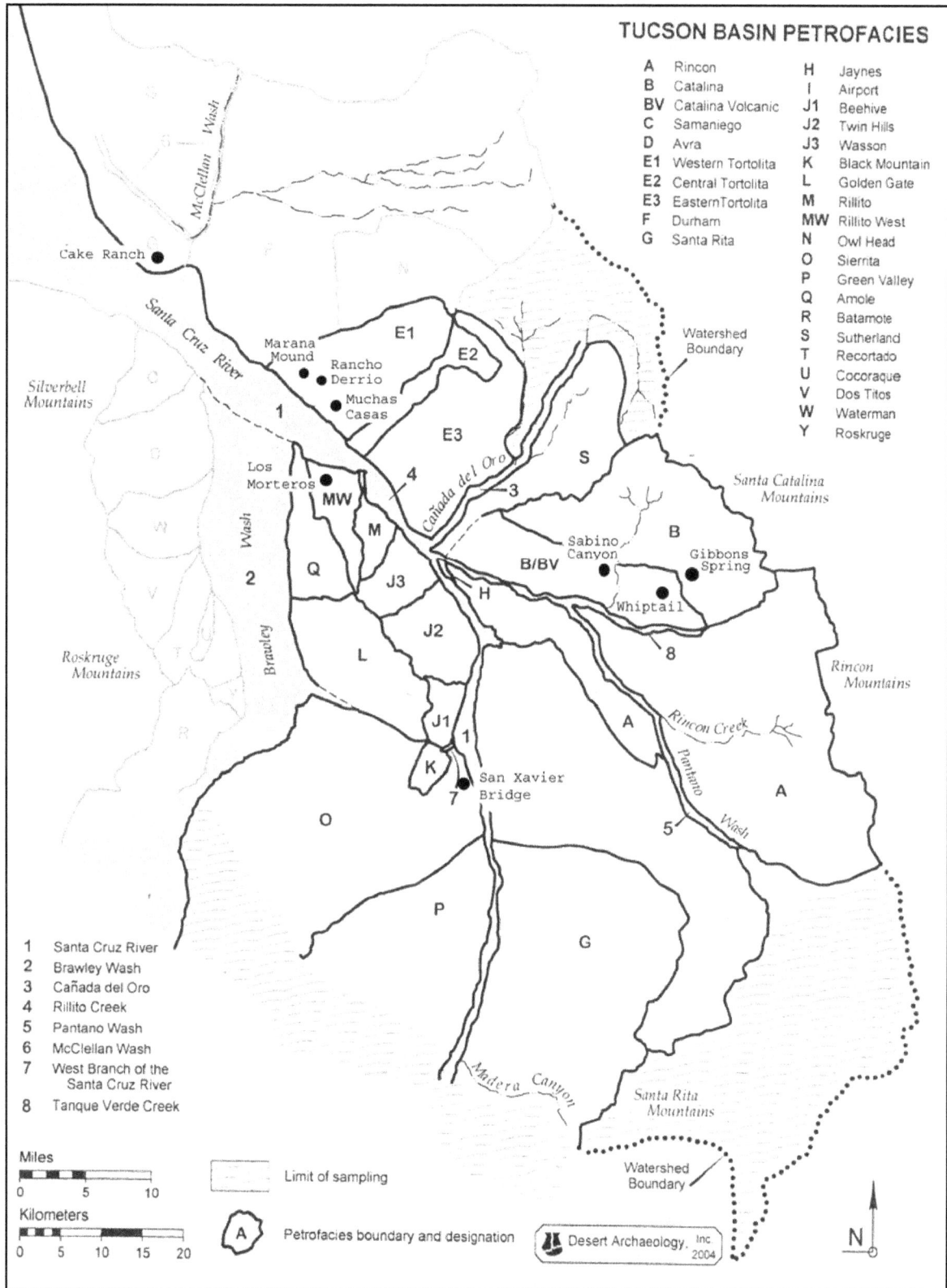

TUCSON BASIN PETROFACIES

A	Rincon	H	Jaynes
B	Catalina	I	Airport
BV	Catalina Volcanic	J1	Beehive
C	Samaniego	J2	Twin Hills
D	Avra	J3	Wasson
E1	Western Tortolita	K	Black Mountain
E2	Central Tortolita	L	Golden Gate
E3	Eastern Tortolita	M	Rillito
F	Durham	MW	Rillito West
G	Santa Rita	N	Owl Head
		O	Sierrita
		P	Green Valley
		Q	Amole
		R	Batamote
		S	Sutherland
		T	Recortado
		U	Cocoraque
		V	Dos Titos
		W	Waterman
		Y	Roskruge

1 Santa Cruz River
2 Brawley Wash
3 Cañada del Oro
4 Rillito Creek
5 Pantano Wash
6 McClellan Wash
7 West Branch of the
   Santa Cruz River
8 Tanque Verde Creek

Miles
0   5   10

Kilometers
0   5   10   15   20

Limit of sampling

A Petrofacies boundary and designation

Desert Archaeology, Inc.
2004

N

Figure 8.2. Petrofacies map of the greater Tucson Basin, with sites sampled for the plain ware study shown.

Table 8.2. Number of Plain Ware Sherds Assigned to each Chemical Group by Site

Site	H	I	Tortolita	Rincon/ Catalina 1	Rincon/ Catalina 2	Black Mountain	Un-assigned	Total
Marana Community								
Marana Mound	50	-	7	8	-	2	14	81
Los Morteros	7	2	-	3	-	17	9	38
Muchas Casas	14	-	-	6	-	-	10	30
Rancho Derrio	15	-	-	3	-	1	12	31
Total Marana Community	86	2	7	20	-	20	45	180
Robles Community								
Cake Ranch	27	-	-	1	-	-	2	30
Southern Tucson Basin								
San Xavier Bridge	-	-	-	-	-	25	-	25
Eastern Tucson Basin								
Gibbons Spring	3	-	-	-	19	2	6	30
Whiptail	-	-	-	-	19	4	8	31
Sabino Canyon	4	-	-	1	21	-	11	37
Total Eastern Tucson Basin	7	-	-	1	59	6	25	98
Total	120	2	7	22	59	51	72	333

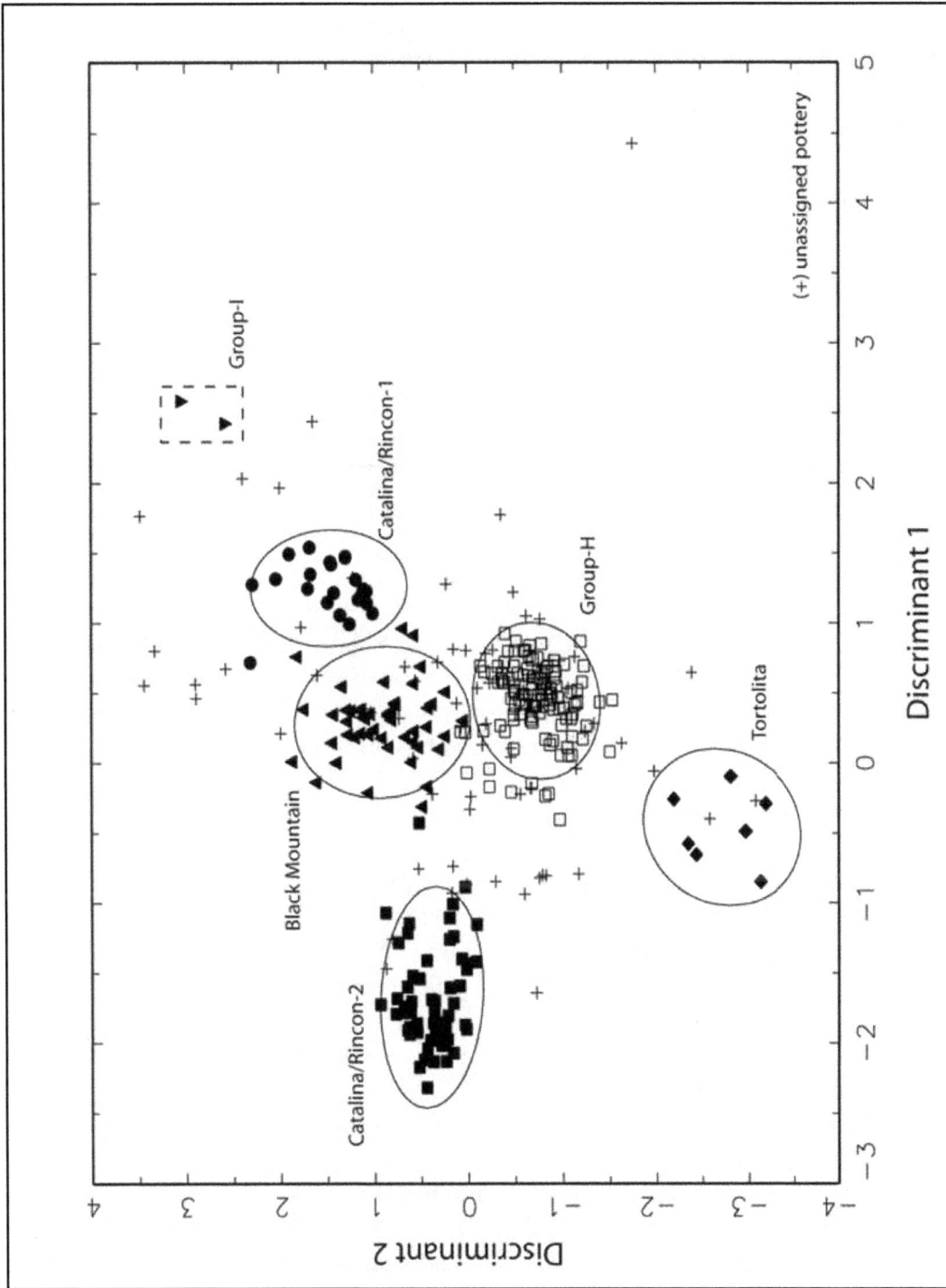

Figure 8.3. Bivariate plot of Discriminant Functions 1 and 2 scores for plain ware compositional groups with unassigned specimens (+). Elipses represent 90 percent conficence level for group membership.

Table 8.3. Results of Petrographic Analysis

Petrographies Assignment	Chemical Group Assignment				
	H	Tortolita	Rincon/ Catalina 1	Rincon/ Catalina 2	Black Mountain
Western Tortolita	2				
Central Tortolita		1			
Eastern Tortolita	1				
Catalina	1		1	2	
Catalina Volcanic	1				
Rincon			2	4	
Black Mountain					4
None (Schist)			1		
Total Analyzed	5	1	4	6	4

from the Marana Mound site, and the sherds containing Catalina Volcanic sands (n = 1) and Catalina sands (n = 1) were recovered from the site of Los Morteros, located not far from these petrofacies. Only the sherd from the Eastern Tortolita petrofacies was from a site located at some distance from the sand source. This sherd was recovered from the Gibbons Spring site, located some 30 km east of that petrofacies. Together, the compositional data and the distributional patterns suggest that Group H sherds were produced within several villages and were made with broadly similar clays, but with compositionally distinct sand sources. Interestingly, Cake Ranch is located well outside of any of the petrofacies represented in the thin-sectioned sherds. This patterning suggests that Cake Ranch may have obtained most of its plain ware pottery from the Marana Community. Alternatively, the ceramics may have been made locally at Cake Ranch with clays that were chemically similar to the other clays

encompassed by Group H. Unfortunately, none of the Cake Ranch sherds assigned to Group H were petrographically analyzed, so the question remains unresolved at this time.

Group I

Only two sherds, both from the site of Los Morteros, were assigned to Compositional Group I. Neither of these sherds was petrographically analyzed. Because of the paucity of information for these sherds, their production source cannot be identified.

Tortolita Group

The Tortolita group contains seven sherds, all of which were recovered from the Marana Mound site. Only one sherd from this group was petrographically analyzed; it contained sands from the Central Tortolita petrofacies (see Table 8.3 and Figure 8.2). Sherds in this group scored low on principal component 1 (Figure 8.4), reflecting low concentrations of As, Sb, Cs and Rb and high concentrations of elements such as Na and Sr. To date, only one clay sample recovered from the Tortolita Mountain area has been chemically analyzed. Perhaps significantly, however, this clay exhibited similar elemental patterns (i.e., low concentrations of As, Sb, Cs and Rb, and high concentrations of Na and Sr) when compared to other analyzed clays (Harry 2003:63-69). Given the concentration of Tortolita group sherds in the Marana Community, the chemical similarities between the Tortolita group and the Tortolita clay sample, and the presence of Tortolita sand temper in the one petrographically analyzed sherd from this group, the likely production locale for this group is somewhere within the Marana Community, most likely at one or more of the villages situated along the flanks of the Tortolita Mountains.

Rincon/Catalina 1 Group

Twenty-two sherds were assigned to the Rincon/Catalina 1 group. Most of these sherds were recovered from sites located in the Marana Community, though single sherds were also identified in the collections recovered from Cake Ranch and Sabino Canyon (see Table 8.2). Four sherds from this group were petrographically analyzed. One of these sherds was found to have only crushed rock (schist) temper, and could therefore not be evaluated with the sand petrofacies model. Of the remaining three sherds, two contained sands from the Rincon petrofacies and one contained sands from the Catalina petrofacies. Based on this information, the Rincon/Catalina 1 group is believed to have been produced somewhere east of the Santa Cruz River, at one or more locations in or near the Catalina and Rincon petrofacies.

Rincon/Catalina 2 Group

The Rincon/Catalina 2 group contained 59 sherds, all of which were recovered from sites in the eastern portion of the Tucson Basin. All three sites containing Rincon/Catalina 2 sherds are believed to have been occupied by recent immigrants from the Mogollon region (Dean et al. 1996; Slaughter and Roberts 1996). Six sherds from this group were petrographically analyzed, of which four contained sands from the Rincon petrofacies and two contained sands from the Catalina petrofacies (see Table 8.3 and Figure 8.2). Although the petrographic results suggest that the Rincon/Catalina 2 sherds were produced in the same general area as the Rincon/Catalina 1 sherds, the compositional patterning exhibited by these groups indicate that they were produced with chemically dissimilar clays (see Figures 8.3 and 8.4). These sherds are believed to have been produced in the Rincon and Catalina petrofacies by the Mogollon newcomers who had settled at eastern communities such as Gibbons Springs, Whiptail, and Sabino Canyon.

Black Mountain Group

Fifty-one sherds were assigned to the group designated Black Mountain. Of these sherds, 25 (49 percent) were recovered from the San Xavier Bridge site located in the southern Tucson Basin. Even more significantly, all of the sherds from the San Xavier Bridge site belong to this group. Petrographic analysis demonstrates that these sherds were produced with sands from the Black Mountain petrofacies (see Table 8.3 and Figure 8.2), located perhaps 3 km to the San Xavier site. Due to the complex alluvial history of the area, the exact distance from the site to the sands with Black Mountain petrofacies composition is somewhat uncertain. Braided, shifting streams on

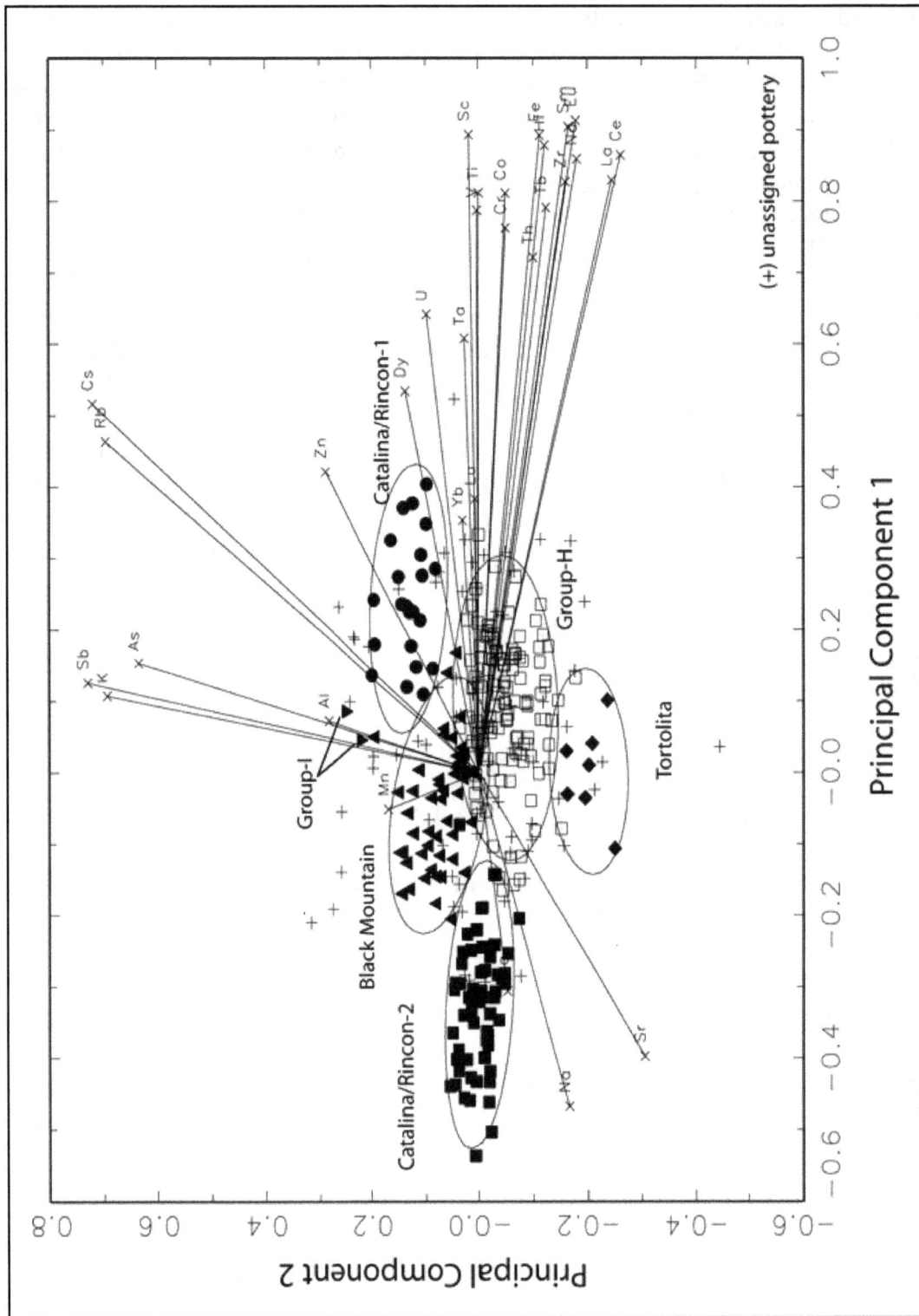

Figure 8.4. Bivariate plot of Principal Components 1 and 2 scores for plain ware compositional groups with unassigned specimens (+) and elemental vectors. Ellipses represent 90 percent confidence level for group membership.

the bajada have resulted in a mixed landscape, where the composition of any individual channel may be similar to either of the bounding petrofacies. There may be up to 1 km of mixing to the east of the mapped line, and up to 500 km of mixing to the west of the line, thus the boundary must be considered gradational (Miksa 2005a,b, 2006). Given the proximity of this petrofacies to the San Xavier Bridge site and the strong association with these sands and San Xavier Bridge sherds, it seems likely that ceramics in the Black Mountain group were produced by potters living at or near the San Xavier Bridge site.

Summary

To summarize, 75 percent of the analyzed plain ware sherds from the Marana Community were assigned to compositional groups. Five groups were identified from this sample, all of which represent newly recognized compositional groups for southern Arizona ceramics. A sixth group was identified in the sample of ceramics that was recovered from sites outside of the Marana Community, but that did not occur in the Marana Community sample.

Of the groups, two (Group H and the Tortolita group) were likely produced within the Marana Community and two (Rincon/Catalina 2 and Black Mountain) were produced outside the community. Of the latter two groups, Rincon/Catalina 2 is believed to have made by puebloan immigrants living in the northeastern portion of the Tucson Basin. The Black Mountain group was almost certainly produced by Hohokam potters from the southern portion of the basin. A fifth group, Catalina/Rincon 1, apparently was produced somewhere in the Rincon and Catalina mountain area, though the production locale cannot be further pinpointed. The production location of Group I sherds is unknown.

RESULTS

Ceramic Production

Compared to Tanque Verde Red-on-brown vessels, plain ware ceramics appear to have been produced at a larger number of settlements. All sites included in this analysis yielded sherds tempered with sands found at or near their respective site, suggesting that plain ware ceramics were produced at most (if not all) settlements. These findings contrast with that obtained from previous studies, which indicated that Tanque Verde Red-on-brown vessels were produced in a limited number of areas. Evidence concerning whether these vessels were produced at the Marana Mound site is contradictory. On the one hand, virtually none of the examined Tanque Verde Red-on-brown sherds contained sands from the any of the Tortolita petrofacies, the petrofacies that encompass and are adjacent to the site. The senior author has interpreted this as evidence that most or all of the Tanque Verde Red-on-brown ceramics found at the mound site were produced elsewhere. This interpretation is based on the fact that other wares contain Tortolita sands, indicating that the potters were not averse to using these sands. In fact, the Tortolita sands contain fewer carbonate inclusions than the sands typically found in the red-on-brown wares, suggesting that they may have been superior for ceramic manufacture. On the other hand, the Marana Mound site contains the greatest concentration of pottery production tools in the Marana Community (see Holeman, this volume). These tools include polishing stones, which are especially necessary for decorated pottery production, their presence suggests the possibility of local manufacture of red ware vessels, red-on-brown vessels, or both. One alternative, considered by Paul Fish and Suzanne Fish, is that the sands used in the Tanque Verde Red-on-brown ceramics were carried (along with other raw materials) to the Marana Mound site and the ceramics manufactured there.

Unlike the ambiguity surrounding the production of red-on-brown ceramics, plain ware vessels were almost certainly produced at the Marana Mound village. This finding is based on the high proportion of Group H sherds found at that site (a group often associated with sands from the Tortolita petrofacies), as well the fact that many of the Group H ceramics are unusually large jars that could not have been transported easily. Although the residents of the Marana Mound settlement may not have produced red-on-brown ceramics, they obviously produced plain ceramics, some of which may have been exported to other settlements.

All of the compositional groups (excluding Group I, which is represented by only two sherds) contained similar proportions of bowls and jars, suggesting that there was no specialization of plain wares by form (Table 8.4). One unique form represented in the assemblage is the *Datura* vessel. Five sherds representing five different *Datura* vessels were submitted for chemical analyses; all of these ceramics were recovered from platform mound proveniences. Of these five samples, three were assigned to compositional Group H, one to the Tortolita compositional group, and one remained unassigned. The association with the *Datura* vessels with Group H and the Tortolita group suggests that the *Datura* vessels were locally produced.

Ceramic Distribution

Table 8.1 and Table 8.2 illustrate the distribution of the plain ware compositional groups between the sites included in the analyzed sample. The distributional patterns indicate that, with the exception of the San Xavier Bridge site, plain ware vessels regularly circulated in

Early Classic period settlements in the Tucson Basin. Regional distribution patterns are similar to those witnessed in the decorated ceramic collection (Table 8.5). In terms of ceramic exchange, the area can be divided into several subregions: the southern Tucson Basin, the eastern Tucson Basin, and the northern Basin area. For both the plain and decorated wares, ceramic exchange occurred frequently between settlements in the same subregion. Although inhabitants of the Marana Community regularly shared ceramic exchange networks with people living in other areas of the northern Tucson Basin and the Los Robles Community, with the exception of the residents of Los Morteros, they appear to have exchanged few vessels with people living in the southern and eastern portions of the basin.

In contrast, intra-community distribution patterns differ between the two types of wares. In the case of the plain ware ceramics, community boundaries appeared to have played little role in structuring exchange networks. Plain ware vessels were transported freely across the community boundaries, with some settlements in the community exchanging pottery more frequently with people living outside of the community than others within it. For example, nearly half of the analyzed plain ceramics from Los Morteros are from the Black Mountain compositional group, made in the southern portion of the Tucson Basin at or near the San Xavier site. However, only trace amounts of these vessels made it to the other Marana Community settlements studied here. Additionally, less than 20 percent of the Los Morteros sample comprises Group H, the most abundant group in the Marana Mound collection. These patterns suggest that, at least in terms of the exchange of utilitarian pottery, the Los Morteros residents maintained a stronger interaction network with the neighbors to their south than they did with other residents of the Marana Community. This contrasts with other lines of evidence

Table 8.4. Vessel Shape Represented by Plain Ware Sherds, by Chemical Group

Chemical Group	Shape					Total
	Bowl	Jar	Datura Vessel	Plate / platter	Indeterminate	
H	26	69	3	2	20	120
I	-	1	-	-	1	2
Tortolita	1	5	1	-	-	7
Rincon/ Catalina 1	6	12	-	-	4	22
Rincon/ Catalina 2	13	43	-	-	3	59
Black Mtn	13	28	-	1	9	51
Unassigned	18	42	-	-	11	72
Total	77	200	4	3	48	333

suggesting that the inhabitants of Los Morteros and the Marana Mound settlement intensively interacted. Intensive interaction between these two settlements is indicated by the presence of a canal linking these two villages (Fish et al. 1992a:21) and by their apparent participation in a shared decorated ceramic exchange sphere (Harry 1997; Harry et al. 2002; Table 8.5).

Intra-community compositional patterns indicate that plain ware ceramics circulated in different exchange spheres and by different mechanisms than did the red-on-brown ceramics. Data from the decorated ceramics suggest the presence of at least two different distribution modes. Compositional diversity for these wares was similar for four of the settlements (i.e., the Marana Mound village and the settlements of Los Morteros, Huntington, and Chicken Ranch; see Table 8.5), which the senior author has elsewhere interpreted as evidence that these residents participated on some form of centralized exchange network, such as might result from centralized trading fairs (Harry and Bayman 2000; Harry et al.

2002:107). Significantly, these are the same settlements in the community that exhibit the highest proportion of Tanque Verde Red-on-brown ceramics, suggesting that the sites near the top of the settlement hierarchy participated in centralized exchange networks from which the smaller sites were excluded. Other settlements were able to acquire Tanque Verde Red-on-brown vessels, but received them through independently maintained trade networks.

Very different patterns are reflected in the plain ware collection. For example, in the decorated ceramic collection shared exchange ties are indicated between the Marana Mound settlement and Los Morteros. Muchas Casas, though located closer to the Marana Mound village than was Los Morteros, obtained most of its decorated ceramics from a different source than did either of the other two settlements. In terms of the plain ware collection, however, Muchas Casas is quite similar to the Marana Mound settlement, and it is the Los Morteros collection that is the most different. This suggests that—as has been observed in Phoenix

Table 8.5. Number of Tanque Verde Red-on-brown Sherds Assigned to each Chemical Group by Site

Site	A	BC	E	F	G	South Tucson	Unass.	Total
Marana Community								
Marana Mound	49	58	6	-	2	1	94	210
Los Morteros	10	12	1	1	-	-	11	35
Huntington	8	7	1	-	-	-	13	29
La Vaca Enferma	-	-	-	-	8	-	11	19
Sueno de Saguaro	1	-	2	-	9	-	7	19
Muchas Casas	1	-	1	17	-	-	12	31
Rancho Derrio	3	1	1	-	-	-	5	10
Chicken Ranch	8	11	2	-	-	1	10	32
Other	3	4	4	-	3	-	17	31
Total Marana Community	83	93	18	18	22	2	180	416
Robles Community								
Robles Mound	1	2	-	1	6	-	17	27
Cerro Prieto	5	1	-	-	4	-	14	24
Hog Farm	5	1	5	1	1	-	17	30
Cake Ranch	2	1	7	-	-	-	20	30
Other	2	-	1	-	4	-	24	31
Total Robles Community	15	5	13	2	15	-	92	142
Northern Tucson Basin								
Hodges	2	6	-	-	1	1	4	14
Como	5	19	-	-	1	-	8	33
Other	1	0			0	0	2	3
Total Northern Tucson Basin	8	25	-	-	2	1	14	50
Southern Tucson Basin								
Salida Del Sol	-	-	-	-	-	7	5	12
A-Mountain	-	-	-	-	-	7	4	11
Other	-	-		-	-	0	7	7
Total Southern Tucson Basin	-	-	-	-	-	14	16	30
Eastern Tucson Basin								
Whiptail	-	-	-	-	-	4	6	10
Tanque Verde Ruin	-	-	-	-	-	2	8	10
Other	-	-	-	-	-	0	4	4
Total Eastern Tucson Basin	-	-	-	-	-	6	18	24
Total	106	123	31	20	39	23	320	662

Basin ceramic collections—the plain wares and decorated wares circulated through different exchange spheres (Abbott 1985, 2000).

CONCLUSIONS

The data obtained from the present study augment the findings of the earlier compositional studies and expand our understanding of economic organization in the Marana Community. The data indicate that the location and organization of production differed between the two types of wares that have been studied. As discussed above, there is virtually no overlap between the compositional groups found in the red-on-brown and plain ware collections. These chemical patterns are supported by the mineralogical information. Of the 20 sherds analyzed here, only four contained felsitic sands found west of the Santa Cruz River (i.e., the four sherds assigned to the Black Mountain petrofacies). The remaining 16 sherds contained granitic sand temper derived to the river's east. These patterns differ from those of the red-on-brown ceramics, nearly all of which contained either felsitic or mixed granitic-felsitic sands (Harry 2003). Together, the chemical and mineralogical data indicate that the red-on-brown ceramics recovered from the Marana Community were produced in different locations and with different materials than were the plain ware vessels. Additionally, the data suggest that there was less specialization in plain ware pottery. It is unclear why potters who produced plain ware vessels would choose not to manufacture red-on-brown pots, particularly when these vessels were evidently much desired and much used. It may be that the clays in the Tortolita region were not suitable for the construction of red-on-brown pots or that the residents of this area were not familiar with the red-on-brown technology. Additional research is needed to resolve this issue.

Despite the strong cultural ties indicated between the residents of the Marana Community and those of the Tucson Basin to the south, the plain ware compositional data indicate that the residents of Marana were also strongly aligned with populations just to the north. For example, the residents of the Marana Mound village and those of Cake Ranch appear to have shared either an exchange network or a common source of ceramic raw materials. In terms of decorated ceramics, however, these two settlements participated in very different exchange spheres (see Harry et al. 2002: Table 8.4). Because red-on-brown and plain ware ceramics have very different social meanings, the differing exchange patterns of these two wares provide information on different types of social relationships. As argued elsewhere (Harry 2003), the Tanque Verde Red-on-brown ceramics likely functioned as items of generalized wealth (sensu Brumfiel and Earle 1987). The plain ware ceramics, by contrast, represent utilitarian items produced by most families and used in everyday contexts. As such, the exchange of plain ware vessels is more likely to inform on social ties maintained by socially close and regularly interacting persons; whereas the movement of Tanque Verde Red-on-brown vessels is more likely to inform on social ties between people that may be more socially distant, but who maintained relationships for political or economic purposes.

If the above assumption is true, the plain ware distributional patterns suggest that the residents of Los Morteros were socially closest to their neighbors on the Santa Cruz River to their south. These neighbors, like the residents of Los Morteros, appear to have descended from generations of Hohokam living in the Tucson Basin and social ties between these settlements may have been in place for generations. In contrast, the inhabitants of the settlements situated on the flanks of the Tortolita Mountains had far less interaction with these long-term Tucson Basin populations, but greater interaction with one another and with residents to the north (such as those living at Cake Ranch).

Community boundaries thus do not appear to have constrained the everyday interaction of community members. Rather, the boundaries appear to have been quite permeable, with some members interacting as much or more with people living outside the community as they did with other community members. Social networks created by the distribution of the red-on-brown ceramics seemingly had little to do with the more common, everyday social ties reflected in the movement of the utilitarian vessels. In this case, interaction appears to be structured not so much by residential proximity or close social ties, but by position in the social hierarchy.

The data presented here support findings from other areas that for the prehistoric Hohokam, different types of ceramics circulated in different spheres of exchange (see Abbott 1985, 2000; Heidke 2000). Which particular exchange sphere(s) a particular individual might have participated in likely depended upon a number of factors, including the value of the item being traded, what pre-existing social ties existed, and what political and other social strategies were at play. These data imply that, like modern-day people, the prehistoric Hohokam simultaneously maintained a number of identities and strategically used those identities and various social ties to try to maintain or alter their social statuses.

Chapter 9

Obsidian Acquisition and (Re)Distribution at the Marana Platform Mound Site

Michael J. Boley

INTRODUCTION

Work on the movement of material goods in the Hohokam world has a long and extensive history (Crown 1991b, Doyel 1991). Unsurprisingly, inquiry has focused on goods that are known to originate in distant locales and/or geographically concentrated areas. Such goods include items thought to be from Mesoamerica (Nelson 1981, 1986), shell from the Gulf of California (Bayman 1996a, McGuire 1985; McGuire and Howard 1987, Nelson 1991, Seymour 1988), intrusive ceramics (Crown 1985, Doyel 1991), and obsidian (see citations above). Interpretations grounded in this work have illuminated the organization of socio-political complexity and exchange networks.

Hohokam archaeologists have long commented on the material differences that accompanied the Preclassic to Classic transition (see Crown 1991a) and speculated upon the concomitant changes in socio-political organization and exchange. McGuire (1985:477; McGuire and Howard 1987), for example, has argued that, while "elites" existed in both the Preclassic and Classic periods, in the latter period they "gained control not only of the distribution of shell, but also of its production." In terms of obsidian, Peterson et al. (1997:236) suggest that it may have been "exchanged between distant elites forging regional alliances [and/or] acquired through elite-sponsored expedi-

tions to the source" (see also Doyel 1996). In fleshing out this argument, Stone (2003:133) writes that "as elites took control over shell procurement expeditions during the Classic period, they also gained control over obsidian raw material. Once at major platform mound sites, the obsidian was redistributed by elites." This quote captures two key dimensions of elite involvement in the context of obsidian, acquisition and (re)distribution. I will assess these issues and explore alternative possibilities that may account for the acquisition and distribution at the Marana Platform Mound site.

THE OBSIDIAN ASSEMBLAGE

The Marana Platform Mound site and larger community in which it is situated have been the focus of an extensive and intensive long-term archaeological project (Bayman 1994; Fish et al. 1992a; Harry 1997). As such, a large number of artifacts of all sorts of materials have been recovered, including flaked stone. While some flaked stone material was available locally, obsidian and cryptocrystalline stone were imported from outside the community. These materials have been collected from the site surface and excavated from a variety of contexts including trash deposits, rooms, and extramural areas.

Thirty-nine obsidian artifacts were surface-collected from an area that measures about 1.50 km east-west by 0.50 km north-south. Twenty-two trashmounds have been tested and 156 obsidian artifacts have been recovered from all but one of these deposits. One hundred and two pieces of obsidian have been collected from the excavation of 21 different rooms on the site. An additional 17 artifacts have been recovered from extra-mural or other excavated contexts. In total, the obsidian assemblage presently consists of 317 artifacts from eight different compounds on the site, which, it should be noted, is a much enlarged sample than the Bayman (1995) study. These numbers indicate that although obsidian is not common on the site, almost every household-level group had access to some.

Each of the obsidian artifacts has been the object of a basic techno-morphological analysis in which attributes such as maximum dimension, weight, and artifact type (i.e., flake, point, core, etc.) were recorded. As a part of this study and the previous study by Bayman (1995), 214 of these have been assigned to one of seven geochemical source areas by Dr. M. Steven Shackley of the Berkeley Archaeological XRF Laboratory at the University of California (Table 9.1). This sourced assemblage is among the largest in Arizona and the largest from any single-component Hohokam site. Like many other Classic period Hohokam assemblages, the one from Marana is dominated by obsidian from a non-local source, the Sauceda Mountains (Figure 9.1).

This collection is unique in three particular ways. First, none of the artifacts are from burial contexts, which thereby may emphasize the more utilitarian aspects of this assemblage over those more explicitly grounded in mortuary ritual, although the site is the center for ritual in the community (Bayman 1994; Fish et al. 1992a) and its higher frequency of obsidian may have ritual implications. Second, the platform mound compound is well represented relative to other compounds on site, something that has been lacking from earlier studies (Bayman 1994, 1995; Peterson 1994; Peterson et al. 1997). Third, about two-thirds of the assemblage has been sourced, thereby strengthening any conclusions that may be drawn.

Table 9.1. Sourced Obsidian Artifacts (n = 214)

Source	Number of Artifacts	Percent of Obsidian Assemblage
Sauceda	148	69
Vulture	25	12
Mule Creek	17	8
Superior	15	7
Cow Canyon	6	3
Unknown A	2	1
Los Vidrios	1	<1
Total	214	100

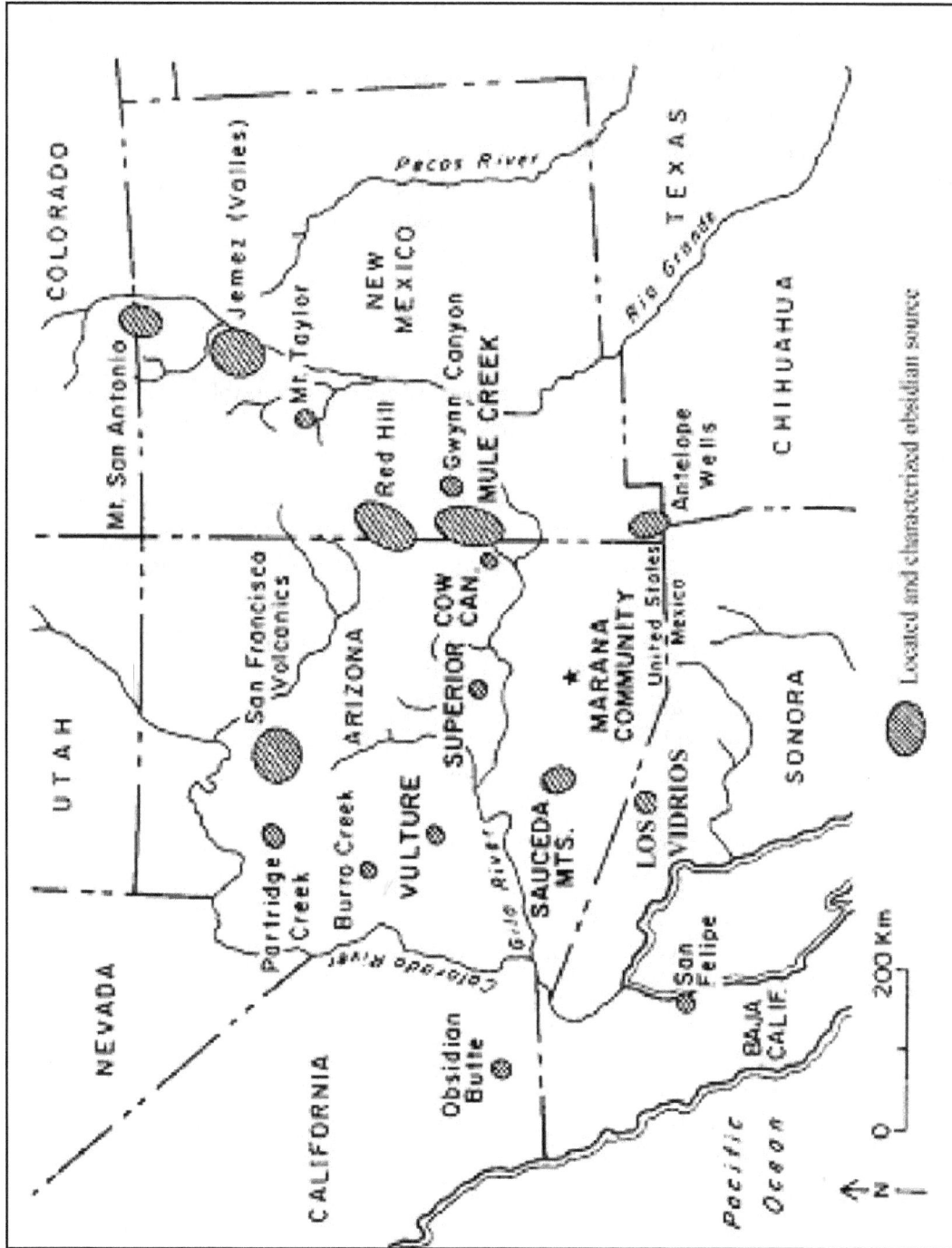

Figure 9.1. Map showing location of Marana and obsidian sources. Sources in capitals indicate those recovered from Marana. Modified from Shackley 1988 and Bayman 1995.

EXCHANGE

David Doyel (1991:241), building upon Colin Renfrew's (1975) work, offered six different strategies by which Hohokam could have procured their goods: (1) expedition to source, (2) acquisition through middlemen, (3) down-the-line acquisition, (4) interaction at or near the source, (5) colonization, and (6) ritual integration or regulation. This paper emphasizes the first three strategies. Additionally, the idea of centralized redistribution will be addressed, because it has played a significant role in examinations of Hohokam exchange (Bayman 1994, 1995; Peterson et al. 1997; Teague 1984).

Centralized Redistribution

Since the pooling of obsidian at the platform mound and its subsequent redistribution to other compounds could potentially mask the archaeological signatures of the three strategies mentioned above, it makes sense to first explore its possible role as a mechanism on the site. Bayman (1994, 1995) has explicitly done so for the obsidian assemblage at the Marana Mound site. He found evidence of centralized redistribution of obsidian within the platform mound site to be lacking, but did argue that the Marana Mound site played a role in the circulation of material at the level of the community, likely during pan-community ceremonies.

Peterson et al. (1997) also found evidence of the centralized redistribution of obsidian to be lacking at the large Hohokam village of Pueblo Grande. But, as with Bayman's study, Peterson et al. (1997) were lacking material from platform mound contexts. Such contexts are not necessarily needed in order to examine the possible role of elites in redistributing material. Pires-Ferreira and Flannery (1976:288), for example, note that if redistribution were an important mechanism we should see a "uniform distribution of obsidian from several sources among [non-elite] households." Still, this study's incorporation of obsidian from platform mound contexts allows for the assessment of other expectations. If the residents of the platform mound were, indeed, pooling and then redistributing obsidian, we might expect: (1) that the platform mound compound's assemblage would be the most diverse, and (2) to see a greater quantity of obsidian at the platform mound compound relative to other residential compounds.

Direct and Embedded Acquisition

As noted above, it is possible in Doyel's (1991) first strategy that obsidian was directly acquired as a result of elite-sponsored expeditions. It has also been suggested that whether elites were involved or not, acquisition of other non-obsidian resources also took place. This idea of "embedded," "secondary," or "parallel" procurement is often proposed as a means by which obsidian could have been conveyed to Hohokam villages in tandem with goods like marine shell. Bayman and Shackley (1999:842) argue that direct acquisition of obsidian, because of its weight, could have been "energetically inefficient" unless it was part of an embedded system of procurement. Mitchell and Shackley (1995:301) state that the "acquisition of [Sauceda, Los Vidrios and Unknown A obsidians were] almost certainly tied to the shell procurement route." David Doyel (1991:241) suggests that "multiple-product trips may have occurred; for instance, shell expeditions could have involved acquisition of Sauceda obsidian and salt, which would have enhanced the payoff for the trip." Mitchell and Shackley more fully elaborate this idea, especially as it relates to obsidian, and "suggest that much of the obsidian found in [Classic period Hohokam sites] was obtained…through direct acquisition related to the acquisition of other resources. In particular, it seems likely that the collection of Sauceda and Los Vidrios obsidian was related to shell expeditions by the Hohokam" (Mitchell and Shackley 1995:298).

Middlemen

Students of the Hohokam have not given too much credence to the idea of itinerant peddlers or middlemen playing a significant role in regional exchange. To the extent they have been considered, it is typically as agents between archaeological cultures, such as Trincheras-Hohokam (McGuire and Howard 1987), Mesoamerican-U.S. Southwestern (Foster 1986) or Mogollon as middlemen between Hohokam and Anasazi (Jernigan 1978). Such traders have not been viewed as important within the Hohokam "sphere," though Doyel (1996:54) suggests that "merchants and entrepreneurs may have independently acquired Sauceda obsidian" during the Classic period. The relative neglect of this concept may be due to the fact that middlemen have been conceived to operate between economically complex European or Euro-American groups and groups native to the region under consideration (Orser 1984, Ray 1978).

The anthropological literature holds that middlemen arise to fill an economic niche created by the regular forces of supply and demand, typically grounded in subsistence goods (Mead 1930, Mintz 1956). Mintz (1956:21) notes that some middlemen may try to supplement income derived from foodstuffs by selling "a few small articles, such as earrings, bangles or tinware"—items that archaeologists are largely forced to focus upon (Orser 1984, Ray 1978).

So, if middlemen existed in Hohokam society, and if they trafficked in obsidian, how might their actions be encoded in the archaeological record? This question largely hinges on the role that obsidian may have played in the economic system. If it were an item of primary exchange and middlemen used it to fulfill some of their everyday subsistence needs, we should expect to see a lot of it at Marana. Alternatively, it may be that obsidian was occasionally "piggy-backing" into the site on top of subsistence goods. Researchers have offered suggestive evidence that certain areas within the larger Hohokam world specialized in certain crops (Gasser and Kwiatkowski 1991) and traded foodstuffs with other groups (Gasser and Miksicek 1985). The residents of the Marana Community specialized in growing agave (Fish et al. 1985, 1992a), producing more food and fiber than they could consume locally, thus indicating that they were part of a larger exchange system. So if obsidian entered the Marana Platform Mound site in this manner, we might expect to see less of it than if it were the primary focus of economic interaction. We might also expect to see a non-patterned spatial distribution. This is because everyone on the site would presumably need the foodstuffs in which the middlemen were primarily trafficking, and any incidental luxuries, such as earrings, bangles, or obsidian, would only occasionally enter the site and be acquired by those who wanted them, perhaps on a "first come, first served" basis.

Down-the-Line Exchange

Winter and Pires-Ferreira (1976:306) formulated two related expectations with respect to what one should witness in instances of down-the-line exchange. These expectations are that variation between households should exist in: (1) the sources used, and (2) the proportions of obsidian from various sources. Barring some over-arching elite involvement in economic transactions, it is clear that not every resident of the site would share the same economic connections as everyone else. Abbott (1996:153) states that compounds "should be associated with imported inventories that differ from one residential unit to the next [and these] differences arise due to the unified manner in which compound-group members associated and exchanged with external parties." An important point in regard to the "external parties" is that they will be associated with disparate geographic locations. Geochemical sourcing studies are particularly well-suited to identify such patterning. Another item to be emphasized is that the repetitive nature of these economic interactions should result in distinctive concentrations of obsidian in various houses or compounds.

ANALYSIS AND DISCUSSION

Centralized Redistribution

If obsidian coming into the site was filtered through the platform mound, we should expect: 1) that the platform mound compound's assemblage would be the most diverse, and 2) to see a greater quantity of obsidian at the platform mound compound relative to other residential compounds. First, the platform mound compound's assemblage would be the most diverse because the less abundant obsidian types would probably not be redistributed equally or uniformly to the other compounds. Table 9.2 is a simple plot of richness by compound and there are two notable patterns. First, the platform mound compound (PM) is no richer in obsidian than five of the other seven compounds. Second, there is no correlation between obsidian sample size and the number of sources represented. Thus, sample size cannot explain the lack of high source diversity at the platform mound compound.

This pattern can be corroborated by exploring another dimension of diversity. Bowbrowsky and Ball (1989:5) define evenness as "the similarity in abundance of several species in the community." For our purposes, "species"

can be replaced with "sources" and "community" with "assemblage." Many quantitative measures of evenness have been developed, but the problem is in comparing the values derived from each measure to one another (see Kintigh 1984, 1989). For example, one can use the reciprocal of Simpson's Index for the four best-represented compounds and come up with the values shown in Table 9.3. We can see a relative ordering, but we cannot determine if any compound is significantly different from any or all of the others.

One way to overcome this problem is to employ the "jackknife technique," as outlined by Kaufman (1998). Table 9.4 displays the reciprocal of the "pseudovalues," values derived by this technique. The ordering of the

Table 9.2. Obsidian Richness in Eight Compounds

Compound	Number of Artifacts	Number of Sources Represented
C1	45	5
C2	22	4
C3	5	5
C4	11	4
C5	46	4
C6	9	2
C7	2	1
PM	18	4

Table 9.3. Source Evenness in Four Obsidian Assemblages Using Reciprocal of Simpson's Index

Compound	Value
PM	3.18
C5	2.45
C1	1.87
C2	1.33

compounds remains the same, but the statistical differences between them have changed.

Evaluation of these differences can be undertaken in two ways. First, 95 percent confidence intervals can be calculated for each of the four pseudovalues; these are presented in Table 9.5. One can see that each compound overlaps with all the others, and this suggests that the differences between them are not particularly notable. A second way to explore these differences is through an analysis of variance (ANOVA). This results in an F-ratio of 3.089 that is significant at 0.064 and therefore warrants further exploration. A Fisher's least significant difference (LSD) test suggests that Compound 2, rather than the platform mound compound, is the most different from the other compounds, particularly from Compound 5 and the platform mound compound (Table 9.6). This inquiry into richness and evenness shows that the platform mound compound does not differ appreciably from the other compounds.

If the platform mound compound were serving as a locus of redistribution we should expect to see more obsidian there than at other compounds. Cryptocrystalline materials are useful for a standardized comparison given their similarities to obsidian in quality and extra-community importation. As shown in Table 9.7, the platform mound compound does not possess appreciably more obsidian relative to cryptocrystallines than do other compounds. It may be, however, that the residents of the platform mound compound were pooling and redistributing these latter materials as well, and that the raw quantities exceed those in any other compound. Table 9.8 shows that this is not the case. Here, raw counts of obsidian and cryptocrystallines are standardized against 100 g of total flaked stone weights by compound. The platform mound compound has no more obsidian than any other compound, and it is not outstanding in its quantity of cryptocrystallines.

Table 9.4. Source Evenness in Four Obsidian Assemblages Using Reciprocal of Kaufman's Jackknife Technique Pseudovalue

Compound	Value
PM	1.80
C5	0.97
C1	0.45
C2	0.31

Table 9.5. Range of 95 percent Confidence Intervals for each Assemblage's Pseudovalue

Compound	Low	High
PM	0.000	1.206
C5	0.460	1.603
C1	1.056	3.381
C2	1.020	5.386

Table 9.6. Matrix of Pairwise Comparison Probabilities from Fisher's LSD Test

	C1	C2	C5	PM
C1	1.000			
C2	0.302	1.000		
C5	0.218	0.043	1.000	
PM	0.093	0.017	0.631	1.000

Table 9.7. Relative Percentages of Two Lithic Materials in Seven Compounds

Compound	Crytocrystalline	N	Obsidian	N
C1	51.8	57	48.2	53
C2	85.6	131	14.4	22
C3	93.1	108	6.9	8
C4	78.5	51	21.5	14
C5	78.0	251	22.0	71
C6	65.5	19	34.5	10
PM	80.5	140	19.5	34

Table 9.8. Number of Cryptocrystalline and Obsidian Artifacts/100g Total Lithics

Compound	Cryptocrystalline	Obsidian
C1	0.23	0.12
C3	0.39	0.03
C5	0.76	0.11
C9	0.50	0.12

Direct and Embedded Acquisition

The lack of any elite involvement in the intra-site redistribution of obsidian casts some doubt on the notion of elite-sponsored treks to procure obsidian. The possibility that entrepreneurs would have taken such tasks upon themselves yet remains. And, as noted above, it has often been suggested that in order to make such a trip "pay off," it would have been necessary to procure more than one type of material. A logical implication of such procurement would be the materials' co-occurrence in the archaeological record.

Perhaps the clearest case for such parallel procurement would consist of caches of two different materials, such as obsidian and marine shell, on the floor of a room. This ideal situation has not been encountered at the Marana Platform Mound site, nor, to my knowledge, anywhere else in the Classic Hohokam world. In the absence of the ideal, we must look elsewhere for such evidence. To this end, it is useful that materials recovered from trash mounds are an accurate reflection of what has been excavated from structures, as indicated by certain aspects of the obsidian assemblage.

For example, the techno-morphological characteristics of the obsidian assemblages, whether recovered from trash mounds or structures, are virtually the same (Table 9.9). Similarly, the percentages of the different sources represented in both the trash mounds and structures are almost identical (Table 9.10). So, in general, social groups at the level of the compound, if not the household, were acquiring

Table 9.9. Relative Percentages of General Techno-Morphological Categories for Two Contexts

	Cores	Debitage	Bifaces	Nodules
Trashmounds	13	64	17	6
Structures	19	63	10	8

Table 9.10. Relative Percentages of Sources for Two Contexts

Source	Trashmounds (%) (n = 127)	Structures (%) (n = 81)
Sauceda	70.1	67.9
Vulture	14.2	7.4
Mule Creek	6.3	9.9
Superior	5.5	8.6
Cow Canyon	2.4	3.7
Unknown A	1.6	1.2
Los Vidrios	0.0	1.2
Total	100.0	100.0

and discarding the same types of materials. We may therefore expect that if an inhabitant of the site was making trips to directly procure multiple resources, we should see this reflected in materials recovered from trash deposits. This is a prickly expectation given that if an individual was undertaking such a venture, the reason he would be doing so would be to distribute his wares to his fellow villagers, which would therefore obfuscate any patterning. Despite this concern, I think it is feasible to expect to discern some degree of co-variation in abundance if two resources were being procured in tandem.

In an attempt to test the "embedded" hypothesis, I regressed counts of shell against counts of Sauceda obsidian, both standardized against counts of plainware sherds. All these materials were recovered from 18 trash deposits at the Marana Platform Mound site (Table 9.11). The result shows that there is no relationship ($r = 0.18$, $p = 0.003$, $r^2 = 0.03$). Further doubt is cast on the hypothesis by noting the virtual absence of obsidian from the two other Papaguerian obsidian sources, Los Vidrios and Unknown A (Shackley 1995).

Evidence for "parallel" resource acquisition is lacking, which hints that the direct acquisition of obsidian, at least, was not practiced by the inhabitants of the Marana Community. This notion is supported by other characteristics of the obsidian assemblage. The ratios of "finished" artifacts, including projectile points and other bifaces, to all other obsidian artifacts demonstrate that the majority of the sources represented, and particularly those most distant

Table 9.11. Standardized Counts (per 1000 plain sherds) of Sauceda Obsidian and Shell Used in Regression Analysis (after Bayman 1994)

TM	Sauceda	Shell
1	9.2	38.6
2	15.2	26.6
3	5.1	54.1
4	4.2	27.5
5	15.5	36.7
6	0.0	23.9
7	0.0	23.3
8	6.1	38.6
9	8.0	51.7
10	7.6	60.5
11	4.2	21.1
12	3.4	45.5
13	0.0	125
14	12.7	22.9
15	5.6	69.8
16	8.3	124
17	13.1	39.4
18	2.2	51.5

from the site, have an inordinately high number of the former (Table 9.12). Projectile points do not, of course, occur naturally at obsidian sources, so this suggests that obsidian from most of the sources, and perhaps all, was being introduced to the site by some means other than direct acquisition.

If an inordinately high number of finished artifacts in any sourced assemblage suggest something other than direct acquisition, then it might be assumed that high ratios of debitage to tools allow the possibility of direct acquisition. At Marana, the two best-represented assemblages (Sauceda and Vulture) possess

such ratios (Table 9.12). But the amounts of the different obsidians when quantified by a measure as simple as weight indicate that direct acquisition was unlikely. The weight of the entire assemblage is 516.8 g, or just over a pound. The assemblage weight of the single best-represented source, Sauceda, is just 133.2 g, or about five ounces. And all of the Vulture obsidian weighs 60.9 g, or just over two ounces. Even if all of the Sauceda material, for example, were procured at the same time, it would have been a negligible addition to any load of shell or salt.

Implications of the above discussion are two-fold. First, the notion of "embedded," "parallel," or "secondary" procurement of obsidian, at least for the people who lived at Marana, is ungrounded. Second, the direct acquisition of obsidian, whether embedded or not, was not an important means by which obsidian was introduced to the site. By extension, the idea that elite-sponsored expeditions were undertaken to procure obsidian, whether to maintain ties with elites at other villages or to reinforce some sort of power or authority over other inhabitants of Marana, is unfounded.

Middlemen, Down-the-Line, Neither?

Three lines of evidence favor the idea of down-the-line exchange over middlemen. First, as statistics concerning the raw quantity of obsidian was used to argue against the notion of direct acquisition, so can it be used to argue against the likelihood of middlemen playing a significant role in the conveyance of obsidian to the site. The entire obsidian assemblage weighs just over a pound and, unless obsidian was extremely valuable, this would not be a quantity from which even a single trader could make a living. Perhaps, then, obsidian was introduced to the site "piggy-backing" with subsistence goods. This hypothetical notion leads to the second line of evidence.

Table 9.12. Relative Percentages of Bifaces and Non-Bifaces by Source

Source	Biface	N	Non-Biface	N
Los Vidrios	100	1	0.0	0
Crow Canyon	85.7	6	14.3	1
Mule Creek	58.8	10	41.2	7
Superior	40.0	6	60.0	9
Vulture	11.5	3	88.5	23
Sauceda	6.9	10	93.1	135
Unknown A	0.0	0	100	3

Using ceramics as a proxy for socio-economic connections with people from areas external to the Marana Community allows us to explore possible associations between the hypothesized primary foodstuffs and secondary "trinkets." As with Sauceda obsidian and shell material, the co-occurrence of these materials in the archaeological record is a logical implication of their paired introduction to the site. To examine this possibility, standardized counts of obsidian from 18 trash mounds on the site were regressed against standardized counts of ceramic types from outside the Tucson Basin that correspond geographically to particular obsidian sources found on the site (Table 9.13).

In the first case, I look toward the Phoenix Basin. If middlemen from the Hohokam "core" were bringing subsistence or other goods in locally made ceramic containers, or even just the vessels themselves, and if they were secondarily complementing these loads with locally obtained obsidian, then we might expect a correlation between such materials at Marana. More specifically, we should expect to see Phoenix Basin sherds and obsidian from the Vulture obsidian source, and perhaps the Superior source, occurring together. It should be mentioned here that Shackley (1995; Mitch-ell and Shackley 1995) has previously noted that the Hohokam's access to Superior obsidian was seemingly restricted. This is reflected in two ways. First, there is a general paucity of this obsidian on Classic period Hohokam sites, despite the source's relative proximity to sites in the Sonoran Desert, especially the Phoenix Basin. Second, there is a relative lack of obsidian from Sonoran Desert sources in areas to the north and east of the Superior source. Taken together, these patterns suggest to Shackley (1995) that a cultural boundary existed between these areas, limiting the movement of obsidian between the Hohokam and Saladoans. Still, if Superior obsidian is present at Marana, it is reasonable to assume that it would have passed through the Phoenix Basin, and therefore that associations of this obsidian and sherds from the Phoenix Basin might co-occur. They do not. In fact, Vulture and Superior obsidians do not co-vary in their abundance with sherds from the Phoenix Basin ($r = 0.12$, $p = 0.09$, $r^2 = 0.01$).

In a second regression, I sought to gauge the potential of obsidian and ceramic relationships between materials from east of Marana. Standardized counts of Cow Canyon and Mule Creek obsidians were regressed against standardized counts of sherds imported from the mountainous region of eastern Arizona.

Table 9.13. Standardized Counts (per 1000 plain sherds) of Obsidians and Non-Local Ceramics Used in Regression Analysis (after Bayman 1994)

TM	Salt-Gila Basin		Mogollon	
	Obsidian	Sherds	Obsidian	Sherds
1	0.0	27.6	0.0	3.7
2	3.8	3.8	0.0	0.0
3	2.6	5.2	0.0	0.0
4	0.0	4.2	0.0	19.0
5	0.0	1.4	0.0	4.2
6	0.9	0.0	1.8	0.0
7	3.3	0.0	0.0	0.0
8	0.0	2.0	4.1	0.0
9	0.0	0.0	1.3	0.0
10	1.1	1.1	0.0	0.0
11	0.0	0.0	0.0	1.4
12	1.0	0.0	1.5	0.0
13	0.0	0.0	0.0	17.9
14	0.0	0.0	0.0	0.0
15	0.0	0.0	0.0	6.8
16	16.5	0.0	0.0	8.3
17	0.0	0.0	0.0	5.3
18	0.0	4.5	0.0	0.0

Again, no correlation was found between these materials ($r = 0.23$, $p = 0.05$, $r^2 = 0.03$). Indeed, only one trashmound contained both types of materials from this region. It is also interesting to note here that there is very little obsidian ($n = 2$) at the contemporaneous site of Gibbon Springs in the eastern Tucson Basin (Myers 1996). If peddlers were moving from east to west in this area and carrying obsidian with them to trade, we might expect to see more of it at this site.

The third line of evidence that weakens the case for middlemen and strengthens the one for down-the-line exchange is grounded in the intra-site spatial distribution of the obsidian. While inquiry into the compounds' evenness in obsidian sources was useful in that it revealed the platform mound compound to be much the same as the other compounds in this regard, it also may have masked some differences that appear real from a simple visual inspection of Table 9.14. Attempts to quantify these differences speak directly to the expectations developed for discerning patterns resulting from middlemen as to those from more casual, but regular, trading partners in a down-the-line exchange system.

Conversion of the values in Table 9.14

Table 9.14. Four Best-Represented Compounds and Five Best-Represented Sources

	C5	C1	C2	C9
Sauceda	26	32	19	6
Vulture	12	4	1	1
Mule Creek	2	2	1	7
Superior	6	0	0	4
Cow Can	0	6	0	0
Total	46	44	21	18

to percentages (Table 9.15) shows an interesting pattern. It shows that at least 50 percent of each of four uncommon obsidian types on the site can be found in one of the same four compounds considered above. Approximately two-thirds of Vulture obsidian, for example, was recovered from Compound 5. Similarly, over half of the Mule Creek obsidian comes from the platform mound compound. A chi-squared test was performed in an attempt to discern if these apparent differences in the obsidian distribution across the site are statistically significant. Because a number of the cells are sparse or empty (Table 9.14), this test was adjusted with Yates' correction for continuity. The result is highly significant ($x^2 = 40.63$, $p < 0.001$), and the more conspicuous associations are displayed in Table 9.16. This result conforms much more closely to the expectations offered for the spatial patterns associated with down-the-line exchange than with middlemen. Specifically, there is a pattern, and it fits the expectation given the idea described above of repetitive interactions with partners from discrete geographic locations.

The result from this chi-squared test can also be used to discount the possibility of middlemen who specialized in gathering obsid-

ian from different sources and then distributing them at a later time. Obsidian from sources in the Sonoran Desert (Sauceda, Vulture, Superior, Unknown A, Los Vidrios), which make up about 90 percent of the Marana assemblage, are macroscopically indistinguishable (Shackley 1988:757). In order for the spatial patterns observable in the obsidian distribution across the site to be maintained in this situation, we would have to expect that such a trader would have kept the obsidians from the different sources separate, and that the residents of the site had a preference for particular obsidians. Given the "extreme variability in color and opacity even within a given source" (Shackley 1988:757) and that the Sonoran Desert sources are all of equal knappability (Shackley 1995:547), it is difficult to imagine that such expectations could be met.

Two issues, then, yet remain to be explored and explained. First, why are the intra-site concentrations of obsidian not even more clear-cut? That is, if the residents of Compound 5, for example, had easier access to Superior and Vulture obsidians than other compounds did (Table 9.15), why is not all of that material in Compound 5? One explanation is that the residents of separate compounds

Table 9.15. Distribution of Uncommon Obsidian Types across Four Compounds

Source	C1	C2	C5	PM
Vulture	22.0	5.5	67.0	5.5
Mule creek	17.0	8.0	17.0	58.0
Superior	0.0	0.0	60.0	40.0
Cow Canyon	100.0	0.0	0.0	0.0

Table 9.16. Standardized Residual Values from X2 (negative, positive, conspicuous)

	C5	C1	C2	PM
Sauceda	0.324047	0.359434	1.841662	2.229488
Vulture	4.022771	0.43783	0.69809	0.407461
Mule Creek	0.739668	0.620012	0.105274	13.90706
Superior	1.049044	2.484148	0.781478	3.174516
Cow Can	1.256383	5.827762	0.232697	0.13582

maintained overlapping external connections. Another explanation is a sort of time-dependent intra-site "trickle down" of obsidian once it was introduced to the site. This idea is supported by examination of Table 9.17, which shows that the larger the assemblage from any given source is, the more compounds from which it is recovered. Reasons for such intra-site exchange are many, but, to invoke ethnographic analogy, may include payment for labor or gambling debt (Underhill 1939). Anecdotally, it is interesting to note the example of Compound 3. Here, five pieces of obsidian have been recovered and each is from a different source. It is unlikely that the residents of this compound maintained ties to each of five different external groups from whom they could have traded for this obsidian. Rather, it seems more likely that they received their obsidian from other site inhabitants.

Second is the question of where, exactly, these interactions may have occurred. While it is fatuous to argue that the site residents never left their village and therefore could not have obtained obsidian from trading partners living elsewhere, there is reason to expect that the obsidian, as well as any number of other goods, was brought directly to the site. Generally, sites at which platform mounds are located have been suggested to have been loci of pan-community events (Abbott 2000:140; Blitz 1993; Doyel 1974:170) at which the exchange of commodities occurred (Lindauer and Blitz 1997:180), and this argument has more specifically been made for the Marana Platform Mound site (Bayman 1994; P. Fish and Fish 2000). Bayman, in fact, found that both shell (1994, 1996a) and obsidian (1994, 1995) do indeed concentrate at the Platform Mound site relative to other contemporaneous

Source	Sample Size	Number of Compounds
Sauceda	99	8
Vulture	24	7
Mule Creek	14	6
Superior	11	3
Cow Canyon	7	2
Unknown A	2	2
Los Vidrios	1	1

Table 9.17. Relationship between Sourced Assemblage Sample Size and Number of Compounds

sites in the larger community. The residents of these smaller sites in the community surely had their own external connections, but the modest amount of obsidian at these sites strongly suggests that the obsidian was imported by residents of the Platform Mound site (Bayman 1994, 1995; see also Teague 1984).

CONCLUSION

The spatial distribution of obsidian at the Marana Platform Mound site, the physical characteristics of the assemblage, and its association with other material classes, or lack thereof, has been used to draw conclusions about how obsidian was introduced to the site, and these have ramifications for obsidian's use in formulations of Classic period socio-political complexity. First, it has been shown that the residents of the platform mound compound played no special role in the circulation of obsidian to other site inhabitants, and neither did autonomous middlemen. Rather, villagers at the level of the compound, if not the household, maintained their own external connections, as suggested by Abbott (1996) for ceramics. If it is true, as Suzanne Fish and

Paul Fish (2006:14) have suggested, that the inhabitants of the platform mound site "almost certainly included households of geographically disparate origin with the Tucson Basin or beyond," then it makes sense that members of these social units had strong ties with other groups in areas from whence they came, and that they maintained these ties upon newly settling at the community center. This can be seen as one "organizational device through which the law of monotonic decrement is circumvented by human exchange systems" (Renfrew 1977:88).

Second, it has been argued that obsidian procurement embedded in trips to procure other resources, particularly shell, was not a common practice for the Hohokam living at the Marana Platform Mound site. Doubt has been cast on the likelihood of direct procurement, embedded or otherwise. If, as has been suggested, elites had the power and authority to organize and sponsor expeditions to procure "exotic" materials (McGuire 1985; Stone 2003), they were not exercising them at this village. Obsidian, therefore, cannot be viewed as important in formulations of political power.

This is not to say, however, that obsidian did not figure into power relations at the site.

Inasmuch as the platform mound site served as the locus for pan-community ritual integration (Bayman 1994; Fish et al. 1992a), and as obsidian at the site was almost certainly possessed of ritual significance (Bayman 1995), and as obsidian is more common at the mound site than other sites in the community, it is likely that obsidian did play some role in the development and maintenance of ritual power.

As the data used herein are specific to one site, so then must be the conclusions. But there are reasons to think these results can be extended to other Classic period villages. For example, the 123 pieces of sourced obsidian from Classic period contexts at Pueblo Grande come from seven different sources. That the number of sources is so similar speaks to a rough equivalence in importance of obsidian to both groups. It also suggests that the areal extents of each group's exchange network were approximately the same. It is worth noting, however, that these networks did not completely overlap, as evidenced by the complete lack of obsidian from northern Arizona in the Marana assemblage.

Chapter 10

Visibility, Perception, and Power at the Marana Platform Mound: A Spatial Analysis

Phillip O. Leckman

Arizona archaeologists have long suspected that Classic period Hohokam society exhibited a degree of political and social asymmetry and inequality in excess of that found in contemporary or historic Southwest societies (Harry and Bayman 2000; McGuire 2000; Wilcox 1991). While Classic Hohokam platform mound centers were once widely interpreted as chiefdoms in the classic, typological sense, in which "big men" achieved and maintained status by managing the production and redistribution of staples (Sahlins 1972) or prestige goods and exotic materials (e.g., Earle 1977), mounting archaeological evidence demonstrates that Classic period Hohokam society largely fails to meet the expectations of traditional chiefdom models (Bayman 1995, 1996a; Rice 1987b).

In tune with other Southwestern archaeologists (Mills 2000), Hohokam researchers are increasingly moving beyond such typologies, recognizing that power and inequality in middle-range societies develop from many sources besides economic status or managerial élan, including kin ties, factional allegiances and rivalries, and, most significantly, ritual (Abbott 2003; Bayman 2001; Elson 1998; S. Fish and Fish 2000).

Discussions of power and politics among archaeologists studying the Hohokam Classic period have long been centered on the interpretation of platform mound architecture. With 120 or more examples known from nearly 100

Classic period sites across southern Arizona (Doelle et al. 1995; Elson 1998), the platform mound phenomenon appears to be strongly linked to political organization and the exercise of power in Hohokam society. Although the structures archaeologists describe as platform mounds subsume a wide range of functional as well as architectural variability, most recognized mounds appear to have functioned as monumental or public architecture. Specifically, their construction probably required the participation of a group (Doelle et al. 1995; Elson 1998) and probably served some integrative function that acted to bring together groups of individuals at a scale beyond the individual household (Doelle et al. 1995). In the words of Bruce Trigger (1990:119), such structures were "intended to perform." This performative aspect of the platform mound, the sense in which the activities that took place there were public events, is a key dimension of the ideas examined in this paper.

Archaeological inquiries from a variety of theoretical perspectives and research objectives have converged on platform mound ceremonialism as a central explanatory principle. Platform mound ritual is portrayed as a key mechanism for the enactment of social processes as diverse as resource redistribution, irrigation management, community integration, and social differentiation (e.g., Craig et al. 1998; Doelle et al. 1995; Elson

1998; Howard 1992; Jacobs 1992; Lindauer and Blitz 1997). This emphasis itself is by no means inappropriate, both ethnographic analogy and the archaeological record strongly suggest that ceremonial activity was one of the central functions of southern Arizona platform mounds, and that this ritualism was of key importance to Hohokam society (e.g., Elson 1998; S. Fish and Fish 2000; Lindauer 1996; Rice and Redman 1993). The chief weakness of most of these analyses, rather, lies in their failure to go beyond this link between ritual and politics. While archaeological investigations of the Hohokam Classic period seem increasingly comfortable with the notion of ceremony as a venue for political action, the potential dynamics of this ritualism itself have typically been left vague and little-discussed. Archaeologists are thus left with something of a paradox: a growing set of archaeological interpretations centered on an explanatory principle that is in some cases left unexplained.

This archaeological Catch-22 is regrettable but immanently correctable. In some ways it is already being corrected, as this volume demonstrates, the social and political implications of activities linked to ritual, such as feasting, are increasingly being examined. But efforts to flesh out our understanding of platform mound ceremonialism can and must go much further. In the remainder of this paper, I address platform mound ceremonialism via two promising routes.

First, theoretical perspectives on performance, visibility, and spectacle (Barrett 1994; Foucault 1977; Inomata and Coben 2006; Moore 1996) are examined as a means of addressing how ritual functions as a social force, how political ideas and ideologies are created and contested therein, and how these forces might manifest themselves materially. Second, methodologies drawn from spatial analysis, architecture, and cognitive research into human perception are utilized to iden-

tify and discuss key dimensions of Classic Hohokam ritual in an archaeological context. This analysis is performed via a consideration of ritual at the Marana Platform Mound, the central site for a large and important Early Classic community that has been the subject of important and intensive archaeological research for more than twenty years. By situating examination of Hohokam ritual at Marana in the context of the platform mound architecture itself, my analysis suggests that ceremonialism at the mound complex operated at multiple scales, simultaneously reinforcing a sense of shared community among members of a large group, even as it emphasized the exalted positions of a select few. Although its elevated prominence probably made it a highly effective venue for large-scale public ritual events, the platform mound complex also created segregated, limited-access spaces where the full comprehension of ritual movement and gesture would have been limited to those privileged with specialized access.

SPACE AND RITUAL

The reticence to engage public ceremonialism in greater depth is not a shortcoming of Southwestern archaeologists alone. As an excellent recent overview of current performance theory in archaeology makes clear, the tendency to ignore the particulars of ritual, in favor of a focus on more structured notions of political or economic organization, is discipline-wide (Inomata and Coben 2006). The absence of a detailed consideration of ritual and performance from most current archaeological inquiry is unfortunate. Inomata and Coben persuasively demonstrate that public performance has played a key role in the enactment and articulation of political and ideological ideas for much of the course of human history. Seeing is indeed very often believing. By communicating simultaneously at a physical, emotional and mental level, performance is often a more persuasive and effective means of expressing an idea than verbal communication alone (Inomata and Coben 2006). Moreover, public rituals and feasts often serve as key venues for both the integration of communities and the creation and maintenance of asymmetrical power relations within human society.

In the former case, Inomata and Coben (2006:23) suggest that performance augments the degree to which members of a community think of themselves as a unified, coherent whole by symbolically dramatizing "the central value of a community and presenting it in sensible forms." Echoing earlier researchers, (such as Durkheim [1965]) Tambiah (1979) and Turner (1972) also argue that ritual uses collective representation, communal emotion, and shared intense experience to both recreate and perpetuate a given set of social values. In opposition to everyday life, when communities larger than a household or small group in regular face-to-face contact may exist primarily in the imagination (Anderson 1991), shared public spectacles allow large numbers of community members to "sense and witness the bodily existence and participation of other members" (Inomata and Coben 2006:24).

With regard to the creation and maintenance of social differentiation and asymmetry, Inomata and Coben (2006) argue that the effectiveness of performance in bringing people together and creating community also gives it a potential to serve as a tool for domination within which ideologies of power and political asymmetry can be reiterated and reinforced without resorting to coercive force. It is valuable here to recall Foucault's (1977:48) notion of spectacle, in which power is manifested and made real by being "deployed before all eyes" in public ritual and symbolically enacted through the bodily actions of the ritual's participants, a group that, by their combined acts

of watching and responding, composes the audience for the spectacle as well. Additional insight into how social control and power asymmetries operate within ritual and public events is also supplied by Foucault's description of panopticism and the disciplined body (Foucault 1977). Foucault's concept of social "discipline" invites investigation into the efforts of some individuals to enforce social orthodoxies, promote dominant ideologies, and utilize other conscious and intentional methods to reinforce particular kinds of behavior. Further, since it operates in terms of surveillance, intervisibility, and other spatial techniques for controlling and constraining individuals, Foucault's concept also provides a basis for investigating discipline through architecture and archaeology.

But how can the political and social dimensions of performance and ritual be effectively operationalized in an archaeological context? While the specific nature of prehistoric ritual behavior is probably beyond the ability of archaeological analysis to precisely reconstruct, many of the material and spatial correlates of performance, such as costuming or ritual accessories, may survive to enter the archaeological record. When such artifacts are examined from a perspective emphasizing their potential roles as symbols to be visually displayed, as epitomized in a recent study of the presentational characteristics of Ancestral Pueblo bowls by Barbara Mills (2004), they may provide insight into the scale of ritual, its intended audience, and, to some extent at least, the political and social dynamics that might have been at play.

A second and even more important avenue for pursuing prehistoric ritual is provided by considering the theatrical aspects of the architectural spaces in which ceremonial events are performed. Ritual architecture should be examined as a venue for music, speech, and other key elements of performance and ceremony in terms of visibility, audibility, access, and human perception. In the remainder of this study, I therefore focus primarily on the platform mound as a setting for performance, a space within which the two central trajectories outlined above, integration and differentiation, would have been enacted, reiterated, and consolidated.

ANALYSIS

My examination of ritual and performance at the Marana Mound is based upon a spatial analysis of the mound precinct and its surroundings, employing two chief components. Building on a similar preliminary study by Douglas Gann and using analysis tools incorporated in the ESRI ARC/Info and ArcGIS software packages, I consider intervisibility within the Marana site, here operationalized in terms of "viewsheds," which indicate an observer's ability to see part or all of a landscape from a given location. A visibility analysis is a powerful means for examining the scale and nature of mound-based ritual performance. How far from the mound itself did its potential audience extend? How effectively did public spectacles enacted atop the raised mound surface transmit into walled compounds hundreds of meters away? Conversely, to what extent could individuals standing atop the mound observe, and thus surveil, the actions of compound residents? And to what extent could site inhabitants without access to the platform mound perceive what transpired within its putatively restricted environs from outside its enclosure wall?

Additionally, I conduct an investigation of the mound's ritual function using techniques drawn from the innovative work of Andean archaeologist Jerry Moore (1996), who applied communicative and perceptive thresholds derived from acoustics and human perception research, particularly the study of proxemics pioneered by Edward Hall (1966, 1972). When used in conjunction with visibility analyses and other computer-based means of measuring distance, slope, and perception, these methodologies offer an insightful way to address the role of platform mounds as ritual staging areas. As both analytical methods are ultimately based on the architecture of the Marana mound complex itself, we will begin by describing the complex in more detail.

PLATFORM MOUND ARCHITECTURE AT MARANA

The Marana Mound is a relatively small platform mound, with an estimated volume of only about 900 m^3 (P. Fish and Fish 2000:260) and a moundtop surface area of approximately 360 m^2 (Figure 10.1). Recent excavations at the site have verified that the mound was constructed by the deposition of clean earthen fill behind massive, straight-sided adobe retaining walls. The moundtop surface was ringed by a perimeter wall that appears, like other compound walls at the site, to have originally stood some 2 m in height. Other documented moundtop features included four adobe rooms built into the corners of the mound perimeter wall. The fourth room stood at the southeast corner of the mound surface, but this portion of the mound was heavily disturbed during the mid-twentieth century by the construction of massive berm and stock pond used for ranching.

The mound itself is situated along the west wall of a larger walled compound with the same orientation, enclosing a space approximately 2,400 m^2 in area. Two additional adobe rooms have been identified and excavated within this larger mound precinct: a massive, thick-walled adobe room in the southeast corner of the outer mound compound and a smaller structure directly to the east of the mound itself. A large number of extramural features, including large

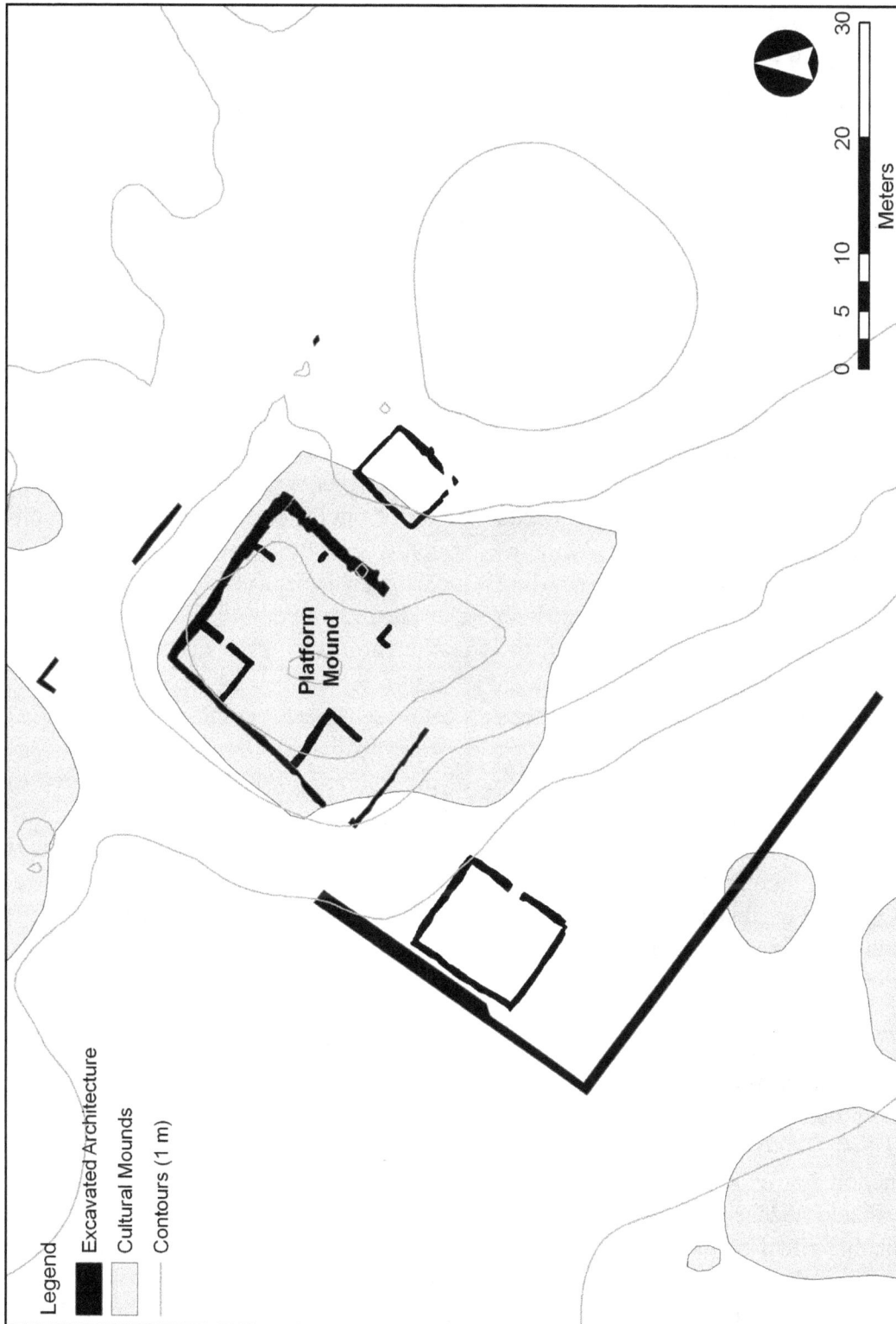

Figure 10.1. The platform mound and associated architecture at the Marana Platform Mound site (AZ AA:12:251).

roasting pits and puddling pits, are situated with remarkably consistent spacing along the southern compound wall. The mound is located near the center of the Marana site (Figure 10.2), and while no formal central plaza has been defined, the areas located to the east and west of the mound complex are noticeably devoid of archaeological features (Fish and Fish, personal communication).

In terms of material culture, only the southwest moundtop room contained a sizeable artifact assemblage, including a large Casa Grande jar, a mountain sheep horn core, and a grooved stone axe (P. Fish and Fish 2000). Both the southwest room and the better-preserved, but largely empty northwest room contained plastered hearths and floors, postholes, and other features typical of residential contexts at the site (P. Fish and Fish 2000). While in-situ assemblages are inconclusive regarding the function of these rooms, Fish and Fish note that trash deposits associated with the mound precinct were virtually identical to trash mounds associated with residential compounds elsewhere in the site. Artifactual support for an elite residence atop the mound is limited, if one assumes such a group would have had preferential access to shell, obsidian, and other valued commodities. Although the mound site as a whole possessed a greater amount of wealth than smaller settlements, artifact assemblages from different residential contexts within the mound site are virtually indistinguishable (P. Fish and Fish 2000; Harry and Bayman 2000). Evidence for intensified production activity within the mound precinct is also lacking (P. Fish and Fish 2000:265; Holeman 2004). A ritual function, however, is strongly supported by the available evidence. A number of artifacts with probable ritual connotations are found almost exclusively within the mound precinct including the mountain sheep horn core and sherds from seven small *Datura* effigy pots (Fish and Fish 2000:266), perhaps testifying to the use of the mound precinct for rituals involving the consumption of hallucinogenic substances.

VISIBILITY: PRINCIPLES, PROCEDURES, PROBLEMS

The principle underlying a visibility analysis, though computationally intensive, is conceptually quite simple. By comparing elevation values between a file containing elevational and locational data for one or more "observer" points and a digital elevation model (DEM) containing elevation values for a grid of cells with a given spatial resolution, the GIS can assess whether or not each cell in the DEM can be seen from the observer point. The resulting visibility grid or "viewshed" contains values indicating whether a cell was visible or not. The viewshed can then be displayed graphically in conjunction with other geographic or spatial datasets, reclassified using a variety of classification schemes, or combined mathematically or statistically with other grid data. A variety of programming options allow the investigator to customize the visibility analysis. Offset heights can be added to either the observer or the features being observed, the range of vertical angles for which visibility is assessed can be modified, and vegetation, buildings or other obstructions within a given cell can be accounted for.

Before performing the visibility analyses that are summarized below, it was first necessary to generate accurate DEMs of the Marana site and community at both a site and regional level. At a site level, the DEM was generated from 1 m contour data derived from hand-drawn 50 m by 50 m maps of the entire site composed during the original full coverage survey of the site area. In addition to elevation data, these maps also included the locations of prehistoric cultural mounds, structural walls,

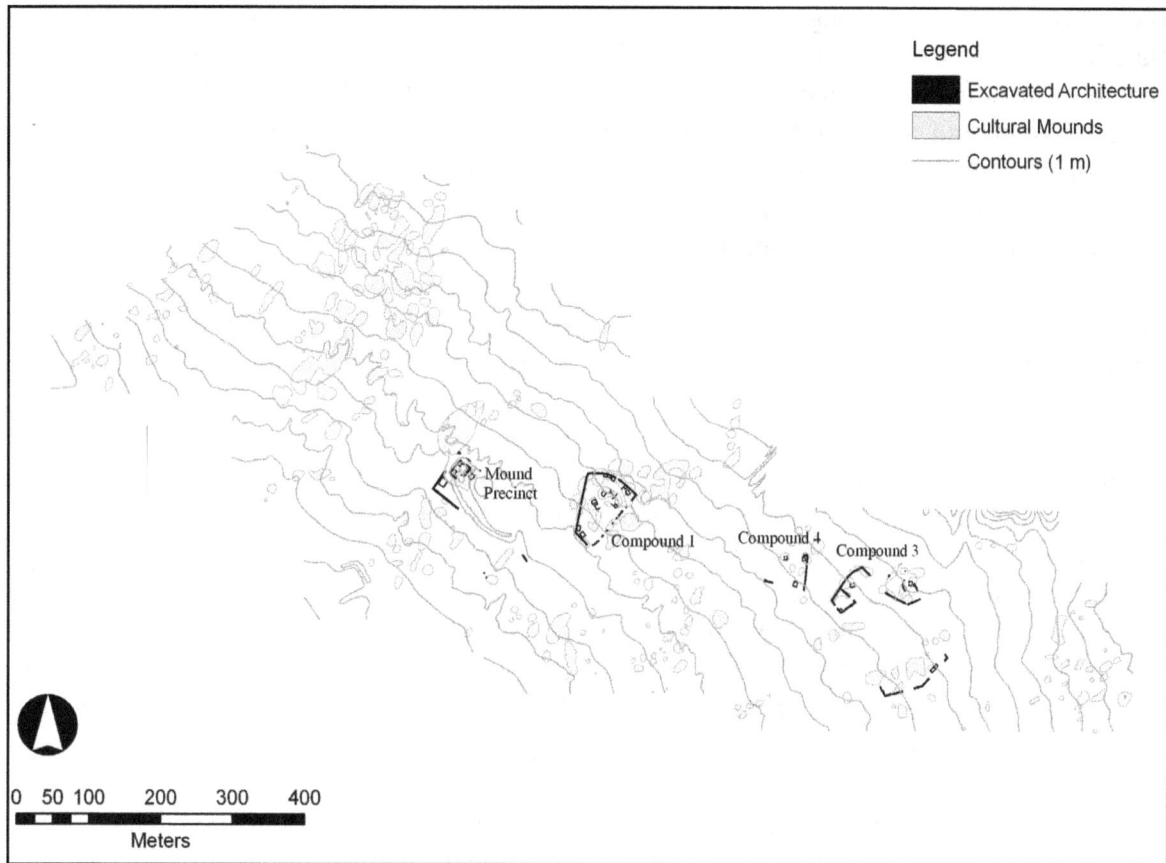

Figure 10.2. The Marana Platform Mound site (AZ AA:12:251) showing structures used in the analysis.

natural drainages, possible canals, architectural cobbles and other surface artifacts, and modern roads and water-retention features. All of these features were hand-digitized and compiled into an overall map of site features. Digital data collected with a Leica Total Station during field mapping of excavated architecture at the Marana site conducted by the author between 2001 and 2004 was also incorporated into the GIS. In addition to a set of several hundred topographical points collected at roughly 2 m intervals on the platform mound itself, the digital dataset also included points taken on newly-discovered architecture, excavation unit corners, surface features, and profiles. Once processed and ground-checked, this archaeological feature data was used to hand-digitize

compound walls, rooms, and other architectural features from original field maps. Together, the topographical points and site contours were used to generate a basic DEM of the site at a 1 m by 1 m resolution. This DEM was in essence a representation of the site's natural topography, as a series of modern water-retention berms were the only cultural features on the site, besides the platform mound, with sufficient elevation to appear.

In the initial run of the data, visibility was assessed at the most basic level: from the perspective of a 1.5 m (roughly 5 feet) tall observer atop the platform mound as it currently exists. When this revealed that the vast majority of documented architectural and refuse mounds at the site would have been visible, I repeated the analysis, this time using a second DEM that incorporated reconstructed prehistoric features, including the mound perimeter wall, the exterior mound compound wall, and three additional compounds whose outlines were delineated well enough to permit reconstruction. Each wall was reconstructed by adding 2 m to base elevations from excavated features that were deemed on the basis of contextual evidence to represent prehistoric ground levels.

Finally, I assumed that at least some community rituals would have been performed atop the mound. Because of the perimeter wall surrounding the mound's surface, this would have meant that rituals intended for community visibility would have been performed from the roofs of the platform mound rooms, in essence using these structures to increase the effective elevation of the mound. Viewsheds calculated from the moundtop were thus generated from the perspective of a 1.5 m-tall observer standing on the roofs of the moundtop structures or atop the mound perimeter wall. In addition to reconstructing the extent to which an observer atop the mound would have been capable of looking across the site and into other compounds, it was also important to compare visibility from the moundtop with the perspectives of observers in non-mound areas. For this reason, I also calculated visibility from the perspective of 1.5 m-tall observers standing within reconstructed compounds and in a number of open areas elsewhere in the site.

INTERPRETATION OF RESULTS

A viewshed based on the reconstructed architecture DEM calculated for an observer atop the platform mound clearly demonstrates the extent to which observers atop the platform mound possessed a commanding view of open areas, as demonstrated by the area west of the mound where no compounds have been excavated (Figure 10.3). On the other hand, the viewshed also illustrates how other compounds fragmented the landscape and restricted visual and spatial access to their interiors (Figures 10.3 and 10.4). Even from the top of the platform mound, only a small portion of the ground surface within Compound 1, the reconstructed compound closest to the mound enclosure would have been visible, and the compound walls would have blocked perception of many areas and access corridors between compounds as well. While many of the activities of the occupants of other compounds could have been at least partially monitored by a moundtop observer, the elevated position of the mound was not sufficient to allow complete surveillance of events in even the closest of its walled neighbors.

While moundtop observers could not fully see into neighboring compounds, ritual activities atop the platform mound would have been visible to observers nearly everywhere else in the site (Figures 10.5, 10.6 and 10.7). Even far downslope or in the middle of an enclosed compound several hundred meters away, individuals would still have been able to see at least a portion of the walled area atop the mound that would have served as a stage for public ritual. Although the degree to which the ability to view a rite equaled meaningful participation in that rite would have varied dramatically given the proximity of the observer to the mound complex, as discussed below, these viewsheds suggest that spectacles conducted atop the Marana Mound would have essentially been inescapable in outdoor contexts, even within an enclosed compound. While an individual's reaction to such a spectacle would, of course, not necessarily have been the one prescribed by the ritual participants, the rite itself and the symbolism that presumably came with it would have been audible and visible even to those

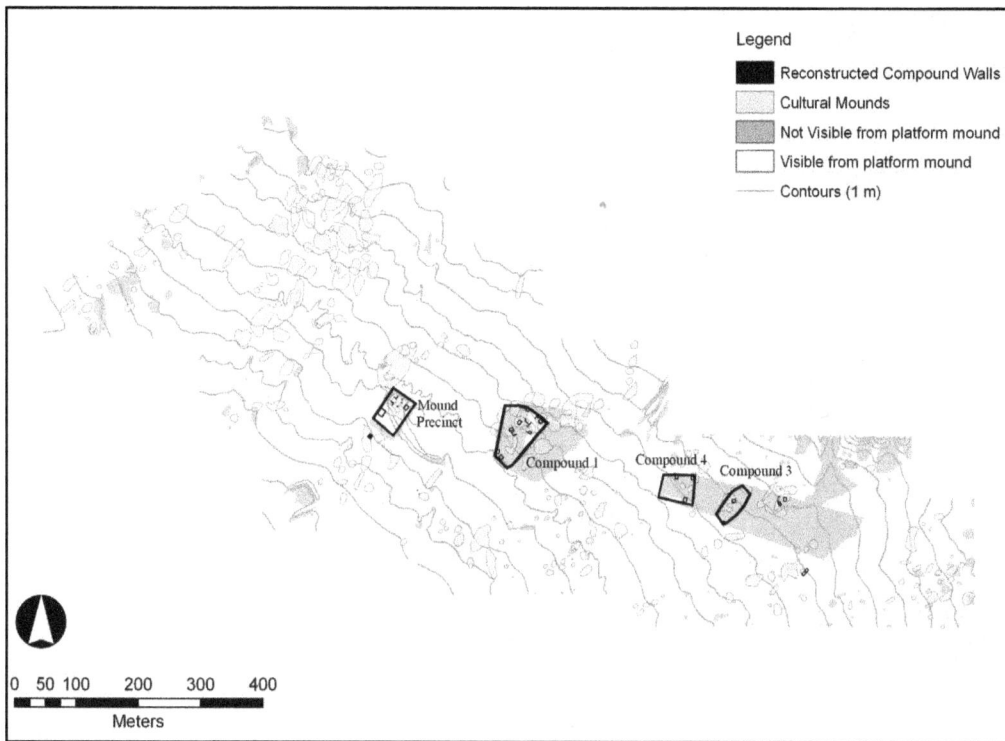

Figure 10.3. Site visibility from atop the platform mound enclosure walls for an observer standing 1.5 m high. Compound walls reconsrtucted to 2 m above documented base heights.

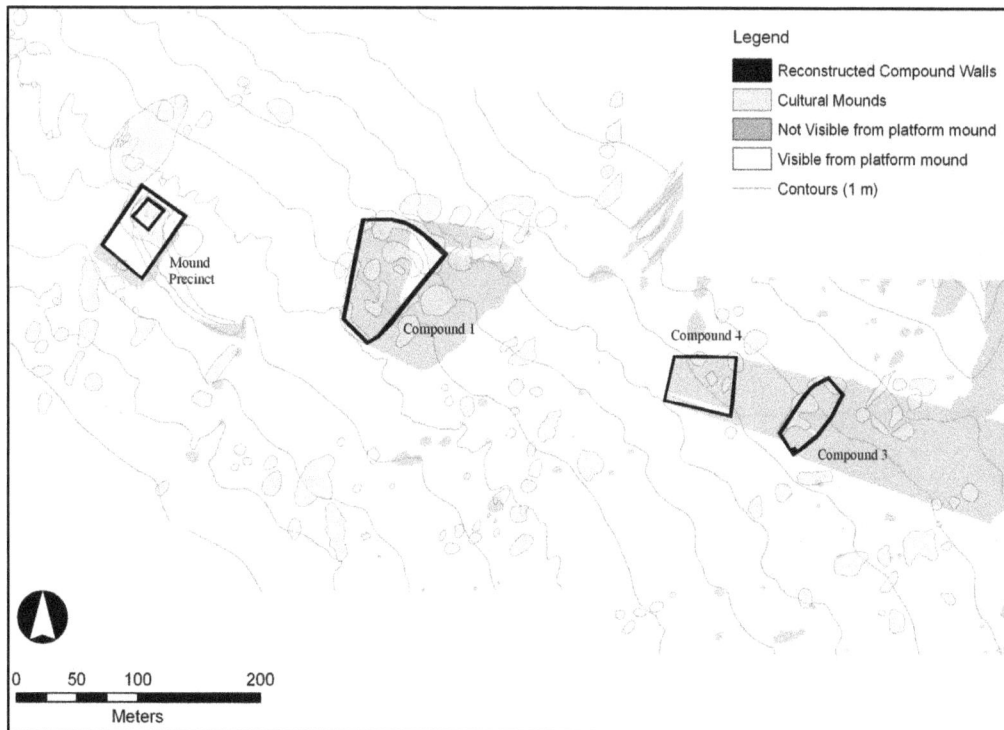

Figure 10.4. Site visibility from atop the platform mound enclosure walls. Close up on reconstructed compounds.

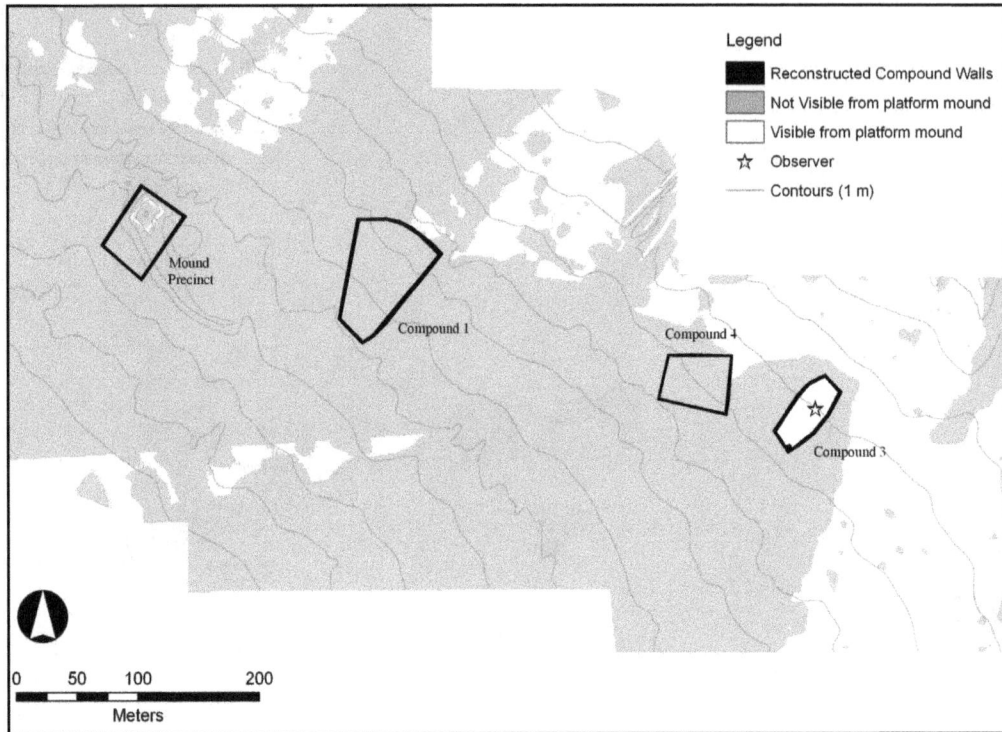

Figure 10.5. Site visibility for a 1.5 m observer standing inside Compound 3. Note continued visibility of platform mound enclosure walls. Compound walls reconstructed to 2 m above documented base heights.

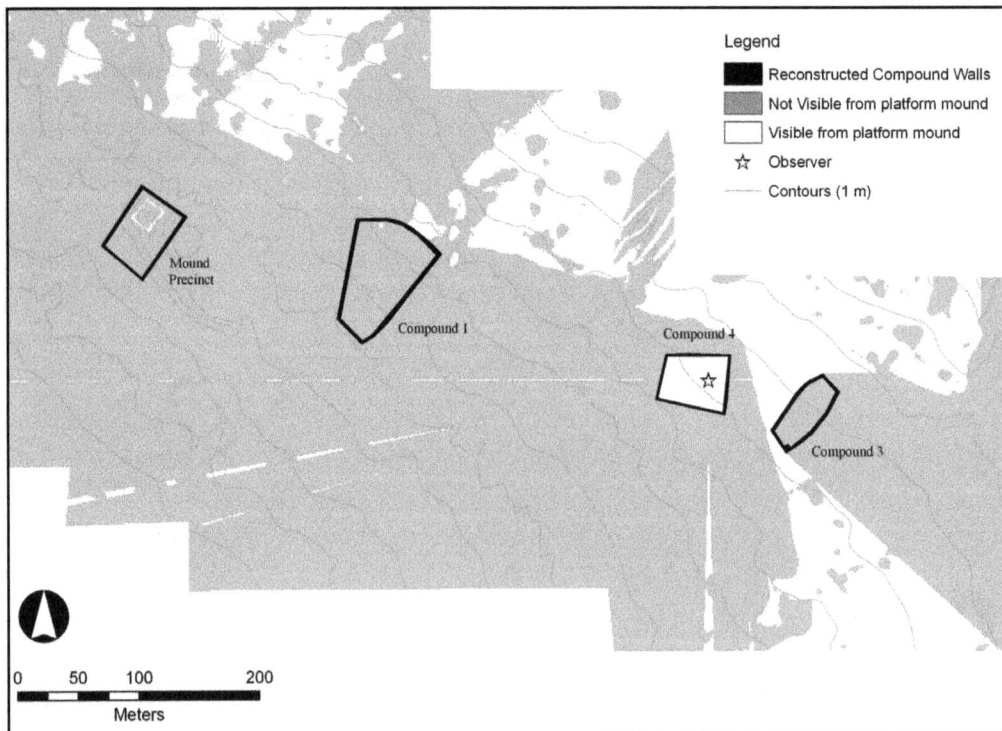

Figure 10.6. Site visibility for a 1.5 m observer standing inside Compound 4. Note continued visibility of platform mound enclosure walls. Compound walls reconstructed to 2 m above documented base heights.

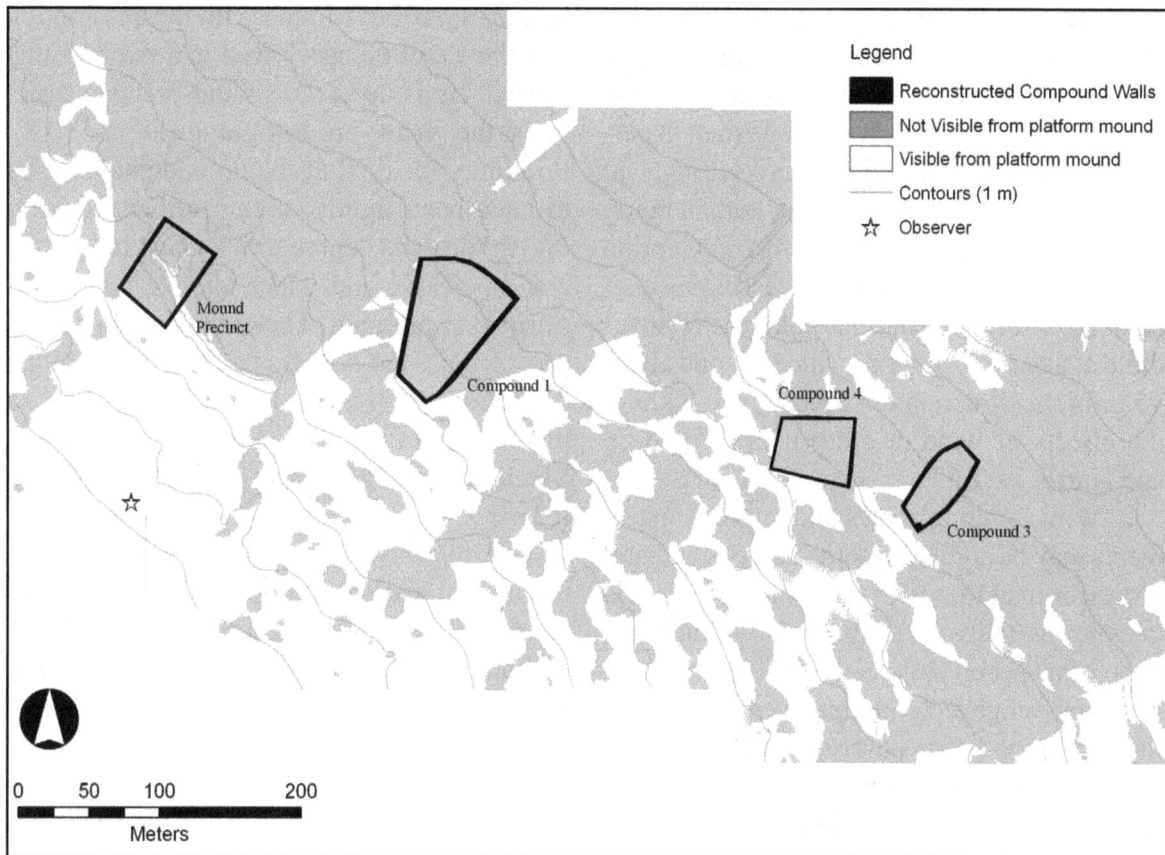

Figure 10.7. Site visibility for a 1.5 m observer standing in an open area approximately 175 m downslope from the platform mound. Note continued visibility of platform mound enclosure walls. Compound walls reconsrtucted to 2 m above documented base heights.

who tried to ignore it. Conversely, it is important to note that both the enclosed compound around the mound and the walled precinct atop it remained sequestered from outside viewers, regardless of their positions.

Although all who observe a performance, even in part, are by some measure themselves participants in that performance, all participants, as noted, are not created equal, and perception and participation in ritual performance have a strong spatial component. To address this more nuanced consideration of perceptivity, I employed the work of psychologist Edward Hall (1972), who divided human perceptive and communicative abilities into four spatial zones: intimate, personal, social, and public distance. Each zone corresponds to

a specific spatial threshold and a particular set of interactive parameters. For the purposes of this analysis, the most significant of these zones are social distance, which extends from about 1 to 4 m, and public distance, which extends from 4 m to the the maximum carrying distance of voice and speech and is further subdivided into close phase (4 m to 10 m) and far phase (from 10 m out) (Hall 1972:142-148; Moore 1996:154-155). At the threshold between social and public distances, speech is audible only if a loud voice is used, while direct personal contact between speaker and audience is impossible. Fine details of facial features disappear, and the entire body of the speaker or speakers is visible in peripheral vision. The threshold between close and far public distance (10 m) marks the onset of even greater perceptive changes: "body stance and gestures are featured, facial expression becomes exaggerated as does the loudness of the voice. . .the whole man is perceived as quite small and he is in a setting. . .at this point, contact with him as a human being begins to diminish (Hall 1972:148). Perception fades even more as distance increases: speaker in the open air, for instance, is likely to be inaudible at a normal speaking voice beyond about 45 m in the direction of speech, even without the effects of wind or other noise (Knudsen and Harris 1978).

While singing voices and musical instruments may be audible to some degree at greater distances than these, the implication is unmistakable: participants or listeners within 10 m or so of a speech or ceremony are much more intimately engaged with that event or speaker than are more distant observers, and additional losses of perception ensue the further one travels from that event or speaker.

As Hall makes clear (1966:131-165), the communicative and perceptive thresholds he identifies are to some extent culturally determined, and should not be treated as rigid categories. While cultural standards of personal space and hygiene certainly operate at the boundaries between "intimate," "personal," and "social" space and, to a lesser degree, perhaps, at the boundary between "social" and "public" space, it should be reiterated that the primary determinates of the social/public boundary are based on the declining ability of the naked eye to perceive detail and the increasing necessity of a loud voice and emphatic gesture, if a message is to be conveyed. These dynamics are therefore subject to the parameters of human physiology rather than cultural taste. The more intimate spatial zones, within which cultural spatial preferences occupy key importance, fall below the minimum scale of the present analysis.

When Hall's thresholds are applied to the Marana Platform Mound with the assumption that the event being viewed is a public ritual enacted atop one of the mound-precinct structures, the results are intriguing (Figure 10.8). Proximity to ritual at the mound site appears to have been tightly circumscribed, restricting, in turn, the degree to which an individual could perceive and understand certain forms of ritual expression. The outer limits of close perception—the borders of Hall's "far public distance"—correspond remarkably well to the borders of the walled moundtop precinct. Much of what unfolded atop the Marana Platform Mound or within its structures would, as a result, have been fully perceptible only within that walled area, an enclosed, spatially restricted space described by Howard (1992) and other authors as "exclusive." The boundary between close and far public distance, a threshold beyond which Hall (1966) suggests an individual speaker or performer begins to fully lose his or her identity as a fellow member of society and merge into their setting or the pageantry of their fellow performers, is also correspondent with a walled boundary, in this case the outer compound wall surrounding the platform mound.

Meaningful and complex participation in the specific ideas and concepts enacted in a platform mound ritual performance was thus closely tied to walled enclosures that presumably served to severely limit access to them. Full participation in the normal-volume speech, complicated nuances, and intimate gestures within a given ritual was limited to those atop the mound. Within the outer mound precinct, perception of a moundtop ritual, although slightly constrained, would still have been within the close public sphere of the performance. Beyond the mound enclosure wall, however, perception would have been limited to highly visible, exaggerated gestures, songs, or dances – still meaningful manifestations of group ritual, perhaps, but quite different than

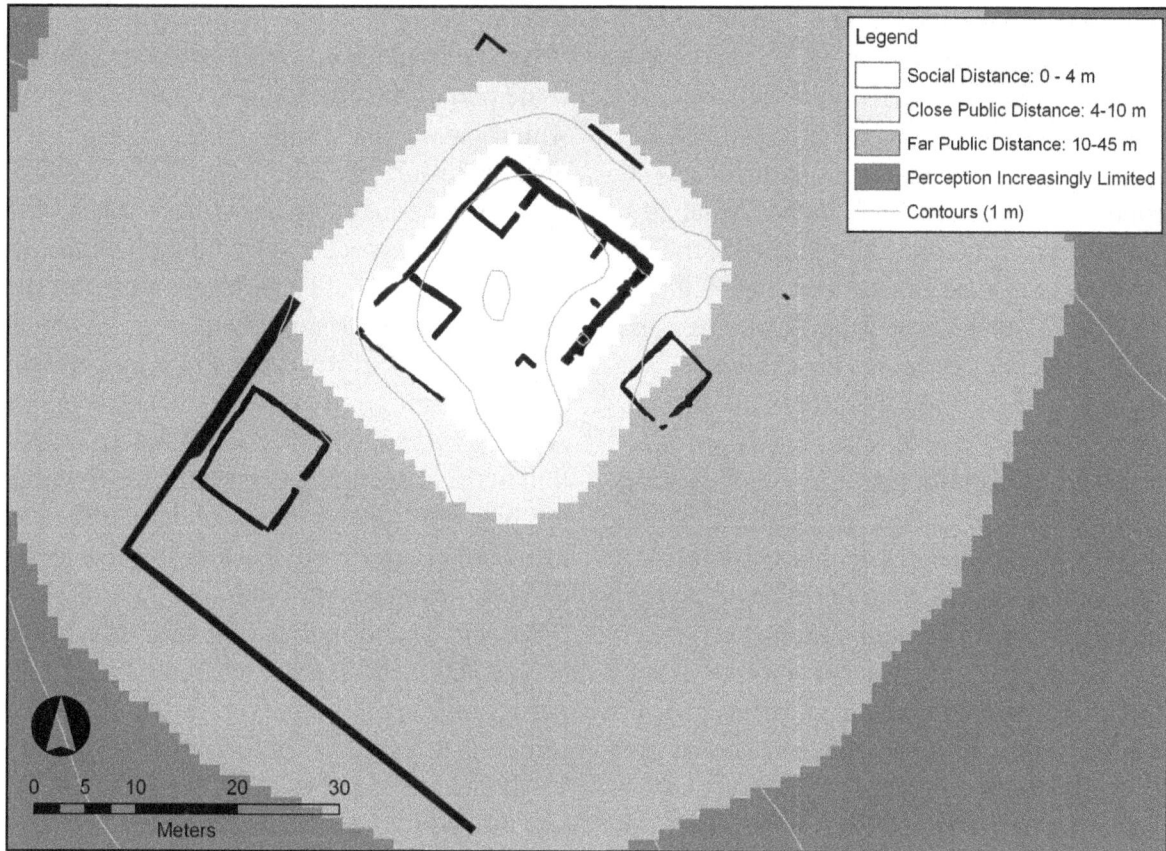

Figure 10.8. Edward Hall's perceptive thresholds applied to a speaker or perfomer standing atop the Marana Platform Mound perimeter wall.

the much more intimate experience of those with access to the inner mound precinct.

DISCUSSION

Platform mounds are widely viewed by archaeologists to have served either as loci for the promotion of social integration and shared group values or as venues for social differentiation within which inequalities between members of a society were created, emphasized, and promoted (Lindauer and Blitz 1997). Recent archaeological interpretations of mound function have, in essence, oscillated between an emphasis on one or the other of these processes (e. g., Craig et al. 1998; Elson and Abbott 2000;

McGuire 1992; Wilcox 1991). The findings documented in this essay suggest that platform mound rituals simultaneously contributed to both processes, bringing large numbers of community members together through highly visible ceremonies conducted atop the mound and, via more exclusive ceremonies conducted within the mound precinct itself, to emphasize the special social and ritual position of, as John C. Barrett (1994) defines them in a similar context at the Neolithic British site of Avebury, a "relatively isolated elect" with full access to ritual spaces.

Such distinctions based on exclusion and access were and are common components of human ceremonialism. Jerry Moore's findings at several Andean mound sites, for instance, led him to posit the existence of "two communicative arenas, and, possibly, two sets of ritual" (1996): one based upon highly visible public gestures such as processions and dances intended for large audiences in the plazas surrounding ritual sites and another centered on "subtle gestures and complex speech" that unfolded atop the mound and was witnessed by only a select few: a body of ritual that, although enacted before an exclusive audience, nonetheless took place within a centrally located, highly visible, and publicly prominent structure. In addition to the clues to access and staging provided by platform mound architecture, artifactual evidence exists to support the notion that a similar ritual dichotomy obtained in Classic period Hohokam society, as well. Ample evidence for communal feasting at Marana (Bayham and Grimstead, this volume) and other sites, as well as the presence in mound contexts of artifacts, such as shell trumpets, shell tinklers, stone batons, and mountain sheep horn cores, which could have served as part of ritual regalia (Lindauer 1996; Rice and Redman 1993:63), suggest that some mound ceremonies may have been characterized by loud music and accentuated gestures visible over large areas. On the other hand, artifacts like *Datura* effigy pots, which, as noted, have been encountered at Marana exclusively within the mound complex (P. Fish and Fish 2000:266), point to the existence of platform mound ritual centered upon small-scale rituals, such as shared hallucinations while under the influence of powerful psychotropic drugs, that would likely have involved only a few participants.

As noted by Barrett (1994) in his discussion of ritual architecture in Britain, the presence of an enclosure creates both exclusion and an awareness of that exclusion on the part of both those inside the enclosure – who perceive a shared membership in something not accessible to others, and those excluded from it. Those who watched from outside that structure's walls might have observed or heard some part of the proceedings within them, but would have been starkly aware both of their own exclusion from these rites and the social distinctions separating them from those with full ceremonial access. The individual inhabitants of Marana would have been aware not only of the existence of individuals or groups with access to the platform mound, but also of their own exclusion from or inclusion in that group. Although visibility, access and direct participation in the rituals and events performed within the platform mound compound was blocked to outsiders, those on the outside, like those excluded from timber or stone circles at Avebury, would have had a partial awareness of the sounds or smells emanating from inside. This partial awareness, however, probably served primarily as a further reinforcement of the reality of enclosure and exclusion and the special status of those who did participate.

However, the possibility of resistance to the centrality of the platform mound in Marana's public life is present in these analyses as well. Compound walls are here demonstrated to be a very effective means of limiting the visual and spatial access of outsiders into the inner workings of whatever social or kinship group inhabited a compound, even if the would-be observers stood atop a 2 m platform mound. As a result, the extent to which individual or compound-group behavior was subject to the scrutiny and surveillance of the community as a whole, a concept related to Foucault's notion of "discipline," but perhaps more akin to the community-wide and inward-looking policing of ethic and action that a recent study of plaza architecture in ancestral Puebloan sites (Graves and Van Keuren 2003) has elegantly described as "the panoptic gaze of the commune," was greatly constrained and effectively limited to the members of an individual compound group. Of course, the Classic period Hohokam were subject to very different historical and social processes than their Puebloan contemporaries. The Early Classic period inhabitants of the Marana site had only recently shifted to residence within high-walled adobe enclosures, and the debut of elevated compounds with restricted access and unparalleled visibility as the chief architectural manifestations of community integration was likewise relatively new. Such a society would have produced ideologies of group identity very different from those at play among the roomblocks, kivas and communal plazas of the Puebloans. Indeed, the rapid rise and proliferation of formalized platform mounds might in some respects be construed as a reaction to the abrupt system-wide changes in social life of the Early Classic, tied, perhaps, to a desire on the part of existing political and religious leaders to emphatically reassert orthodox (sensu Bourdieu) notions of community integration and identity. Of course, since even the very act of platform mound ritual itself served, as we have seen, to differentiate some group members from their peers, such an enterprise would simultaneously have contributed to the centrifugal forces of differentiation it sought to ameliorate.

CONCLUSION

Even without addressing the sticky issue of moundtop residence, this analysis of platform mound ritual at Marana illustrates how it simultaneously contributed to both community integration and the creation of social and political asymmetries. By limiting access to areas that archaeologists typically agree were the central loci of the platform mound's ceremonial role, the Early Classic Hohokam at Marana created distinctions between groups and individuals even as they brought the community as a whole together in shared feasts, dances, and other ritual performances.

As this essay has repeatedly emphasized, the broad diversity in platform mound form and function across time and space means that these conclusions can be only cautiously extended beyond the borders of the Marana Community. But platform mounds across the Southwest share crucial similarities, giving room for optimism that the observations made here might indeed be more broadly applicable. Earlier manifestations of platform mound-style architecture also seem to have practiced a form of exclusion behind their wooden palisades (Haury 1976). Similarly, distinctions between individuals on the basis of access and membership, akin to what has been outlined above, are likely to have existed at other Early Classic platform mound settlements as well. Ceremonial dynamics like those discussed here may also have continued to have wide currency among the peoples of the Arizona desert long after the Hohokam era. The ceremonial system suggested here has important parallels with the historic O'odham *viikita* and saguaro wine rituals as well. Both were large-scale ritual performances and community gatherings that were conceptually centered on key rituals and ceremonies that took place out of the public eye in enclosed structures accessible only to elders (Hayden 1937; Lumholtz 1990).

References Cited

Abbott, David R.

1985　Spheres of Intra-Cultural Exchange and the Ceramics of the Salt-Gila Aqueduct Project. In *Proceedings of the 1983 Hohokam Symposium*, Part II, edited by A.E. Dittert, Jr. and D.E. Dove, pp. 419-438. Arizona Archaeological Society Occasional Paper No. 2. Phoenix.

1996　Ceramic Exchange and a Strategy for Reconstructing Organizational Developments Among the Hohokam. In *Interpreting Southwestern Diversity: Underlying Principles and Overarching Patterns*, edited by Paul R. Fish and J. Jefferson Reid, pp. 147-158. Anthropological Research Paper No. 48. Arizona State University, Tempe.

2000　*Ceramics and Community Organization Among the Hohokam*. University of Arizona Press, Tucson.

2003　*Centuries of Decline During the Hohokam Classic Period at Pueblo Grande*. Publications in Archaeology, Soil Systems, Inc., Phoenix.

Ackerly, Neal W.

1982　Irrigation, Water Allocation Strategies, and the Hohokam Collapse. *Kiva* 47 (3): 91-106.

Adler, Michael

1994　Population aggregation and community organization. In *The Ancient Southwestern Community: Models and Methods for the Study of Prehistoric Social Organization*, edited by W. H. Wills and Robert D. Leonard, pp. 85-102. The University of New Mexico Press, Albuquerque.

2003　Architecture and Ancestral Pueblo Migrations: Recent Research at Chaves-Hummingbird Pueblo (LA 578), New Mexico. Poster paper presented at the 68th Annual Meetings of the Society for American Archaeology, Milwaukee, WI, April 9-13.

Allison, L. E., and C. D. Moodie

1965　Carbonate. In *Methods of Soil Analysis*. Part 2 (2nd ed.), edited by C.A. Black, et al., pp. 1379-1400. Agronomy Monograph No. 9. American Society of Agronomy, Crop Science Society of America, and Soil Science Society of America, Madison, WI.

Ames, Kenneth M.

1995　Chiefly Power and Household Production on the Northwest Coast. In *Foundations of Inequality*, edited by T. D. Price and G. M. Feinman. Plenum Press, New York.

Anderson, Benedict

1991　*Imagined Communities: Reflections on the Origin and Spread of Nationalism*. 2nd ed. Verso, London.

Barrett, John C.

1994　*Fragments from Antiquity: An Archaeology of Social Life in Britain, 2900-1200 BC*. Blackwell, Oxford.

150

Bayham, Frank E.
1979   Factors Influencing the Archaic Pattern of Animal Exploitation. *The Kiva* 44:219-235.

1982   *A Diachronic Analysis of Prehistoric Animal Exploitation at Ventana Cave*. Unpublished Ph.D. dissertation, Department of Anthropology, Arizona State University, Tempe.

1990   Effects of a Sedentary Lifestyle on the Utilization of Animals in the Prehistoric Southwest. In *Agriculture: Origins and Impacts of a Technological Revolution*, edited by C. Cameron, pp. 54-78. Occasional Papers of the Archaeological Research Facility, CSU Fullerton No. 5. Museum of Anthropology, Fullerton.

Bayham, Frank E. and Pamela H. Hatch
1985a   Archaeofaunal Remains from the New River Area. In *Hohokam Settlement and Economic System in the Central New River Drainage, Arizona*, edited by D. E. Doyel and M. D. Elson, pp. 405-433. Soil Systems Publications in Archaeology 4, Phoenix.

1985b   Hohokam and Salado Animal Utilization in the Tonto Basin. In *Studies in the Hohokam and Solado of the Tonto Basin*, edited by G. Rice, pp. 191-210. Office of Cultural Resource Management, Arizona State University, Tempe.

Bayman, James M.
1994   *Craft Production and Political Economy at the Marana Platform Mound Community*. Ph.D. Dissertation, Department of Anthropology, Arizona State University, Tempe.

1995   Rethinking "Redistribution" in the Archaeological Record: Obsidian Exchange at the Marana Platform Mound. *Journal of Anthropological Research* 51(1):37-63.

1996a   Shell Ornament Consumption in a Classic Hohokam Platform Mound Community Center. *Journal of Field Archaeology* 23:403-420.

1996b   Hohokam craft production and platform mound community organization in the Tucson Basin. In *Interpreting Southwestern Diversity: Underlying Principles and Overarching Patterns*, edited by Paul R. Fish and J. Jefferson Reid, pp. 159-172. Anthropological Papers No. 48. Department of Anthropology, Arizona State University, Tempe.

2002   Hohokam Craft Economies and the Materialization of Power. In *Journal of Anthropological Method and Theory* 9: 69-95.

Bayman, James M. and Guadalupe Sanchez
1998   The surface archaeology of Classic period Hohokam community organization. In *Surface Archaeology*, edited by Alan Sullivan, pp. 75-88. University of New Mexico Press, Albuquerque.

Bayman, James M., and M. Steven Shackley
1999   Dynamics of Hohokam Obsidian Circulation in the North American Southwest. *Antiquity* 73:836-845

Beals, Ralph L.
1934   *Material Culture of the Pima, Papago, and Western Apache*. U.S. Department of the Interior. University of California Press, Berkeley.

Beck, Margaret E.
2003   *Ceramic Deposition and Midden Formation in Kalinga, Philippines*. Unpublished Ph.D. dissertation, Department of Anthropology, University of Arizona, Tucson.

Beck, Margaret E., and Matthew E. Hill, Jr.
2004 Rubbish, Relatives, and Residence: The Family Use of Middens. *Journal of Archaeological Method and Theory* 11(3):297-333.

2005 Midden Ceramics and Their Sources: Ceramic Deposition in Kalinga, Philippines. In *Archaeology as Anthropology: Theoretical and Methodological Approaches*, edited by James M. Skibo, Michael Graves, and Miriam Stark. Accepted for publication by University of Arizona Press.

Blitz, John H.
1993 Big Pots for Big Shots: Feasting and Storage in a Mississippian Community. *American Antiquity* 58(1):80-96.

Bloch, Maurice
1995 The Resurrection of the House Amongst the Zafimaniry. In *About the House: Levi-Strauss and Beyond*, edited by J. Carsten and S. Hugh-Jones. Cambridge University Press, Cambridge.

Bocek, Barbara
1986 Rodent Ecology and Burrowing Behavior: Predicted Effects on Archaeological Site Formation. *American Antiquity* 51:589-603.

1992 The Jasper Ridge Reexcavation Experiment: Rates of Artifact Mixing by Rodents. *American Antiquity* 57:261-269.

Bohrer, Vorsila
1991 Recently Recognized Cultivated and Encouraged Plants Among the Hohokam. *Kiva* 56:227-235.

Bostwick, Todd W.
1987 A descriptive summary of the excavation results at Locus D, AZ AA:12:2 (ASU), Muchas Casas. In *Field Investigations at the Marana Community Complex*, edited by T. Kathleen Henderson, pp. 85-120. Anthropological Field Studies No. 14. Department of Anthropology, Arizona State University, Tempe.

Bostwick, Todd W. and Christian E. Downum
1994 *Archaeology of the Pueblo Grande Platform Mound and Surrounding Features, Vol. 2: Features in the Central Precinct of the Pueblo Grande Community*. Anthropological Papers 1. Pueblo Grande Museum, Phoenix.

Bowbrowsky, Peter T., and Bruce F. Ball
1989 The Theory and Mechanics of Ecological Diversity in Archaeology. In *Quantifying Diversity in Archaeology*, edited by Robert D. Leonard and George T. Jones, pp. 4-12. Cambridge University Press, Cambridge.

Bradford, Joe E.
1986 Penetrability. In *Methods of Soil Analysis, Part One: Physical and Mineralogical Methods, 2nd ed* edited by Arnold Klute, pp. 463-478. American Society of Agronomy and Soil Science Society of America, Madison.

Bradford, Joe E. and S. C. Gupta
1986 Compressibility. In *Methods of Soil Analysis, Part One: Physical and Mineralogical Methods, 2nd ed.* Edited by Arnold Klute, pp. 479-492. American Society of Agronomy and Soil Science Society of America, Madison.

Bradley, Richard, and Michael Fulford
1980 Sherd Size in the Analysis of Occupation Debris. *Bulletin of the Institute of Archaeology* 17:85-94.

152

Bray, Tamara L.(editor)
  2003   *The Archaeology and Politics of Food and Feasting in Early States and Empires.* Plenum Press, New York.

Broughton, Jack M.
  1994   Declines in Mammalian Foraging Efficiency During the Late Holocene, San Francisco Bay, California. *Journal of Anthropological Archaeology* 13:371-401.

Broughton, Jack M. and Frank E. Bayham
  2003   Showing Off, Foraging Models, and the Ascendance of Large Game Hunting in the California Middle Archaic. *American Antiquity* 68:783-789.

Brumfiel, Elizabeth and Timothy K. Earle
  1987   Specialization, Exchange, and Complex Societies: An Introduction. In *Specialization, Exchange, and Complex Societies*, edited by E. Brumfiel and T. Earle, pp. 1-9. Cambridge University Press, Cambridge.

Brunson, Judy L.
  1989   *The Social Organization at the Los Muertos Hohokam: A Reanalysis of Cushing's Hemenway Expedition Data.* Ph.D. dissertation, Department of Anthropology, Arizona State University.

Bubemeyer, Trixi D.
  1993   *Implications of Ceramic Variability at a Hohokam Platform Mound Village.* M.A. Thesis, Department of Anthropology, University of Arizona, Tucson.

Burton, Robert J., Nancy E. Knoob, Chad Phinney, Maria Shrock, and C. Duane Spears
  1972   *Excavations at Pueblo Grande, AZ, AZ U:9:1(PGM): A Report on Caliche Pits at Pueblo Grande.* Unpublished Ms., on file, Pueblo Grande Museum, Phoenix.

Buskirk, Winfred
  1986   *The Western Apache: Living wth the Land before 1950.* University of Oklahoma Press, Norman.

Cameron, Judi L.
  1995   *Sociopolitical and Economic Roles of Faunal Resources in the Prehistory of the Tonto Basin, Arizona.* Unpublished Ph.D. dissertation, Department of Anthropology, University of Arizona.

  1998   The Faunal Resource Use in the Prehistoric Tonto Basin. In *Environment and Subsistence Change in the Classic Period Tonto Basin: The Roosevelt Archaeology Studies, 1989 to 1998*, edited by Katherine A. Spielmann, pp. 133-188. The Roosevelt Monograph Series, vol. 10, Anthropological Field Studies 39. Arizona State University, Tempe.

Cannon, Michael D.
  2000   Large Mammal Relative Abundance in Pithouse and Pueblo Period Archaeofaunas from Southwestern New Mexico: Resource Depression among the Mimbres-Mogollan? *Journal of Anthropological Archaeology* 19: 317-347.

  2001   Archaeofaunal Relative Abundance, Sample Size, and Statistical Methods. *Journal of Archaeological Science* 28:185-195.

Carsten, Janet and Stephen Hugh-Jones
  1995   Introduction: About the House - Levi-Strauss and Beyond. In *About the House: Levi-Strauss and Beyond*, edited by J. Carsten and S. Hugh-Jones. Cambridge University Press, Cambridge.

Castetter, Edward F. and Willis Harvey Bell
    1942   *Pima and Papago Indian Agriculture*. University of New Mexico Press, Albuquerque.

    1951   *Yuman Indian Agriculture*. University of New Mexico Press, Albuquerque.

Castetter, Edward F. and Morris E. Opler
    1935   *The Ethnobiology of the Papago Indians.* Ethnobiological Studies in the American Southwest. Vol. II. University of New Mexico Bulletin, Biological Series 4 (3).

    1936   *The Ethnobiology of the Chiricahua and Mescalero Apache.* Ethnobiological Studies in the American Southwest III. University of New Mexico Bulletin 4(5):1-63.Castetter, E. F. and R. Underhill

Castro-Reino, Sergio and Elizabeth J. Miksa
    2005   *Provenance Analysis of Twenty Sherds from the Tucson Basin for the Marana Mound Study*. Petrographic Report No. 2005-03. Desert Archaeology, Inc., Tucson.

Ciolek-Torrello, Richard, Joseph A. Ezzo, and Jeffrey H. Altschul
    1999   Summary and Conclusions. In *Investigations at Sunset Mesa Ruin*, edited by R. Ciolek-Torrello, E. K. Huber, and R. E. Neily, pp. 203-219. SRI Technical Series, No. 66. SRI, Tucson.

Clark, John E.
    1991   Flintknapping and Debitage Disposal Among the Lacondon Maya of Chiapas, Mexico. In *The Ethno-archaeology of Refuse Disposal*, edited by Edward Staski and Livingston D. Sutro, pp. 63-78. Arizona State University Anthropological Research Papers No. 42. Tempe, Arizona.

Colwell, Chip
    1995   *An Example of Deceased Animals and Their Bones as Ritual Paraphernalia.* Ms. on file, Arizona State Museum Library, University of Arizona, Tucson.

Cordell, Linda S.
    2012   *The Archaeology of the Southwest*, Third Edition. Left Coast Press, San Francisco.

Costin, Cathy L.
    1991   *Craft Specialization: Issues in Defining, Documenting, and Explaining the Organization of Production.* Archaeological Method and Theory Vol. 3:1-56.

Craig, Douglas B., and Jeffery J. Clark
    1994   The Meddler Point Site, AZ V:5:4/26 (ASM/TNF). In *The Roosevelt Community Development Study: Vol. 2. Meddler Point, Pyramid Point, and Griffin Wash Sites*, by Mark D. Elson, Deborah L. Swartz, Douglas B. Craig, and Jeffery J. Clark, pp. 1-198. Anthropological Papers No. 13. Center for Desert Archaeology, Tucson.

Craig, Douglas B., James P. Holmlund and Jeffery J. Clark
    1998   Labor Investment and Organization in Platform Mound Construction: a Case Study from the Tonto Basin of Central Arizona. *Journal of Field Archaeology* 25(3):245-259.

Craig, Douglas B. and Henry D. Wallace
    1992   The Role of Formation Process Studies in Prehistoric Research. In *Research Design for the Roosevelt Community Development Study*, edited by W. H. Doelle, H. D. Wallace, M. D. Elson and M. T. Stark, pp. 35-56. Anthropological Papers. vol. 12. Center for Desert Archaeology, Tucson.

Craig, Douglas B. and Mary Walsh-Anduze
    2001   *The Grewe Archaeological Research Project: Synthesis*. Anthropological Papers 99-1(3). Northland Research, Tempe.

Crown, Patricia L.
    1985   Intrusive Ceramics and the Identification of Hohokam Exchange Networks. In *Proceedings of the 1983 Hohokam Symposium, Part II*, edited by Alfred E. Dittert and Donald E. Dove, pp. 439-458. Phoenix Chapter, Arizona Archaeological Society, Occasional Paper 2.

    1987   Classic Period Hohokam Settlement and Land Use in the Casa Grande Ruinds Area, Arizona. *Journal of Field Archaeology* 14: 147-162.

    1991a The Hohokam: Current Views of Prehistory and the Regional System. In *Chaco and Hohokam: Prehistoric Regional Systems in the American Southwest*, edited by Patricia L. Crown and W James Judge, pp. 135-157. School for American Research Press, Santa Fe, New Mexico.

    1991b The Role of Exchange and Interaction in Salt-Gila Basin Hohokam Prehistory. In *Exploring the Hohokam: Prehistoric Desert Peoples of the American Southwest*, edited by George J. Gumerman, pp. 383-416. University of New Mexico Press, Albuquerque.

Crown, Patricia L. and Suzanne K. Fish
    1996   Gender and status in the Hohokam pre-Classic to Classic transition. *American Anthropologist* 98(4):803.

Cushing, Frank Hamilton
    1890   Preliminary Notes on the Origin, Working Hypothesis and Primary Researches of the Hemenway Southwestern Archaeological Expedition. *Congres International des Americanistes*, pp. 151-194.

Deal, Michael
    1985   Household Pottery Disposal in the Maya Highlands: An Ethnoarchaeological Interpretation. *Journal of Anthropological Archaeology* 4:243-291.

    1998   *Pottery Ethnoarchaeology in the Central Maya Highlands*. University of Utah Press, Salt Lake City.

Dean, Jeffrey S., Mark C. Slaughter, and Dennie O. Bowden III
    1996   Desert Dendrochronology: Tree-Ring Dating Prehistoric Sites in the Tucson Basin. *Kiva* 62(1):7-26.

Dean, Walt E.
    1974   Determination of Carbonate and Organic Matter in Calcareous Sediments and Sedimentary Rocks by Loss On Ignition: Comparison with Other Methods. *Journal of Sedimentary Petrology* 44(1): 242-248.

Diehl, Michael
    2001   Macrobotanical Remains and Land Use: Subsistence and Strategies for Food Acquisition. In *Excavations in the Santa Cruz River Floodplain: The Early Agricultural Component at Los Pozos*, edited by D.A. Gregory, pp. 195-208. Anthropolocial Papers No. 21. Center for Desert Archaeology, Tucson.

Dietler, Michael
    1996   Feasts and Commensal Politics in the Political Economy: Food, Power, and Status in Prehistoric Europe. In *Food and the Status Quest*, edited by Polly Wiessner and Wulf Schienfenhovel, pp 87-126. Berghan Books, Providence.

Dietler, Michael and Brian Hayden (editors)
  2001   *Feasts: Archaeological and Ethnographic Perspectives.* Smithsonian Institution Press, Washington.

Doebley, John F.
  1984   "Seeds" of Wild Grasses: A Major Food of Southwestern Indians. *Economic Botany* 38(1): 52-64.

Doelle, William H.
  1985   The Southern Tucson Basin Rillito-Rincon Subsistence, Settlement, and Community Structure. In *Proceedings of the 1983 Hohokam Symposium*, edited by A. E. Dittert and D. E. Dove, pp. 183-198. Occasional Paper. vol. 2. Arizona Archaeological Society, Phoenix.

Doelle, William H., David A. Gregory, and Henry D. Wallace
  1995   Classic Period Platform Mound Systems in Southern Arizona. In *The Roosevelt Community Development Study: New Perspectives on Tonto Prehistory*, edited by Mark D. Elson, Miriam T. Stark, and David A. Gregory, pp. 385-440. Anthropological Papers No. 15. Center for Desert Archaeology, Tucson.

Doelle, William H., Frederick W. Huntington and Henry D. Wallace
  1987   Rincon Phase Reorganization in the Tucson Basin. In *The Hohokam Village: Site Structure and Organization*, edited by D. E. Doyel, pp. 71-96. Southwestern and Rocky Mountain Division of the American Association of the Advancement of Science, Ft. Collins.

Doelle, William H. and Henry D. Wallace
  1991   The Changing Role of the Tucson Basin in the Hohokam Regional System. In *Exploring the Hohokam: Prehistoric Desert Peoples of the American Southwest*, edited by G. J. Gumerman, pp. 279-345. University of New Mexico Press, Albuquerque.

Doolittle, Christopher J.
  1993   *A Design Element Analysis of Tanque Verde Red-on-Brown: Sherds from the Marana Mound.* M.A. thesis, Department of Anthropology, University of Arizona, Tucson.

Doolittle, William E.
  1990   *Canal Irrigation in Prehistoric Mexico: The Sequence of Technological Change.* University of Texas Press, Austin.

Downum, Christian
  1993   *Between Desert and River: Hohokam Settlement and Land Use in the Los Robles Community.* Anthropological Papers of the University of Arizona No. 57. University of Arizona Press, Tucson/

Downum, Christian and John Madsen
  1993   Classic Period Platform Mounds South of the Gila River. In *The Northern Tucson Basin Survey: Research Directions and Background Studies* edited by John H. Madsen, Paul R. Fish, and Suzanne K. Fish, pp 125-142. Arizona State Museum Archaeological Series 182. Univeristy of Arizona, Tucson.

Doyel, David E.
  1974   *Excavations in the Escalante Ruin Group, Southern Arizona.* Arizona State Museum Archaeological Series 37. Arizona State Museum, Tucson.

  1980   Hohokam Social Organization and the Sedentary to Classic Transition. In *Current Issues in Hohokam Prehistory: Proceedings of a Symposium*, edited by D. E. Doyel and F. T. Plog, pp. 23-40. Anthropological Research Paper. vol. 23. Arizona State University, Tempe.

Doyel, David E., cont'd

1981 *Late Hohokam Prehistory in Southern Arizona.* Contributions to Archaeology 2. Gila Press, Scottsdale.

1991a Hohokam Exchange and Interaction. In *Chaco and Hohokam: Prehistoric Regional Systems in the American Southwest*, edited by Patricia L. Crown and W. James Judge, pp. 225-252. School for American Research Press, Santa Fe, New Mexico.

1991b Hohokam cultural evolution in the Phoenix Basin. In *Exploring the Hohokam: Prehistoric Desert People of the American Southwest*, edited by George Gumerman, pp. 231-278. University of New Mexico Press, Albuquerque.

1996 Resource Mobilization and Hohokam Society: Analysis of Obsidian Artifacts from the Gatlin Site, Arizona. *Kiva* 62(1):45-60.

2000 Salado in the Sonoran Desert. In *Salado*, edited by J. S. Dean, pp. 295-314. University of New Mexico Press. Albuquerque.

Doyel, David E., Suzanne K. Fish, and Paul R. Fish, (editors)

2000 *The Hohokam Village Revisited.* Southwestern and Rocky Mountain Division of the American Association for the Advancement of Science, Ft. Collins, Colorado.

Doyel, David E. and Stephen Lekson

1993 Regional organization in the American Southwest. In *Anasazi Regional Organization and the Chaco System,* edited by David E. Doyel, pp. 15-22. Anthropological Papers 5. Maxwell Museum, University of New Mexico, Albuquerque.

Dozier, Edward P.

1966 *Mountain Arbiters: The Changing Life of a Hill People.* University of Arizona Press, Tucson.

Dreimanis, Aleksis

1962 Quantitative Gasometric Determination of Calcite and Dolomite by Using the Chittick Apparatus. *Journal of Sedimentary Petrology* 32:520-529.

Drucker, Phillip

1941 *Culture Element Distributions: XVI Yuman-Piman.* Anthropological Records 6. University of California Press, Berkeley.

Durkheim, Emile

1965 *The Elementary Forms of the Religious Life.* Free Press, New York.

Earle, Timothy K.

1977 A Reappraisal of Redistribution: Complex Hawaiian Chiefdoms. In *Exchange Systems in Prehistory*, edited by T. K. Earle and J. E. Ericson, pp. 213-219. Academic Press, New York.

1997 *How Chiefs Come to Power: The Political Economy in Prehistory.* Stanford University Press, Palo Alto.

2002 *Bronze Age Economics: The Beginnings of Political Economies.* Westview Press, Boulder.

Effland, Richard W.
   1988   An Examination of Hohokam Mortuary Practice from Casa Buena. In *Excavations at Casa Buena: Changing Hohokam Land Use along the Squaw Peak Parkway*, edited by Jerry B. Howard, pp. 693-794. Publications in Archaeology, No. 11. Soils Systems, Inc., Phoenix.

Elson, Mark D.
   1986   *Archaeological Investigations at the Tanque Verde Wash Site, a Middle Rincon Settlement in the Eastern Tucson Basin.* Anthropological Papers 7. Institute for American Research, Tucson.

   1998   *Expanding the View of Hohokam Platform Mounds: An Ethnographic Perspective.* Anthropological Papers of the University of Arizona 63. University of Arizona Press, Tucson.

Elson, Mark D. and David R. Abbott
   2000   Organizational Variability in Platform Mound-Building Groups of the American Southwest. In *Alternative Leadership Strategies in the Prehispanic Southwest*, edited by B. J. Mills, pp. 117-135. University of Arizona, Tucson.

Feinman, Gary M.
   1999   Rethinking Our Assumptions: Economic Specialization at the Household Scale in Ancient Ejutla, Oaxaca, Mexico. In *Pottery and People: A Dynamic Interaction*, edited by J. M. Skibo and G. M. Feinman, pp. 81-98. The University of Utah Press, Salt Lake City.

Feinman, Gary M. and Linda M. Nicholas
   2004 Unraveling the Prehispanic Highland Mesoamerican Economy: Production, Exchange, and Consumption in the Classic Period Valley of Oaxaca. In *Archaeological Perspectives on Political Economies*, edited by G. M. Feinman and L. M. Nicholas, pp. 167-188. The University of Utah Press, Salt Lake City.

Fewkes, Jesse Walter
   1912   Casa Grande, Arizona. *28th Annual Report of the Bureau of Ethnology*, 1906-1907, 25-179. Washington, D.C.

Field, John, Keith Katzer, Jim Lombard and Jeanette Schuster
   1993   A Geomorphic Survey of the Picacho and Northern Tucson Basins. In *The Northern Tucson Basin Survey: Research Directions and Background Studies*, edited by John H. Madsen; Paul R. Fish and Suzanne K, Fish, pp. 33-50. Arizona State Museum Archaeological Series 182. University of Arizona, Tucson.

Fish, Paul R. and Suzanne K. Fish
   1989   Hohokam Warfare from a Regional Perspective. In *Cultures in Conflict: Current Archaeological Perspectives*, edited by D. C. Tkaczuk and B. C. Vivian, pp. 112-129. University of Calgary Archaeological Association, Calgary.

   1991   Hohokam Political and Social Organization. In *Exploring the Hohokam: Pehistoric Desert People of the American Southwest*, edited by G. J. Gumerman, pp. 151-175. University of New Mexico Press, Albuquerque.

   1994   Southwest and Northwest: Recent Research at the Juncture of the United States and Mexico. *Journal of Archaeological Research* 2: 3-44.

   2000   The Marana Mound Site: Patterns of Social Differentiation in the Early Classic Period. In *The Hohokam Village Revisited*, edited by David Doyel, Suzanne Fish, and Paul Fish, pp. 373-384 American Association for the Advancement of Science, Ft. Collins, Colorado.

Fish, Paul R., Suzanne K. Fish, C. Brennan, Doug Gann, and James Bayman
  1992   Marana: Configuration of an Early Classic Period Hohokam Platform Mound Site. In *Proceedings of the Second Salado Conference*, Globe, AZ 1992, edited by Richard C. Lange and S. Germick, pp. 62-68. Arizona Archaeological Society, Phoenix.

Fish, Paul R., Suzanne K. Fish, Stephanie Whittlesey, Hector Neff, Michael D. Glascock, and J, Michael Elam
  1992   An Evaluation of the Production and Exchange of Tanque Verde Red-on-brown Ceramics in Southern Arizona. In *Chemical Characterization of Ceramic Pastes in Archaeology*, edited by Hector Neff, pp. 233-254. Monographs in World Archaeology No. 7. Prehistory Press, Madison.

Fish, Suzanne K.
  1995   Mixed Agricultural Strategies in Southern Arizona and their implications. In *Soil, Water, Biology and Belief in Prehistoric and Traditional Southwestern Agriculture*, edited by H. Wolcott Toll, pp. 101-116. New Mexico Archaeological Council Special Publication No. 2. Albuquerue.

  2000   Hohokam Impacts on Sonoran Desert Environments. In *Imperfect Balance: Landscape Transformations in the Precolumbian Americas*, edited by D. Lentz, pp. 251-281. Columbia University Press, New York.

  2004   Corn, Crops, and Cultivation in the North American Southwest. In *People and Plants in Ancient Western North America*, edited by Paul E. Minnis, pp. 115-166. Smithsonian Books, Washington.

Fish, Suzanne K. and M. Donaldson
  1991   Production and Consumption in the Archaeological Record: A Hohokam Example. *The Kiva* 56: 255-276.

Fish, Suzanne K. and Paul R. Fish
  1990   An archaeological assessment of ecosystem in the Tucson Basin of southern Arizona. In *The Ecosystem Concept in Anthropology*, edited by Emilio Moran, pp. 159-169. University of Michigan Press, Ann Arbor.

  1994   Multisite communities as measures of Hohokam aggregation. In *The Ancient Southwestern Community*, edited by W. Wills and R. Leonard, pp. 119-130. University of New Mexico Press, Albuquerque.

  2000   The Institutional Contexts of Hohokam Complexity and Inequality. In *Alternative Leadership Styles in the Prehispanic Southwest,* edited by Barbara Mills, pp. 154-167. University of Arizona Press, Tucson.

  2006   Reorganization and Realignment: The Classic Period in the Tucson Basin. In *The Hohokam in World Perspective*, edited by Suzanne K. Fish and Paul R. Fish. University of Arizona Press, Tucson. Ms. on file, Arizona State Museum Library. University of Arizona, Tucson.

Fish, Suzanne K., Paul R. Fish, and John Madsen
  1989   Differentiation and integration in a Tucson Basin Classic period community. In *The Sociopolitical Structure of Prehistoric Southwestern Societies*, edited by Steadman Upham, Kent Lightfoot, and Roberta Jewett, pp. 237-267. Westview Press, Boulder.

  1992a   *The Marana Community in the Hohokam World*. Anthropological Papers of the University of Arizona No. 56. The University of Arizona Press, Tucson.

  1992b   Evolution and Structure of the Classic Period Marana Community, Chapter 3. In *The Marana Community in the Hohokam World*. Eds Suzanne K. Fish; Paul R. Fish; and John H. Madsen, pp. 20-40. Anthropological Papers of the University of Arizona, no 56. University of Arizona Press, Tucson.

1992c Early Sedentism and Agriculture in the Northern Tucson Basin, Chapter 2. In *The Marana Community in the Hohokam World.* Eds Suzanne K. Fish; Paul R. Fish; and John H. Madsen, pp. 1-19. Anthropological Papers of the University of Arizona, no 56. University of Arizona Press, Tucson.

Fish, Suzanne K., Paul R. Fish, Charles H. Miksicek, and John H. Madsen
1985 Prehistoric Agave Cultivation in Southern Arizona. *Desert Plants* 7(2):100, 107-112.

Fish, Suzanne K. and Norman Yoffee
1996 The State of Hohokam. In *Debating Complexity: Proceedings of the 26th Annual Chacmool Conference*, edited by D. Meyer, P. Dawson, and D. Hanna, pp. 61-67. University of Calgary, Calgary.

Foster, Michael S.
1986 The Mesoamerican Connection: A View from the South. In *Ripples in the Chichimec Sea: New Considerations of Southwestern-Mesoamerican Interactions*, edited by Frances J. Mathien and Randall H. McGuire, pp. 154-182. Southern Illinois University Press, Carbondale.

Foucault, Michel
1977 *Discipline and Punish: The Birth of the Prison.* Vintage Books, New York.

Fox, James J.
1993 Comparative Perspectives on Austronesian Houses: An Introductory Essay. In *Inside Austronesian Houses, Perspectives on Domestic Designs for Living*, edited by J. J Fox, pp. 1-24. Research School of Pacific Studies, The Australian National University, Canberra.

Fritz, Gayle J.
2007 Pigweeds for the Ancestors: Cultural Identities and Archaeobotanical Identification Method. In *Archaeology of Food and Identity*, edited by K. Twiss, pp. 288-307. Occasional Paper # 34, Center for Archaeological Investigations, Southern Illinois University, Carbondale.

Gabel, Norman
1931 *The Martinez Hill Ruin.* M.A. thesis, Department of Anthropology, University of Arizona, Tucson.

Gasser, Robert E., and E. Charles Adams
1981 Aspects of Deterioration of Plant Remains in Archaeological Sites: The Walpi Archaeological Project. *Journal of Ethnobiology* 1 (1): 182-192.

Gasser, Robert E., and Scott M. Kwiatkowski
1991 Food for Thought: Recognizing Patterns in Hohokam Subsistence. In *Exploring the Hohokam*, edited by George J. Gumerman, pp. 417-459. Amerind Foundation Publication. University of New Mexico Press, Albuquerque.

Gasser, Robert E., and Charles H. Miksicek
1985 The Specialists: A Reappraisal of Hohokam Exchange and the Archaeobotanical Record. In *Proceedings of the 1983 Hohokam Symposium, Part II*, edited by Alfred E. Dittert and Donald E. Dove, pp. 483-498. Phoenix Chapter, Arizona Archaeological Society, Occasional Paper 2. Phoenix.

Gifford, Edward Winslow
1932 *The Southwestern Yavapai.* University of California Publications in American Archaeology and Ethnology, volume 29. University of California Press, Berkeley.

1936 *Northeastern and Western Yavapai.* University of California Publications in American Archaeology and Ethnography 34:247-354.

Gifford-Gonzalez, Diane P., David B. Damrosch, Debra D. Damrosch, John Pryor, and Robert L. Thunen
    1985   The Third Dimension in Site Structure: An Experiment in Trampling and Vertical Dispersal. *American Antiquity* 50:803-818.

    1966   Morphological and Genetic Sequences of Carbonate Accumulation in Desert Soils. *Soil Science* vol. 101, pp. 347-360.

Gile, Leland H., John W. Hawley, and Robert B. Grossman
    1981   *Soils and Geomorphology in the Basin and Range Area of Southern New Mexico: Guidebook to the Desert Project.* New Mexico Bureau of Mines & Mineral Resources, Socorro, New Mexico.

Gillespie, Susan D.
    2000   Beyond Kinship: An Introduction. In *Beyond Kinship: Social and Material Reproduction in House Societies*, edited by S. D. Gillespie and R. A. Joyce, pp. 1-21. University of Pennsylvania Press, Philadelphia.

Girard, I and R. A. Klassen
    2001   A Comparison of Seven Methods for Analysis of Carbon in Soils. *Geological Survey of Canada, Current Research* 2001-E11. Available online at http://dsp-psd.communication.gc.ca/Collection/M44-2001-E11E.pdf Accessed 11.20.04

Gladwin, Harold S., N. Gladwin, Emil Haury, and Edmond B. Sayles
    1938   *Excavations at Snaketown: Material Culture.* Medallion Papers No XXV. Tucson.

    1965   *Excavations at Snaketown: Material Culture.* Medallion Papers 25. University of Arizona Press, Tucson.

Glascock, Michael
    1992   Neutron Activation Analysis. In *Chemical Characterization of Ceramic Pastes in Archaeology*, edited by Hector Neff, pp. 11-26. Monographs in World Archaeology No. 7. Prehistory Press, Madison.

Goudie, Andrew S.
    1973   *Duricrusts in Tropical and Subtropical Landscapes.* Clarendon Press, Oxford.

Graves, William M. and Scott Van Keuren
    2003   Ancestral Pueblo Villages and the Panoptic Gaze of the Commune. Paper presented at the Complex Society Group Conference, Cotsen Institute of Archaeology, University of California, Los Angeles, CA.

Grayson, Donald
    1984   *Quantitative Zooarchaeology: Topics in the Analysis of Archaeological Faunas.* Academic Press, Inc, Orlando.

    2001   The Archaeological Record of Human Impacts on Animal Populations. *Journal of World Prehistory* 15(1): 1-68.

Greenleaf, J. Cameron
    1975   *Excavations at Punta de Agua.* Anthropological Papers 26 of the University of Arizona. Tucson.

Gregonis, Linda M. and Gayle H. Hartmann
    2011   *Whiptail Ruin (AZ BB:10:3-ASM): A Classic Period Community in the Northeastern Tucson Basin.* Arizona State Museum Archaeological Series 203. University of Arizona, Tucson.

Gregory, Chris A.
1982   *Gifts and Commodities*. Academic Press, London.

Gregory, David A.
1984   Excavations at the Siphon Draw Site. In *Hohokam Archaeology Along the Salt-Gila Aqueduct*, edited by Lynn Teague and Patricia Crown, pp. 15-218. Arizona State Museum Archaeological Series 150(4). University of Arizona, Tucson.

1987   The Morphology of Platform Mounds and the Structure of Classic Period Hohokam Sites. In *The Hohokam Village: Site Structure and Organization*, edited by D. E. Doyel, pp. 183-210. Southwestern and Rocky Mountain Division of the American Association of the Advancement of Science, Ft. Collins.

Gregory, David A. and David Abbott
1988   Stages of Mound Construction and Architectural Details. In *The 1982-1984 Excavations at Las Colinas: The Mound 8 Precinct*, edited by David A. Gregory, pp. 25-50. Arizona State Museum Archaeological Series 162. University of Arizona, Tucson.

Gross, M. Grant
1971   Carbon Determination. In *Procedures in Sedimentary Petrology*, edited by Robert E. Carver, pp. 573-596. Wiley Interscience, New York.

Grossman, R. B., and T. G. Reinsch
2002   Bulk Density and Linear Extensibility. In *Methods of Soil Analysis. Part 4. Physical Methods*, edited by Jacob H. Dane and G. Clarke Topp, pp. 201-228. Soil Science Society of America Book Series, no. 5, Madison, Wisconsin.

Hackbarth, Mark
1987   A Descriptive Summary of the Excavation Results at Locus E, AZ AA:12:2 (ASU), Muchas Casas. In *Field Investigations at the Marana Community Complex*, edited by T. Kathleen Henderson, pp. 151-158. Anthropological Field Studies No. 14. Department of Anthropology, Arizona State University, Tempe.

Hall, Edward T.
1966   *The Hidden Dimension*. Doubleday, New York.

1972   Silent Assumptions in Social Communication. In *People and Buildings,* edited by R. Gutman, pp. 135-151. Basic Books, New York.

Hammack, Laurens C. and Alan P. Sullivan (editors)
1981   *The 1968 Excavations at Mound 8, Las Colinas Ruin Group, Phoenix, Arizona.* Arizona State Musuem Archaeological Series 154. University of Arizona, Tucson.

Hammond, Gawain, and Norman Hammond
1981   Child's Play: A Distorting Factor in Archaeological Distribution. *American Antiquity* 46:634-636.

Hansen-Speer, Karla
2006   *Subsistence and Economy of a Classic Hohokam Site in Southern Arizona: A Paleoethnobotanical Analysis of the Marana Mound Site*. Ph.D. dissertation, Department of Anthropology, Washington University in St. Louis.

Harry, Karen G.

1997   *Ceramic Production, Distribution, and Consumption in Two Classic Period Hohokam Communities.* Ph.D. dissertation, Department of Anthropolgy, University of Arizona, Tucson. UMI Microfilms, Ann Arbor.

2000   Community-Based Craft Specialization: The West Branch Site. In *The Hohokam Village Revisited,* edited by D. E. Doyel, S. K. Fish, and P. R. Fish, pp. 197-220. Southwestern and Rocky Mountain Division of the American Association for the Advancement of Science. Ft. Collins, Colorado.

2003   *Economic Organization and Settlement Hierarchies: Ceramic Production and Exchange Among the Hohokam.* Praeger Press, Westport.

Harry, Karen G. and James M. Bayman

2000   Leadership Strategies among the Classic Period Hohokam: A Case Study. In *Alternative Leadership Strategies in the Prehispanic Southwest,* edited by Barbara J. Mills, pp. 136-153. University of Arizona Press, Tucson.,

Harry, Karen G., Paul R. Fish, and Suzanne K. Fish

2002   Ceramic Production and Distribution in Two Classic Period Hohokam Communities. In *Ceramic Production and Circulation in the Greater Southwest: Source Determination by INAA and Complementary Mineralogical Investigations,* edited by Donna M. Glowacki and Hector Neff, pp. 99-110. The Cotsen Institute of Archaeology Monograph 44, University of California, Los Angeles.

Haury, Emil W.

1945   *The Excavation of Los Muertos and Neighboring Ruins in the Salt River Valley, Southern Arizona.* Papers of the Peabody Museum of American Archaeology and Ethnology 24(1).

1976   *The Hohokam: Desert Farmers and Craftsmen.* University of Arizona Press, Tucson.

Hayden, Brian

1995   Pathways to Power: Principles for Creating Socio Economic Inequalities. In *Foundations of Social Inequality,* edited by T. D. Price and G. M. Feinman, pp. 15-86. Pleneum Press, New York.

1996   Feasting in Prehistoric and Traditional Societies. In *Food and the Status Quest: An Interdisciplinary Perspective,* edited by P. Wiessner and W. Schiefenhovel, pp. 129-147. Berghahn Books, Oxford.

Hayden, Brian, and Aubrey Cannon

1983   Where the Garbage Goes: Refuse Disposal in the Maya Highlands. *Journal of Anthropological Anthropology.* 2:117-163.

Hayden, Julian D.

1957   *Excavations, 1940, at University Indian Ruin.* Southwestern Monuments Association Technical Series 5. Globe, Arizona.

Hayden, Julian D.

1937   The Vikita Ceremony of the Papago. *Southwestern Monuments Monthly Report* Supplement for April 1937:263-283.

1957   *Excavations, 1940, at University Indian Ruin, Tucson,* Arizona. Southwestern Monuments Association. Globe, Arizona.

1972 Hohokam Petroglyphs of the Sierra Pinacate, Sonora and the Hohokam Shell Expeditions. *The Kiva* 37:74-83.

Heidke, James M.
1995   Ceramic Analysis. In *Archaeological Investigations at Los Morteros, a Prehistoric Settlement in the Northern Tucson Basin*, Part I, by Henry Wallace, pp. 263-442. Anthropological Papers No. 17. Center for Desert Archaeology, Tucson, Arizona.

1996   Production and Distribution of Rincon Phase Pottery: Evidence from the Julian Wash Site. In *A Rincon Phase Occupation at Julian Wash*, AZ BB:13:17 (ASM), by J. B. Mabry, pp. 47-71. Technical Report No. 96-7. Center for Desert Archaeology, Tucson.

2000   Middle Rincon Phase Ceramic Artifacts from Sunset Mesa. In *Excavations at Sunset Mesa Ruin*, by M. W. Lindeman, pp. 69-118. Technical Report No. 2000-02. Desert Archaeology, Inc., Tucson.

Heidke, James M., Elizabeth J. Miksa, and Henry D. Wallace
2002   A Petrographic Approach to Sand-Tempered Pottery Provenance Studies: Examples from Two Hohokam Local Systems. In *Ceramic Production and Circulation in the Greater Southwest: Source Determination by INAA and Complementary Mineralogical Investigations*, edited by Donna M. Glowacki and Hector Neff, pp. 152-178. The Cotsen Institute of Archaeology Monograph 44, University of California, Los Angeles.

Heiri, Oliver, André F. Lotter and Gerry Lemcke
2001   Loss of Ignition as a method for estimating organic and carbonate content in sediments: Reproducibility and comparability of results. *Journal of Paleolimnology* 25(1):101-110.

Helms, Mary W.
1993   *Craft and the Kingly Ideal: Art, Trade, and Power.* University of Texas Press, Austin.

1998   *Access To Origins: Affines, Ancestors, and Aristocrats.* University of Texas Press, Austin.

Henderson, T. Kathleen
1987a *Structure and Organization at La Ciudad.* Arizona State University Anthropological Field Studies 18. Office of Cultural Resource Management, Department of Anthropology, Arizona State University, Tempe.

1987b The Growth of a Hohokam Village. In *The Hohokam Village: Site Structure and Organization*, edited by D. E. Doyel, pp. 97-126. Southwestern and Rocky Mountain Division of the American Association of the Advancement of Science, Ft. Collins, Colorado.

Hendon, Julia A.
1999   Multiple Sources of Prestige and the Social Evaluation of Women in Prehispanic Mesoamerica. In *Material Symbols: Culture and Economy in Prehistory*, edited by J. E. Robb. Center for Archaeological Investigations Southern Illinois University, Occasional Paper No. 26, Carbondale.

Hackett, Brian Scott
1998   Sociopolitical Meaning of Faunal Remains From Baker Village. *American Antiquity* 63:289-302.

Hodgson, Wendy C.
2001   *Food Plants of the Sonoran Desert.* University of Arizona Press, Tucson.

Holeman, Abigail
2004   Polishing Stones and their Story: A Look at Production at the Marana Platform Mound Site. Paper presented at the 70th Annual Meeting of the Society for American Archaeology, 3 April 2004, Montreal.

Holliday, Vance T. and Julie K. Stein

1989   Variability of Laboratory Procedures and Results in Geoarchaeology. *Geoarchaeology: An International Journal* 4(4):347-358.

Hovezak, Mark J.

1988   Adobe Wall Material Analysis. In *Hohokam Settlement Along the Slopes of the Picacho Mountains: Synthesis and Conclusions*, Tucson Aqueduct Project, edited by R. Ciolek-Torrello and D. R. Wilcox, pp. 315-328. MNA Research Paper No. 35, Vol. 6. Museum of Northern Arizona, Flagstaff.

Howard, Jerry B.

1985   Courtyard Groups and Domestic Cycling: A Hypothetical Model of Growth. In *Proceedings of the 1983 Hohokam Symposium*, edited by A. E. Dittert and D. E. Dove, pp. 311-326. Occasional Paper. vol. 2. Arizona Archaeological Society, Phoenix.

1988   *Excavations at Casa Buena: Changing Hohokam Land Use along the Squaw Peak Parkway*. Publications in Archaeology, No. 11. Soil Systems, Inc., Phoenix.

1992   Architecture and Ideology: An Approach to the Functional Analysis of Platform Mounds. In *Proceedings of the Second Salado Conference, Globe, AZ 1992,* edited by R. C. Lange and S. Germick, pp. 69-77. Arizona Archaeological Society, Phoenix.

2000   Quantitative Approaches to Spatial Patterning in the Hohokam Village: Testing the Village Segment Model. In *The Hohokam Village Revisited*, edited by David E. Doyel, Suzanne K. Fish, and Paul R. Fish, pp. 167-195. Southwestern and Rocky Mountain Division of the American Association for the Advancement of Science, Fort Collins, Colorado.

Huntington, Fred W.

1986   *Archaeological Investigations at the West Branch Site: Early and Middle Rincon Occupation in the Southern Tucson Basin*. Anthropological Papers 5. Institute for American Research, Tucson.

Inomata, Takeshi and Lawrence S. Coben

2006   Overture: An Invitation to the Archaeological Theater. In *Archaeology of Performance: Theatres of Power, Community and Politics* edited by T. Inomata and L. S. Coben, pp. 11-46. University of Pennsylvania, Philadelphia.

Jacobs, David

1992   A Procession Route: Accessibility and Architecture at Three Salado Mounds. In *Proceedings of the Second Salado Conference, Globe, AZ 1992*, edited by R. C. Lange and S. Germick, pp. 57-61. Arizona Archaeological Society, Phoenix.

James, Steven R.

1987   Hohokam Patterns of Faunal Exploitation at Muchas Casas. In *Studies in the Hohokam Community of Marana*, edited by G. E. Rice, pp. 171-196. Submitted to the U. S. Department of the Interior Bureau of Reclamation Lower Colorado Region Boulder City, Nevada.

Jernigan, Wesley

1978   *Jewelry of the Prehistoric Southwest*. University of New Mexico Press, Albuquerque.

Kaufman, Daniel

1998   Measuring Archaeological Diversity: An Application of the Jackknife Technique. *American Antiquity* 63(1):73-85.

Kearney, Thomas H., and Robert H. Peebles
1969 *Arizona Flora*. University of California Press, Berkeley.

Kelly, Lucreta S.
2001 A Case of Ritual Feasting at the Cahokia Site. In *Feasts: Archaeological and Ethnographic Perspectives on Food, Politics, and Power*, edited by M. Dieter and B. Hayden, pp. 334-367. Smithsonian University Press, Washington.

Kelly, William H.
1977 *Cocopa Ethnography*. Anthropological Papers 29 of the University of Arizona, Tucson.

Kendall, James
2002 *Faunal Remains from the Hohokam Community of Marana*. M.A. Thesis, Department of Anthropology, University of Arizona, Tucson.

Kintigh, Keith W.
1984 Measuring Archaeological Diversity by Comparison with Simulated Assemblages. *American Antiquity* 49:44-54.

1989 Sample Size, Significance, and Measures of Diversity. In *Quantifying Diversity in Archaeology*, edited by Robert D. Leonard and George T. Jones, pp. 25-36. Cambridge University Press, Cambridge.

Knudsen, Vern O. and Cyril M. Harris
1950 *Acoustical Designing in Architecture*. Acoustical Society of America, Melville, New York.

Kolb, Michael F. and Jeffrey A. Homburg
1991 Soil and Sediment Analysis. In *The Lower Verde Archaeological Project, Laboratory Manual*, edited by Carol J. Ellick and Stephanie M. Whittlesey, pp 43-62. Statistical Research, Inc., Tucson.

Lekson, Stephen
2009 *A History of the Ancient Southwest*. SAR Press, Santa Fe.

Lesure, Richard and Michael Blake
2002 Interpretive Challenges in the Study of Early Complexity: Economy, Ritual, and Architecture at Paso de la Amada, Mexico. *Journal of Anthropological Archaeology* 21:1-24.

Limbrey, Susan
1975 *Soil Science and Archaeology*. Academic Press, London.

Lindauer, Owen
1992 Architectural engineering and variation among Salado platform mounds. In *Proceedings of the Second Salado Conference: Globe, AZ 1992*, edited by Richard Lange and S. Germick, pp. 50-66. Occasional Paper. Arizona Archaeological Society, Phoenix.

1996 *The Place of the Storehouses: Roosevelt Platform Mound Study, Report on the Schoolhouse Platform Mound, Pinto Creek Complex*. Roosevelt Monograph Series 6 No. 35. Office of Cultural Resource Management, Arizona State University, Tempe.

Lindauer, Owen, and John H. Blitz
1997 Higher Ground: The Archaeology of North American Platform Mounds. *Journal of Archaeological Research* 5(2):169-207.

Littmann, Edwin R.
  1967   *Southwestern Mortars and Plasters from Casa Grande, Montezuma Castle, and Walnut Canyon.* Unpublished Ms. On file, Western Archeological Center, National Park Service, Tucson.

Longacre, William A.
  1974   Kalinga Pottery Making: The Evolution of a Research Design. In *Frontiers of Anthropology: An Introduction to Anthropological Thinking,* edited by Murray Leaf, pp. 51-67. D. Van Nostrand Company, New York.

  1981   Kalinga Pottery: An Ethnoarchaeological Study. In *Pattern of the Past: Studies in Honor of David Clarke,* edited by Ian Hodder, Glynn Issac, and Norman Hammond, pp. 49-66. Cambridge University Press, Cambridge.

Longacre, William A., and James M. Skibo
  1994   An Introduction to Kalinga Ethnoarchaeology. In *Kalinga Ethnoarchaeology: Expanding Archaeological Method and Theory,* edited by William A. Longacre and James M. Skibo, pp. 1-11. Smithsonian Institution Press, Washington.

Longacre, William A., and Miriam T. Stark
  1992   Ceramics, Kinship, and Space: A Kalinga Example. *Journal of Anthropological Archaeology* 11: 125-136.

Lowery, Birl, and John E. Morrison, Jr.
  2002   Soil penetrometers and penetrability. In *Methods of Soil Analysis. Part 4. Physical Methods,* edited by J. H. Dane and G. Clarke Topp, pp. 363-388. Soil Science Society of America Book Series, No. 5, Madison, Wisconsin.

Lumholtz, Carl
  1990   *New Trails In Mexico: An Account of One Year's Exploration in North-Western Sonora, Mexico and South-Western Arizona, 1909-1910.* The Southwest Center Series. University of Arizona Press, Tucson.

Machette, Michael N.
  1985   Calcic soils of the southwestern United States. In *Soils and Quaternary Geology of the Southwester United States* edited by David L. Weide. Geological Society of America Special Paper 203, Boulder.

Madsen, John H., Paul R. Fish, and Suzanne K. Fish (editors)
  1993   *The Northern Tucson Basin: Research Questions and Background Studies.* Arizona State Museum Archaeological Series 182. University of Arizona, Tucson.

Martin, Alexander C., and William D. Barkley
  1961   *Seed Identification Manual.* University of California Press, Berkeley.

Martin, Alexander C., and Ronald E. Reeve
  1955   A rapid manometric method for determining soil carbonate. *Soil Science.* 79:187-197.

Mauss, Marcel
  1990 [1925]   *The Gift: The Form and Reason for Exchange in Archaic Societies.* W.W. Norton, New York.

McClelland, John
  2003   Compound 3 Inhumation Excavation Report, Ms. on file. Arizona State Museum, University of Arizona, Tucson.

McFadden, Leslie D. and John C. Tinsley

1985   Rate and depth of pedogenic-carbonate accumulation in soils: Formulation and testing of a compartment model. In *Soils and Quaternary Geology of the Southwestern United States,* edited by David L. Weide, pp. 23-41. Geological Society of America Special Paper 203, Boulder.

McGuire, Randall H.

1985   The Role of Shell Exchange in the Explanation of Hohokam Prehistory. In *Proceedings of the 1983 Hohokam Symposium, Part II,* edited by Alfred E. Dittert and Donald E. Dove, pp. 473-482. Phoenix Chapter, Arizona Archaeological Society, Occasional Paper 2.

1987   The Papaguerian Periphery: Uneven Development in the Prehistoric Southwest. In *Polities and Partitions: Human Boundaries and the Growth of Complex Societies,* edited by Kathryn M. Trinkaus, pp. 123-139. Anthropological Research Papers, Arizona State University, Tempe.

1991   On the Outside Looking In: The Concept of Periphery in Hohokam Archaeology. In *Exploring the Hohokam: Prehistoric Desert Peoples of the American Southwest,* edited by George J. Gumerman, pp. 347-382. University of New Mexico Press, Albuquerque.

1992   *Death, Society, and Ideology in a Hohokam Community.* Westview Press, Boulder.

2000   Alternative Models, Alternative Strategies: Leadership in the Prehispanic Southwest. In *Alternative Leadership Strategies in the Prehispanic Southwest,* edited by B. J. Mills, pp. 3-18. University of Arizona Press, Tucson.

McGuire, Randall H., and Ann V. Howard

1987   The Structure and Organization of Hohokam Shell Exchange. *The Kiva* 52(2):113-146.

McKinnon, Susan

1995   Houses and Hierarchy: The view from a South Moluccan Society. In *About the House: Lévi-Strauss and Beyond,* edited by J. Carsten and S. Hugh-Jones, pp.170-188. Cambridge University Press, Cambridge.

2000   Domestic Exceptions: Evans-Pritchard and the Creation of Nuer Patrilineality and Equality. *Cultural Anthropology* 15(1):35-83.

Mead, Margaret

1930   Melanesian Middlemen. *Natural History* 30(2):115-130.

Miksa, Elizabeth J.

2005a (Draft Report) A Revised Petrofacies Model for the Tucson Basin. In *Craft Specialization in the Southern Tucson Basin: Archaeological Excavations at the Julian Wash Site, AZ BB:13:17 (ASM), Part 2, Synthetic Studies,* edited by Henry D. Wallace, pp. 170-188. Anthropology Papers No. 40. Center for Desert Archaeology, Tucson.

2005b Technological and Provenance Variation in Native American Pottery from the Spanish Period to the American Territorial Period, Tucson, Arizona. Paper presented at the 70th Annual Meeting of the Society for American Archaeology, Salt Lake City, Utah.

2006   A Revised Petrofacies Model for the Tucson Basin. In *Craft Specialization in the Southern Tucson Basin: Archaeological Excavations at the Julian Wash Site, AZ BB:13:17 (ASM), Part 2, Synthetic Studies,* edited by Henry D. Wallace, pp. 250-258. Anthropology Papers 40. Center for Desert Archaeology, Tucson.

Miksa, Elizabeth J. and James M. Heidke

2001   It all Comes out in the Wash: Actualistic Petrofacies Modeling of Temper Provenance, Tonto Basin, USA. *Geoarchaeology* 16(2):177-222.

Miksicek, Charles H.

1983   Archaeobotanical Aspects of Las Fosas: A Statistical Approach to Prehsitoric Plant Remains. In *Hohokam Archaeology Along the Salt Gila Aqueduct, Central Arizona Project. Parts V and VI*. Appendix B, pp. 671-698. Arizona State Museum Archaeological Series 150. University of Arizona, Tucson.

1987   Late Sedentary-Early Classic Period Hohokam Agricutlture: Plant Remains from the Marana Community Complex. In *Studies in the Hohokam Community of Marana*, edited by Glen E. Rice, pp. 197-216. Anthropological Field Studies Number 15. Office of Cultural Resource Management, Department of Anthropology, Arizona State University, Tempe.

Mills, Barbara J.

1991   Ceramics from the Box B Site. In *Archaeology of the San Juan Breaks: The Anasazi Occupation*, edited by Patrick Hogan and Lynne Sebastian, pp. 51-88. Office of Contract Archaeology, University of New Mexico, Albuquerque.

2000   *Alternative Leadership Strategies in the Prehispanic Southwest*. University of Arizona Press, Tucson.

2004   Performing the Feast: Visual Display and Suprahousehold Commensualism in the Puebloan Southwest. Paper presented at the 70th Annual Meeting of the Society for American Archaeology, 3 April 2004, Montreal.

Mindeleff, Cosmos

1989   Navajo Houses. In *17th Annual Report of the Bureau of American Ethnology*, pp. 469-517. Smithsonian Institution, Washington D.C.

Minnis, Paul

1989   The Casas Grandes polity in the International Four Corners. In *The Sociopolitical Structure of Prehistoric Southwestern Societies*, edited by Steadman Upham, Kent Lightfoot, and Roberta Jewett, pp. 269-306. Westview Press, Boulder.

Mintz, Sidney W.

1956   The Role of the Middleman in the Internal Distribution System of a Caribbean Peasant Economy. *Human Organization* 15:18-23.

Mitchell, Douglas R.

1988a Results of Data Recovery. In *Excavations at La Lomita Pequena: A Santa Cruz/Sacaton Phase Hamlet in the Salt River Valley*, edited by D. R. Mitchell, pp. 25-94. Publications in Archaeology, No. 10. Soil Systems, Inc., Phoenix.

1988b Site Structure and Chronology. In *Excavations at La Lomita Pequena: A Santa Cruz/Sacaton Phase Hamlet in the Salt River Valley*, edited by D. R. Mitchell, pp. 351-394. Publications in Archaeology, No. 10. Soil Systems, Inc., Phoenix.

1990   *The La Lomita Excavations: 10th Century Hohokam Occupation in South-central Arizona*. Publications in Archaeology, No. 15. Soil Systems, Inc., Phoenix.

1992   Burial Practices and Paleodemographic Reconstructions at Pueblo Grande. *Kiva* 58:89-105.

Mitchell, Douglas R., and M. Steven Shackley
  1995   Classic Period Hohokam Obsidian Studies in Southern Arizona. *Journal of Field Archaeology* 22:291-304.

Mitchell, Douglas R., and Michael S. Foster
  1994   Habitation area and burial group descriptions. In *The Pueblo Grande Project*, Volume 2: *Feature Descriptions, Chronology, and Site Structure*, edited by Douglas Mitchell, pp. 50-32. Soil Systems Publications in Archaeology No. 20. Phoenix.

  2000   Hohokam Shell Middens along the Sea of Cortez, Puerto Peñasco, Sonora, Mexico. *Journal of Field Archaeology* 27-41.

Mitchell, Douglas R., T. Michael Fink, and Wilma Allen
  1989   Disposal of the Dead: Explorations of Mortuary Variability and Social Organization at the Grand Canal Ruins. In *Archaeological Investigations at the Grand Canal Ruins: A Classic Period Site in Phoenix, Arizona*, edited by D. R. Mitchell, pp. 705-773. Publications in Archaeology, No. 12. Soil Systems, Inc., Phoenix.

Mooers, Howard D.
  1999   Comparison of Loss on Ignition and Coulometric Titration for Determining Carbonate Content of Till. *Glacial Geology and Geomorphology*, tn01/1999. http://ggg.qub.ac.uk/ggg/papers/full/1999/tn011999/tn01.html. Accessed 11.20.04.

Moore, Jerry D.
  1996   *Architecture and Power in the Ancient Andes: The Archaeology of Public Buildings.* Cambridge University Press, Cambridge.

Munsell Color
  1994   *Munsell Soil Color Chart.* Kollmorgen Instruments Corporation, New Windsor New York.

Myers, Laural
  1996   Flaked Stone. In *Excavation of the Gibbon Springs Site: A Classic Period Village in the Northeastern Tucson Basin*, edited by Mark C. Slaughter and Heidi Roberts, pp. 331-372. SWCA Archaeological Report 94-87, Tucson.

National Geographic
  2002   *Field Guide to the Birds of North America*, 4th edition. National Geographic Society, Washington D.C.

Needham, Stuart, and Tony Spence
  1997   Refuse and the Formation of Middens. *Antiquity* 71:77-90.

Neff, Hector
  2002   Quantitative Techniques for Analyzing Ceramic Compositional Data. In *Ceramic Production and Circulation in the Greater Southwest: Source Determination by INAA and Complementary Mineralogical Investigations*, edited by Donna M. Glowacki and Hector Neff, pp. 15-36. The Cotsen Institute of Archaeology Monograph 44, University of California, Los Angeles.

Neitzel, Jill
  1991   Hohokam material culture and behavior: the dimensions of organizational change. In *Exploring the Hohokam: Prehistoric Desert Peoples of the American Southwest*, edited by George Gumerman, pp. 177-230. University of New Mexico Press, Albuquerque.

Nelson, Richard E.
   1982   Carbonate and Gypsum. In *Methods of Soil Analysis, Part 2: Chemical and Microbioloigcal Methods* (2nd ed.). Edited by A.L. Page, pp. 181-197. American Society of Agronomy and Soil Science Society of America, Madison.

Nelson, Richard S.
   1981   *The Role of a Pochteca System in Hohokam Exchange.* Unpublished Ph.D. Dissertaton, Department of Anthropology, New York University, New York.

   1986   Pochtecas and Prestige: Mesoamerican Artifacts in Hohokam Sites. In *Ripples in the Chichimec Sea: New Considerations of Southwestern-Mesoamerican Interactions*, edited by Frances J. Mathien and Randall H. McGuire, pp. 154-182. Southern Illinois University Press, Carbondale.

   1991   *Hohokam Marine Shell Exchange and Artifacts.* Arizona State Museum Archaeological Series 179. University of Arizona, Tucson.

Nielsen, Axel E.
   1991   Trampling the Archaeological Record. *American Antiquity* 56:483-503.

   1993   Formation Processes of Ceramic Assemblages: Examples from the San Juan Basin, Upper Puerco River, and Little Colorado River Regions. In *Across the Colorado Plateau: Anthropological Studies for the Transwestern Pipeline Expansion Project, Volume XVI: Interpretation of Ceramic Artifacts*, by Barbara J. Mills, Christine E. Goetze, and Maria Nieves Zedeño, pp. 151-174. Office of Contract Archaeology and Maxwell Museum of Anthropology, University of New Mexico, Albuquerque.

Orser, Charles E., Jr.
   1984   Trade Good Flow in Arikara Villages: Expanding Ray's "Middleman Hypothesis." *Plains Anthropologist* 29(103):1-12.

Parsons, Jeffrey R. and Mary H. Parsons
   1990   *Maguey Utilization in Highland Central Mexico: An Archaeological Ethnography.* Anthropological Papers No. 82, Museum of Anthropology, University of Michigan, Ann Arbor.

Pauketat, Timothy R., Lucreta S. Kelly, Gayle J. Fritz, Neal H. Lopinot, Scott Elias, and Eve Hargrave
   2002   The Residues of Feasting and Public Ritual at Early Cahokia. *American Antiquity* 67(2): 257-279.

Pearsall, Deborah
   1989   *Paleoethnobotany: a Handbook of Procedures.* Academic Press, San Diego.

Peterson, Jane E
   1994   Chipped Stone. In *The Pueblo Grande Project, Volume 4: Material Culture*, edited by Michael S. Foster, pp. 49-118. Soil Systems Publicatons in Archaeology No. 20. Soil Systems, Inc., Phoenix.

Peterson, Jane E., Douglas R. Mitchell, and M. Steven Shackley
   1997   The Social and Economic Contexts of Lithic Procurement: Obsidian from Classic-Period Hohokam Sites. *American Antiquity* 62(2): 231-259.

Pires-Ferreira, Jane W., and Kent V. Flannery
   1976   Ethnographic Models for Formative Exchange. In *The Early Mesoamerican Village*, edited by Kent V. Flannery, pp. 286-292. Academic Press, New York.

Plog, Stephen
  2008   *Ancient Peoples of the American Southwest*, second edition. Thames and Hudson, London.

Potter, James A.
  1997   Communal Ritual and Faunal Remains: An Example from the Dolores Anasazi. *Journal of Field Archaeology* 24:353-364.

Preucel, Robert W.
  1996   Cooking Status: Hohokam Ideology, Power, and Social Reproduction. In *Interpreting Southwestern Diversity: Underlying Principles and Overarching Patterns*, edited by Paul R. Fish and J. Jefferson Reid, pp. 125-131. Anthropological Research Papers. vol. 48. Arizona State University, Tempe.

Rader, Lloyd F. and F. S. Grimaldi
  1961   *Chemical Analysis for Selected Minor Elements in Pierre Shale*. US Geological Survey Professional Paper 391-A.

Ray, Arthur J.
  1978   History and Archaeology of the Northern Fur Trade. *American Antiquity* 43(1):26-34.

Rea, Amadeo
  1997   *At the Desert's Green Edge: An Ethnobotany of the Gila River Pima*. University of Arizona Press.

Reid, Jefferson and Stephanie Whittlesey
  1997   *The Archaeology of Ancient Arizona*. University of Arizona Press, Tucson.

Renfrew, Colin
  1975   Trade as Action at a Distance: Questions of Integration and Communication. In *Ancient Civilization and Trade*, edited by Jeremy A. Sabloff and C.C. Lamberg-Karlovsky, pp. 3-59. University of New Mexico Press, Albuquerque.

  1977   Alternative Models for Exchange and Spatial Distribution. In *Exchange Systems in Prehistory*, edited by Timothy K. Earle and Jonathon E. Ericson, pp. 71-90. Academic Press, New York.

Rice, Glen E.
  1987a *Studies in the Hohokam Community of Marana*. 15. Office of Cultural Resource Management, Department of Anthropology, Arizona State University, Tempe.

  1987b The Marana Community Complex: a Twelfth Century Chiefdom. In *Studies in the Hohokam Community of Marana*, edited by G. E. Rice, pp. 249-253. Anthropological Field Studies. vol. 15. Arizona State University Office of Cultural Resource Management, Tempe.

Rice, Glen E. and Charles L. Redman
  1993   Platform Mounds of the Arizona Desert: An Experiment in Organizational Complexity. In *Expedition*, pp. 53-63. vol. 35.

Roos, Christopher I.
  2002   *Formation Processes, Sampling, and Comparability: Independent Archaeological Theory and Archaeological Practice at the Marana Platform Mound Site (AZ AA:12:251 [ASM])*. Unpublished Master's paper, Department of Anthropology, University of Arizona, Tucson.

Ruhe, Robert V.

  1967   *Geomorphic Surface and Surficial Deposits in Southern New Mexico.* Memoir 18, State Bureau of Mines and Mineral Resources, New Mexico Institute of Mining and Technology, Socorro, New Mexico.

Ruscavage, Samantha

  1992a   Ceramic Variability and Refuse Disposal Patterns at the Verde Bridge Sites. In *Prehistoric and Historic Occupation of the Lower Verde River Valley: The State Route 87 Verde Bridge Project*, by Mark D. Hackbarth, pp. 145-184. Report submitted to the Arizona Department of Transportation, Contract No. 89-28. Northland Research, Inc., Flagstaff, Arizona.

  1992b   *Refuse Disposal Patterns in Hohokam Pit Structures.* Unpublished Master's thesis, Department of Anthropology, Arizona State University, Tempe.

Sahlins, Marshall S.

  1972   *Stone Age Economics.* Aldine Publishing Company, Chicago.

  1990   Monumental Architecture: A Thermodynamic Explanation of Symbolic Behavior. *World Archaeology* 22(2):119-132.

Saitta, Dean

  1999   Prestige, Agency, and Change in Middle-Range Societies. In *Material Symbols: Culture and Economy in Prehistory*, edited by J. E. Robb. Center for Archaeological Investigations Southern Illinois University, Occasional Paper, No. 26, Carbondale.

Schiffer, Michael B.

  1972   Archaeological Context and Systemic Context. *American Antiquity* 37:156-165.

  1987   *Formation Processes of the Archaeological Record.* University of New Mexico Press, Albuquerque.

Schlanger, Sarah

  1990   Artifact Assemblage Composition and Site Occupation Duration. In *Perspectives on Southwestern Prehistory*, edited by Paul E. Minnis and Charles L. Redman, pp. 103-121. Westview Press, Boulder.

Schroeder, Albert H.

  1953   The Problem of Hohokam, Sinagua, and Salado Relations in Southern Arizona. *Plateau* 26(2):75-83.

Seymour, Deni J.

  1988   An Alternative View of Sedentary Period Hohokam Shell Ornament Production. *American Antiquity* 53(4):812-828.

Seymour, Deni J. and Michael B. Schiffer

  1987   A Preliminary Analysis of Pithouse Assemblages from Snaketown, Arizona. In *Method and Theory for Activity Area Research: An Ethnoarchaeological Approach*, edited by S. Kent. Columbia University, New York.

Shackley, M. Steven

  1988   Sources of Archaeological Obsidian in the Southwest: An Archaeological, Petrological, and Geochemical Study. *American Antiquity* 53:752-772.

  1995   Sources of Archaeological Obsidian in the Greater American Southwest: An Update and Quantitative Analysis. *American Antiquity* 60(3):531-551.

Shemie, Bonnie
    1995   *Houses of Adobe: Native Dwellings of the Southwest*. Tundra Books, Montréal.

Sires, Earl W.
    1987   Hohokam architectural variability and site structure during the Sedentary to Classic transition. In *The Hohokam Village: Site Structure and Organization*, edited by David Doyel, pp. 171-182. Southwestern and Rocky Mountain Division of the American Association for the Advancement of Sciences, Glenwood Springs, CO.

Slaughter, Mark C. and Heidi Roberts (editors)
    1996   *Excavation of the Gibbon Springs Site: A Classic Period Village in the Northeastern Tucson Basin.* SWCA Archaeological Report 94-87. SWCA, Inc., Tucson.

Soil Science Society of America
    1996   *Glossary of Soil Science Terms*. Soil Science Society of America, Madison, Wisconsin.

Soil Survey Staff
    1999   *Soil Taxonomy: A Basic System of Soil Classification for Making and Interpreting Soil Surveys, Second Edition*. United States Department of Agriculture, Natural Resources Conservation Service. Agricultural Handbook Number 436.

Spensley, Ellen
    2004   Micromorphology of Construction and Culture at La Trinidad, Peten, Guatemala. Paper Presented at the Archaeological Sciences of the Americas Symposium, Septmember 22-25, Tucson, Arizona.

Speth, John and Katherine A Spielmann
    1983   Energy Source, Protein Metabolism, and Hunter-Gatherer Subsistence Strategies. *Journal of Anthropological Archaeology* 2:1-31.

Spielmann, Katherine A.
    2002   Feasting, Craft Specialization, and the Ritual Mode of Production in Small-Scale Societies. *American Anthropologist* 104(1):195-207.

Spier, Leslie
    1928   *Havasupai Ethnography*. Anthropology Paper, No. 3. American Museum of Natural History, New York.

    1933   *Yuman Tribes of the Gila River*. University of Chicago Press, Chicago.

Stark, Miriam
    1991a Ceramic Change in Ethnoarchaeological Perspective: A Kalinga Case Study. *Asian Perspectives* 30:193-216.

    1991b Ceramic Production and Community Specialization: A Kalinga Ethnoarchaeological Study. *World Archaeology* 23: 64-78.

    1992   From Sibling to Suki: Social Relations and Spatial Proximity in Kalinga Pottery Exchange. *Journal of Anthropological Archaeology* 11:137-151.

    1993   *Pottery Economics: A Kalinga Ethnoarchaeological Study.* Unpublished Ph.D. dissertation, Department of Anthropology, University of Arizona, Tucson.

Stark, Miriam, cont'd

1994   Pottery Exchange and the Regional System: A Dalupa Case Study. In *Kalinga Ethnoarchaeology: Expanding Archaeological Method and Theory*, edited by William A. Longacre and James M. Skibo, pp. 169-197. Smithsonian Institution Press, Washington.

1995   Economic Intensification and Ceramic Specialization: A View from Kalinga. *Research in Economic Anthropology* 16:179-226.

1999   Social Dimensions of Technical Choice in Kalinga Ceramic Traditions. In *Material Meanings: Critical Approaches to the Interpretation of Material Culture*, edited by E. S. Chilton, pp. 24-43. University of Utah Press, Salt Lake City.

Stark, Miriam T., and William A. Longacre

1993   Kalinga Ceramics and New Technologies: Social and Cultural Contexts of Ceramic Exchange. In *The Social and Cultural Context of New Ceramic Technologies*, edited by W. D. Kingery, pp. 1-32. The American Ceramic Society, Westerville.

Stark, Miriam T., Ronald L. Bishop, and Elizabeth Miksa

2000   Ceramic Technology and Social Boundaries: Cultural Practices in Kalinga Clay Selection and Use. *Journal of Archaeological Method and Theory* 7:295-331.

Stebbins, Robert C.

2000   *Peterson Field Guide to Western Reptiles and Amphibians, Third Edition.* Houghton Mifflin Company, New York.

Stephen, Alexander M.

1898   Pigments in the Ceremonials of the Hopi. In *International Folk-Lore Association, Archives*, pp. 260-265. The International Folk-Lore Congress of the World's Columbian Exposition ed. International Folklore Congress, 3rd, Chicago, 1893. vol. 1.

1936   *Hopi Journal of Alexander M. Stephen 1 & 2.* 2 vols. Columbia University Press, New York.

Steward, Julian H.

1933   *Archaeological Problems of the Northern Periphery of the Southwest.* Bulletin No. 5. Museum of Northern Arizona, Flagstaff.

Stone, Tammy

2003   Hohokam Exchange in Social Context. In *Centuries of Decline during the Hohokam Classic Period at Pueblo Grande*, edited by David R. Abbott, pp. 128-147. University of Arizona Press, Tucson.

Sullivan, Alan P., III, James M. Skibo, and Mary Van Buren

1991   Sherds as Tools: The Role of Vessel Fragments in Prehistoric Succulent Plant Processing. *North American Archaeologist* 12:243-255.

Szuter, Christine R.

1989   *Hunting by Prehistoric Horticulturalists in the American Southwest.* Unpublished Ph. D. dissertation, Department of Anthropology, University of Arizona.

Szuter, Christine R. and Frank E. Bayham

1989   Sedentism and Prehistoric Animal Procurement Among Desert Horticulturalists of the North American Southwest. In *Farmers as Hunters: The Implications of Sedentism*, edited by S. Kent, pp. 80-95. Cambridge University Press, Cambridge.

1997   Faunal Exploitation during the Late Archaic and Early Ceramic/Pioneer Periods in the south-central Arizona. In *Early Formative Adaptations in the southern Southwest*, edited by B. J. Roth, pp. 65-72. Monographs in World Archaeology No. 25. Prehistory Press, Madison.

Takaki, Michiko
1977   *Aspects of Exchange in a Kalinga Society, Northern Luzon*. Unpublished Ph.D. dissertation, Department of Anthropology, Yale University, New Haven.

Talayesva, Don A. and Leo Simmons
1942   *Sun Chief: The Autobiography of a Hopi Indian*. Yale University Press, New Haven.

Tambiah, Stanley J.
1979   A Performative Approach to Ritual. *Proceedings of the British Academy* 65: 113-169.

Teague, Lynn S.
1984   The Organization of the Hohokam Economy. In *Hohokam Archaeology along the Salt-Gila Aqueduct, Central Arizona Project*, Volume 9: *Synthesis and Conclusions*, edited by Lynn S. Teague and Patricia L. Crown, pp. 187-250. Arizona State Museum, Archaeological Series 150.University of Arizona, Tucson.

Thomas, David S.G.
1989   *Arid Zone Geomorphology*. Belhaven Press, London.

Trigger, Bruce
1990   Monumental Architecture: A Thermodynamic Explanation of Symbolic Behavior. *World Archaeology* 22(2):119-132.

Turner, Victor W.
1972   *The Ritual Process*. Cornell University Press, Ithaca.

Twiss, Katherine
2004   Home is Where the Hearth Is: Exploring Food and identity in the Neolithic Levant. We Are What We Eat: Archaeology, Food, and Identity, organized by Katherine Twiss. Visiting Scholar Conference, Southern Illinois University, Carbondale. March 12-13, 2004.

Ugan, A.
2004   The Big Deal About Small Animals. Paper presented at the 29th annual Great Basin Anthropology Conference. Sparks.

Underhill, Ruth M.
1939   *Social Organization of the Papago Indians*. Columbia University Press, New York.

1946   *Papago Indian Religion*. Columbia University Press, New York.

Van Buren, Mary, James M. Skibo, and Alan P. Sullivan, III
1992   The Archaeology of an Agave Roasting Location. In *The Marana Community in the Hohokam World*, edited by Suzanne K. Fish, Paul R. Fish, and John H. Madsen, pp. 88-96. University of Arizona Press, Tucson.

Van Slyke, Donald D. and Jordi Folch
1940   Manomentric carbon determination. *Journal of Biological Chemistry*. 136:509-541.

Vestal, Paul A.
    1952   *The Ethnobotany of the Ramah Navaho.* Papers of the Peabody Museum of American Archaeology and Ethnology 40(4):1-94.

Walker, William H.
    1995   Ceremonial Trash? In *Expanding Archaeology*, edited by J. M. Skibo, W. H. Walker, and A. E. Nielsen, pp. 67-79. University of Utah Press, Salt Lake City.

Wallace, Henry D.
    1986a *Rincon Phase Decorated Ceramics in the Tucson Basin: A Focus on the West Branch Site.* Institute for American Research Anthropological Papers No. 1. Tucson, Arizona.

    1986b Decorated Ceramics: Introduction, Methods, and Rincon Phase Seriation. In *Archaeological Investigations at the West Branch Site: Early and Middle Rincon Occupation in the Southern Tucson Basin* by Frederick Huntington, pp. 127-164. Institute for American Research Anthropological Papers No. 5. Tucson, Arizona.

    1995   *Archaeological Investigations at Los Morteros: A Prehistoric Settlement in the Northern Tucson Basin.* Anthropological Papers No. 17. Center for Desert Archaeology, Tucson.

Wallace, Henry D. and James Holmlund
    1984   The Classic period in the Tucson Basin. *The Kiva* 49: 167-194.

Wallace, Henry D., Douglas B. Craig, Mark D. Elson, Miriam T. Stark, and James M. Heidke
    1992   The Interpretation of Archaeological Context: The Role of Formation Process Studies in Prehistoric Research. In *The Rye Creek Project: Archaeology in the Upper Tonto Basin. Volume 2: Artifact and Specific Analyses*, by Mark D. Elson and Douglas B. Craig, pp. 3-16. Anthropological Papers No. 11. Center for Desert Archaeology, Tucson, Arizona.

Wasley, William W.
    1960   A Hohokam platform mound at the Gatlin site, Gila Bend, Arizona. *American Antiquity* 26: 242-262.

Wasley, William W. and Alfred E. Johnson
    1965   *Salvage Archaeology in Painted Rocks Reservoir Western Arizona.* Anthropological Papers of the University of Arizona 9. University of Arizona Press, Tucson.

Wasley, William W. and David E. Doyel
    1980   Classic Period Hohokam. *The Kiva* 45(4):33-352.

Waterson, Roxana
    1990   *The Living House: An Anthropology of Architecture in Southeast Asia.* Thames and Hudson, Singapore.

Watson, Andrew
    1989   Desert Crusts and Rock Varnish. In *Arid Zone Geomorphology* edited by David S. G. Thomas, pp. 25-55. Belhaven Press, London.

Watts, N. L.
    1980   Quaternary Pedogenic Calcretes from the Kalahari (South Africa): Minerology, Genesis and Diagenesis. *Sedimentology* 27:661-686.

Wegener, Robert, Richard Ciolek-Torrello, and William Deaver
    2002   *Preliminary Report of Archaeological Investigations along U.S. 60 at Florence Junction, Pinal County, Arizona*. Draft Technical Report 02-51. Statistical Research, Inc., Tucson.

Whitaker, John O.
    1996   *National Audubon Society Field Guide to North American Mammals*. Alfred A. Knopf, New York.

Whittlesey, Stephanie M.
    1997   Rethinking the Core-Periphery Model of the Pre-Classic Period Hohokam. In *Vanishing River: Landscapes and Lives of the Lower Verde Valley: The Lower Verde Archaeological Project, Overview, Synthesis, and Conclusions*, edited by Stephanie M. Whittlesey, Richard Ciolek-Torrello, and Jeffrey H. Altschul, pp. 597-628. SRI Press, Tucson.

Wiessner, Pauline Wilson and Wulf Schiefenhovel (editors)
    1995   *Food and the Status Quest: An Interdisciplinary Perspective*. Berghahn Books, Oxford.

Wilcox, David R.
    1987a   *Frank Midvale's Investigation of the Site of La Ciudad*. Office of Cultural Resource Management, Anthropological Field Studies, No. 19. Arizona State University, Tempe.

    1987b   New Models of Social Structure at the Palo Parado Site. In *The Hohokam Village: Site Structure and Organization*, edited by David E. Doyel, pp. 223-248. Southwestern and Rocky Mountain Division of the American Association of the Advancement of Science, Ft. Collins.

    1991   Hohokam Social Complexity. In *Chaco and Hohokam: Prehistoric Regional Systems in the American Southwest*, edited by Patricia L. Crown and W. James Judge, pp. 253-276. School of American Research, Santa Fe.

Wilcox, David R., and Charles Sternberg
    1983   *Hohokam Ballcourts and their Interpretation*. Arizona State Museum Archaeological Series 160. University of Arizona, Tucson.

Wilcox, David R, Thomas R. McGuire and Charles Sternberg
    1981   *Snaketown Revisited: A Partial Cultural Resource Survey, Analysis of Site Structure and an Ethnohistoric Study of the Proposed Hohokam-Pima National Monument*. Arizona State Museum Archaeological Series 155. University of Arizona, Tucson.

Wilcox, David R. and Lynette O. Shenk
    1977   *The Architecture of Casa Grande and Its Interpretation*. Arizona State Museum Archaeological Series 115. University of Arizona, Tucson.

Wilk, Richard R., and Robert McC. Netting
    1984   Household: Changing Forms and Functions. In *Households: Comparative and Historical Studies of the Domestic Group*, edited Netting, R. McC., Wilk, R., and Arnould, E. J., pp. 1-28. University of California Press, Berkeley

Wilk, Richard R., and Michael B. Schiffer
    1979   The Archaeology of Vacant Lots in Tucson, Arizona. *American Antiquity* 44:530-536.

Wilson, Douglas C.
   1994   Identification and Assessment of Secondary Refuse Aggregates. *Journal of Archaeological Method and Theory* 1(1):41-68.

Winter, Marcus C., and Jane W. Pires-Ferreira
   1976   Distribution of obsidian among households in two Oaxacan villages. In *The Early Mesoamerican Village*, edited by Kent V. Flannery, pp. 306-311. Academic Press, New York.

Winterhalder, Bruce and Smith, Eric A.
   2000   Analyzing Adaptive Strategies: Human Behavioral Ecology at Twenty-Five. *Evolutionary Anthropology* 9:51-72.

Wood, W. Raymond, and Donald Lee Johnson
   1978   A Survey of Disturbance Processes in Archaeological Site Formation. *Advances in Archaeological Method and Theory* 1:315-381.

Woodbury, Richard B.
   1961   A Reappraisal of Hohokam Irrigation. *American Anthropologist* 63:550-560.

Zyniecki, Mark (editor)
   1993   *Pueblo Viejo: Archaeological Investigations at a Classic Period Cemetery in El Reposo Park, Phoenix, Arizona.* 92-75. SWCA, Tucson.

www.ingramcontent.com/pod-product-compliance
Lightning Source LLC
Chambersburg PA
CBHW080554270326
41929CB00019B/3309